1. efficiency
2. embarrassed
3. grievance
4. lieutenant
5. exaggerated
6. fascination
7. hypocrisy
8. fulfilled
9. irrelevant
10. irresistible

Improving College Reading

Improving College Reading

LEE A. JACOBUS

Danbury State College

HARCOURT, BRACE & WORLD, INC.

New York / Chicago / San Francisco / Atlanta

Library of Congress Catalog Card Number: 67–14189

Printed in the United States of America

Preface

This book has been designed to help students improve their reading ability. Its forty selections have been chosen to interest them, and its exercises have been planned to develop and test their retention, comprehension, and vocabulary knowledge.

I have tried to include selections a reader might choose for himself, to find anecdotes or articles or essays stimulating or exciting to a young adult. There are selections on automobiles, television, exploration, space travel, movies, and on human relationships. Selections are always reprinted as they were originally written; they are not watered-down or insipid as many artificially produced or rewritten passages are. A number of the selections are from the kind of books used as supplementary reading in many college courses.

Each selection is followed by exercises which enable the student to evaluate and test his retention, comprehension, and vocabulary. Charts at the back of the book help measure his reading speed, although the book does not emphasize speed as much as it emphasizes the more demanding skill of concentration and the student's understanding of what he has read.

The selections are grouped in five sections of increasing difficulty. The student should work from Section I to Section V in as orderly a fashion as possible. Within a given section, however, the selections are approximately equal in difficulty and may be read or assigned in any order which individual interest or need requires.

The exercises are to be scored on the basis of a 100-point total. This scoring is designed for the convenience of the student—that is, it makes use of the kind of testing and test scores with which he is probably familiar. Using this consistent scoring plan and the graphs at the end of the book, he can measure his progress throughout. Any progress in point totals from the first to final sections is, of course, an indication of the development of skills. In fact, even a constant point total throughout indicates progress because the selections and test exercises become progressively more difficult.

Many people have helped me with this book. Miss Luella Clancy and Mr. William Bauserman of the New Milford Library and Mr. George Theissen and Mr. Walter Lilly of Danbury State College gave special assistance. My colleagues in the English Department at Danbury State College, in particular its chairman, Mrs. Elizabeth James, have been continually helpful. My wife Joanna, who read the manuscript in all its phases, also deserves special thanks.

Improving College Reading is dedicated to those people who will use it. I hope it will be of interest and use to them.

LEE JACOBUS

Contents

Improving College Reading

1 · The Latins' Oldest Pawnshop

JACK RUTLEDGE

*Founded with the approval of a king, this old pawnshop still oper-
ates, giving loans at low interest and good terms to the poor and
the not-so-poor.*

After every holiday thousands of people line up in front of a grimy,
four-story building facing the Zócalo or main square. Every day you'll see
tourists seeking bargains.

The Nacional Monte de Piedad, Latin America's oldest pawnshop, has its
main headquarters in the old building. It operates 25 branches—12 in Mexico
City, and the others scattered over the country.

It was founded Feb. 25, 1775, under authority of Spanish King Charles III,
and has been active ever since.

Those long lines after holidays are of Mexicans who have spent their last cent
celebrating and want to pawn their valuables until their finances straighten out.

But loans are made all the time, and the pawnshop averages about $56,000
daily. The main office and its branches have 1,250 employes.

Founder Romero de Terreros, with a fortune from gold and silver mining in
Mexico, had the money to organize the much-needed pawnshop.

Its favorite legend is about Pancho Villa. When the bandit came in triumph
to Mexico City during the revolution, he asked for a list of banks and rich
persons to whom he could turn for money. When he came to the name of the
pawnshop, he marked it out, saying he would not get funds from the bank of
the poor.

Today it is operated as a foundation by Dr. Gustavo A. Uruchurtu, brother
of the mayor of Mexico City; Antonio E. Canale, a lawyer; and Manuel Romero

THE LATINS' OLDEST PAWNSHOP   Reprinted by permission of the Associated Press.

de Terreros, a descendant of the founder. A descendant must always be on the board, according to the founder's decision.

The Monte de Piedad also is a charitable organization providing free breakfasts to hundreds, and operating a primary school for about 1,500 orphan girls.

Like most pawnshops, it loans money and gives the borrower a certain time limit to repay and pick up the item.

When this deadline arrives, the borrower can repay, and pay a small interest rate—lower than in most banks. If he defaults, the pawnshop can sell the item, hence the tourists and others who drop in to find bargains.

It also makes small loans. No interest is charged on amounts up to $1.60.

LENGTH: 365 WORDS

VOCABULARY

founded   established
pawn   offer an item in exchange for money
Pancho Villa   famous Mexican bandit of the early 1900's
default   fail to claim an item that has been pawned

1 · The Latins' Oldest Pawnshop

SCORING: Reading time: _____ Rate from chart: _____ W.P.M.

RETENTION	number right _____ × 4 equals _____ points	
INFERENCES	number right _____ × 3 equals _____ points	
COMPLETION	number right _____ × 4 equals _____ points	
DEFINITIONS	number right _____ × 3 equals _____ points	

(Total points: 100)   **total** _____ points

RETENTION   Based on the passage, which of the following statements are True (T), False (F), or Not answerable (N)?

1. _____ The author borrowed money at the Nacional Monte de Piedad.

2. _____ The pawnshop averages loans of a total of $56,000 daily.

3. _____ Pancho Villa would not take money from the pawnshop during the revolution.

4. _____ Tourists can sometimes find a bargain at the pawnshop.

5. _____ Mexicans don't like the attitude Americans have toward pawnshops.

6. _____ The university in Mexico City has a great respect for the pawnshop.

7. _____ Dr. Gustavo Uruchurtu is the founder of the pawnshop.

8. _____ The pawnshop is more than 150 years old.

9. _____ The Zócalo is where Pancho Villa died.

10. _____ Most borrowing seems to take place after great holidays.

INFERENCES

1. _____ Which of the following statements is probably most accurate?
   (a) The people who operate the pawnshop are money-hungry public officials.
   (b) Much of the good the pawnshop does is performed in its role as an organization of charity.
   (c) King Charles III had long dreamed of such a pawnshop for his people.

2. _____ Which of the following statements is probably inaccurate?
   (a) The pawnshop charges no interest on very small loans.
   (b) Wealthy people, more than the poor, patronize the pawnshop.
   (c) Poor but ambitious Mexicans operate the pawnshop.

Choose the best answer for each question.

1. _____ Pancho Villa called the pawnshop the: (a) bank of the poor. (b) home of the brave. (c) king of the charities. (d) pawn of the rich.

2. _____ Today the Monte de Piedad is operated as: (a) a bank. (b) a foundation. (c) a restaurant. (d) an orphanage.

3. _____ In Mexico City alone the branches of the pawnshop number: (a) 1. (b) 2. (c) 5. (d) 12.

4. _____ The pawnshop is described as: (a) "a building resembling an orphanage." (b) "a silver-colored institution." (c) "an immaculate, sun-swept Mexican villa." (d) "a grimy, four-story building."

5. _____ Loans are made: (a) only on feast days. (b) all the time. (c) only after holidays. (d) only to orphans.

6. _____ The Spanish name for the pawnshop is: (a) Mexicali Loanaria. (b) Banca de Zócalo. (c) Monte de Piedad. (d) El Pancho Villa.

DEFINITIONS Choose the definition from Column B that best matches each word in Column A.

Column A		*Column B*
1. holiday	_____	a. dirty
2. organize	_____	b. money
		c. story
3. grimy	_____	d. main office
4. funds	_____	e. festival, day of celebration
5. triumph	_____	f. time limit
		g. difficulties
6. legend	_____	h. get together, set up
7. headquarters	_____	i. victory
8. deadline	_____	j. working, ongoing
		k. having too good a time
9. active	_____	l. vacationer
10. tourist	_____	m. dullness
		n. insistence

2 · Wheels Within Wheels

SHIRLEY JACKSON

In her book, Life Among the Savages, *Shirley Jackson writes humorously about her home and family. This selection tells of her vain attempt to simplify life by throwing things away.*

Our house is old and noisy and full. When we moved into it we had two children and about five thousand books; I expect that when we finally overflow and move out again we will have perhaps twenty children and easily half a million books; we also own assorted beds and tables and chairs and rocking horses and lamps and doll dresses and ship models and paint brushes and literally thousands of socks. This is the way of life my husband and I have fallen into, inadvertently, as though we had fallen into a well and decided that since there was no way out we might as well stay there and set up a chair and a desk and a light of some kind; even though this *is* our way of life, and the only one we know, it is occasionally bewildering, and perhaps even inexplicable to the sort of person who does not have that sort of swift, accurate conviction that he is going to step on a broken celluloid doll in the dark. I cannot think of a preferable way of life, except one without children and without books, going on soundlessly in an apartment hotel where they do the cleaning for you and send up your meals and all you have to do is lie on a couch and—as I say, I cannot think of a preferable way of life, but then I have had to make a good many compromises, all told.

I look around sometimes at the paraphernalia of our living—sandwich bags, typewriters, little wheels off things—and marvel at the complexities of civilization with which we surround ourselves; would we be pleased, I wonder, at a wholesale elimination of these things, so that we were reduced only to necessities (coffeepot, typewriters, the essential little wheels off things) and then—this happening usually in the springtime—I begin throwing things away, and it turns out that although we can live agreeably without the little wheels off things, new little wheels turn up almost immediately. This is, I suspect, progress. They can make new little wheels, if not faster than they can fall off things, at least faster than I can throw them away.

LENGTH: 350 WORDS

VOCABULARY

inadvertently by accident
inexplicable impossible to explain
paraphernalia things, materials, furnishings

2 · Wheels Within Wheels

SCORING: Reading time: _____ Rate from chart: _____ W.P.M.

RETENTION	number right _____ × 4 equals _____ points
INFERENCES	number right _____ × 3 equals _____ points
COMPLETION	number right _____ × 4 equals _____ points
DEFINITIONS	number right _____ × 3 equals _____ points

(Total points: 100)   **total** _____ points

RETENTION   Based on the passage, which of the following statements are True (T), False (F), or Not answerable (N)?

1. _____ The author carefully planned the kind of life she lives.

2. _____ The little wheels off things came primarily from the typewriter.

3. _____ No one would want to live the way the author does.

4. _____ All told, the author has had to make a good many compromises.

5. _____ The author usually throws things out in the springtime.

6. _____ The author cannot think of a preferable way of life.

7. _____ The author's books are mostly nontechnical.

8. _____ The author lives in a new house with five hundred books.

9. _____ The author has two children.

10. _____ The life the author and her husband lead is occasionally bewildering.

INFERENCES

1. _____ Which of the following statements is probably most accurate?
   (a) Sometimes people can plan their lives a little too carefully.
   (b) Nobody likes to throw things out, though everyone has to sometimes.
   (c) New things seem to replace the old almost before they have been thrown out.

2. _____ Which of the following statements is probably inaccurate?
   (a) The author finds it impossible to throw anything away.
   (b) The author can live agreeably without the little wheels of things.
   (c) This is the only way of life the author knows.

COMPLETION Choose the best answer for each question.

1. ___ Stepping on a celluloid doll in the dark: (a) is actually impossible. (b) is noisy and highly annoying. (c) can only happen to a tired mother. (d) demands one's utmost attention.

2. ___ The first sentence of the passage is: "Our house is old and noisy and: (a) dull." (b) large." (c) vacant." (d) full."

3. ___ When the author overflows out of her present house, she expects to: (a) have twenty children and half a million books. (b) be able to clean all the useless things out of her life. (c) make a better start than she did before. (d) have her husband set up a chair and desk and light.

4. ___ The essential things, the "necessities," are: (a) rocking horses and lamps. (b) assorted beds, tables, and chairs. (c) paint brushes and ship models. (d) coffeepots and typewriters.

5. ___ A wholesale elimination of things is: (a) one way of simplifying one's life. (b) probably best to try in late fall. (c) the only way to get rid of 5,000 books. (d) necessary in large, old houses.

6. ___ When the author throws things away: (a) they stay thrown away. (b) the children rescue them. (c) new things take their places. (d) she marvels at the complexities of civilization.

DEFINITIONS Choose the definition from Column B that best matches each word in Column A.

Column A		*Column B*
1. bewildering	___	a. culture
2. agreeably	___	b. correct
		c. confusing
3. immediately	___	d. by mistake
4. preferable	___	e. substantially
5. inadvertently	___	f. pleasantly
		g. more desirable
6. inexplicable	___	h. without explanation
7. civilization	___	i. completely unexpected
8. compromise	___	j. now, right away
		k. giving in, making agreements
9. accurate	___	l. actually, exactly
10. literally	___	m. unhappily
		n. less pleasant

3 · Hollywood and TV

PENELOPE HOUSTON

> *This note from a book about the movies shows that the motion
> picture and television industries help each other in strange ways.
> Television uses the old Hollywood production methods even bet-
> ter than Hollywood did, and old Hollywood movies have become
> valuable on TV screens.*

At any given moment, there are likely to be more television series
than movies in active production at a big Hollywood studio. Three-quarters of
Hollywood's studio population, it has been estimated, now work in television
and not in films. In the old days, small companies turning out cut-price Westerns made them two at a time—same bar-room set, same actors, a frugal minimum of changes in clothes and dialogue. Now TV companies, no less brisk
and more efficient, turn out the same kind of Westerns, in the same studios,
as likely as not with the same technicians.

Television did more than this: it supplied the film companies with a market
for their old films and enabled them to realize on assets which had previously
added up, commercially if not historically, to so many cans of dead celluloid.
In Britain, the film industry has come together rather effectively to keep films
as far as possible off the television screens, the fear being that if the movies
shown on TV are not too decrepit, they keep people at home who might
otherwise be in the cinemas. In America the barriers fell with a crash in 1955,
when R.K.O.-Radio ceased production and was sold to a company whose
interest lay at least partly in the acquisition of TV rights in the old movies.
(The studio itself was bought by Desilu, the TV production company which

HOLLYWOOD AND TV   Reprinted from *The Contemporary Cinema* by Penelope Houston by permission of Penguin Books Ltd. Copyright © 1963.

had made a fortune out of *I Love Lucy*.) If one company had opened the doors to television, others might as well do the same; and by 1957 it could be estimated that more than 10,000 cinema films had become available to TV. An expanding industry, desperate for any material it could lay its hands on, had come to terms with a contracting one, equally hard up for cash to see it through the worst years.

LENGTH: 320 WORDS

VOCABULARY

frugal   thrifty, designed to save money
decrepit   very old, worn out
cinemas   movie theaters
acquisition   gaining possession of, gaining ownership

Length (# words)
time in minutes

3 · Hollywood and TV

SCORING: Reading time: _____ Rate from chart: _____ W.P.M.

RETENTION	number right _____ × 4 equals _____ points
INFERENCES	number right _____ × 3 equals _____ points
COMPLETION	number right _____ × 4 equals _____ points
DEFINITIONS	number right _____ × 3 equals _____ points

(Total points: 100) **total** _____ points

RETENTION Based on the passage, which of the following statements are True (T), False (F), or Not answerable (N)?

1. __T__ More than half of Hollywood's production goes to the TV industry.
2. __N__ Old films appear more frequently on British TV than on American TV.
3. __F__ Desilu did not purchase R.K.O.-Radio.
4. __T__ It is cheaper to make two movies at the same time than to make one at a time.
5. __T__ Newer movies will appear on American TV more often than on British TV.
6. __N__ The British film industry is making a fortune.
7. __F__ Westerns are not so popular on TV as they were in the movies.
8. __T__ The sale of R.K.O.-Radio began a new era in TV.
9. __T__ TV helped the film industry make money from its old films.
10. __F__ British film makers want newer films to appear on British TV.

INFERENCES

1. __B__ Which of the following statements is probably most accurate?
    (a) TV companies like Desilu can make a fortune from old films.
    (b) Film companies contributed to the success of TV.
    (c) Ten thousand films were available to TV in 1957.

2. __B__ Which of the following statements is probably inaccurate?
    (a) When one film company opened its door to TV, many others did also.
    (b) American and British film companies opened their doors to TV at the same time.
    (c) In 1955, TV was desperate for any material it could get.

COMPLETION   Choose the best answer for each question.

1. _D_ If the TV industry was expanding in 1955, then the movie industry in 1955 was: (a) dull.   (b) thinking.   (c) swelling.   (d) contracting.

2. _B_ TV companies today are more: (a) concerned about the quality of films than they used to be.   (b) efficient in the production of films than Hollywood was.   (c) anxious to follow the pathways of Desilu than R.K.O.   (d) anxious to make money than Hollywood companies were.

3. _A_ When the film industry was having its worst years: (a) Desilu bought out R.K.O.   (b) Westerns were made two at a time.   (c) British TV showed the oldest films it had.   (d) TV was having its best years.

4. _C_ The English would probably stay away from cinemas if: (a) TV would show *I Love Lucy*.   (b) more Westerns were made in the studios.   (c) newer films showed up on TV.   (d) R.K.O. had not sold out in 1955.

5. _D_ Three-quarters of Hollywood's studio production is earmarked for: (a) Britain.   (b) Westerns.   (c) Desilu.   (d) TV.

6. _B_ Before the introduction of TV old films were: (a) being shown with success in Britain.   (b) just cans of dead celluloid.   (c) being shown in place of new ones.   (d) hard up for cash.

DEFINITIONS   Choose the definition from Column B that best matches each word in Column A.

Column A		*Column B*
1. barrier	E	a. film
2. desperate	H	b. workers
3. celluloid	A	c. stop
		d. conversation
4. realize on assets	G	e. obstacle
5. technicians	K	f. obtain
6. cease	C	g. make money
7. dialogue	D	h. needy
8. minimum	J	i. make believe
		j. least
9. estimate	N	k. cameramen
10. contracting	M	l. begin
		m. shrinking
		n. guess

4 · The Bogart Cult

RICHARD GEHMAN

The movie actor Humphrey Bogart is even more popular today than he was in his lifetime. College students identify with the lonely tough guy he portrays and flock to see his movies.

"**I** made more lousy pictures than any other actor in history," Humphrey DeForest Bogart used to say, looking challengingly around his living room in Hollywood in the last year of his life. Those of us who sat there used to nod, more in indulgence of the dying man's statement than in agreement with it, for he also had made some very, very good ones, including "The Treasure of the Sierra Madre," "African Queen," "The Maltese Falcon" and many others.

How Bogart would laugh if he could know what is going on today! Even the "lousy" ones are being shown all over the country, treasured by moviegoers everywhere. *In fact, the country is in the spasms of a Bogart Boom, and the star, dead since January 14, 1957, is more popular in movie houses and on television reruns of old films than he ever was when he was alive.* All three major networks report that ratings zoom up when a Bogart film is announced for showing.

At Harvard, there is a student who has seen "Casablanca" no fewer than 19 times. Other students there can claim to have seen "High Sierra" or "Across the Pacific" at least nine or ten times. At the University of New York at Buffalo, the eminent critic-novelist Leslie A. Fiedler, in response to a question about a possibility of there being a Bogart revival there, replied at once that one of his students was doing a term paper on Bogart, and that he himself personally had just arranged a private showing of a Bogart film.

THE BOGART CULT From "Bogey's New Boom." Reprinted from *This Week Magazine.* Copyright © 1965 by the United Newspapers Magazine Corporation.

It generally is agreed that the new Bogart Boom began at the Brattle Theater, in Cambridge, Mass., in February 1953, when the management converted the house into what is called an "art theater" and began playing Bogart revivals. Seven years later, in 1960, it instituted a regular policy of Bogart Weeks. Soon word began to get out across the nation, and students in other college towns were asking local theaters to put in Bogart Weeks at around examination time.

That the Bogart Weeks occur at that particular time could be said to be symbolic of the students' identification with the star. In his films, he always was walking into a situation, either as gangster or as defender of the law, in which he had to rely entirely on himself. In students' examinations, they must walk into a classroom and rely entirely on themselves. So one Harvard instructor explains the current Bogart craze. . . .

Near-campus theaters do incredible business on Bogart nights at examination times. "It's bedlam on a Bogart night," says Mrs. John W. Pratt, of The Brattle in Cambridge. "I wouldn't go near the theater myself on one of those nights, and I would hate to try to catch dialogue I didn't already know."

The students, she explains, "Sing Along with Bogey," saying all the dialogue-lines as he says them from the screen. Thus, in "Casablanca," when Bogart says to piano player Dooley Wilson, "Play it again, Tham," (Bogart had a pronounced lisp), everybody shouts the line right along with him. Similar echoes are heard for lines in "Beat the Devil," another Bogart film that enjoys tremendous popularity at The Brattle.

LENGTH: 540 WORDS

VOCABULARY

cult   religious devotion
indulgence   giving in, pampering
spasm   sudden effort or sudden motion
eminent   famous
revival   renewal of interest, bringing back to life
symbolic   representative of
bedlam   noisy confusion, a madhouse
dialogue   spoken lines as in a play or movie

4 · The Bogart Cult

SCORING:	Reading time: _____ Rate from chart: _____ W.P.M.

RETENTION	number right _____ × 4 equals _____ points
INFERENCES	number right _____ × 3 equals _____ points
COMPLETION	number right _____ × 4 equals _____ points
DEFINITIONS	number right _____ × 3 equals _____ points

(Total points: 100)   **total** _____ points

RETENTION   Based on the passage, which of the following statements are True (T), False (F), or Not answerable (N)?

1. _____ Harvard students study about Bogart in some of their classes.

2. _____ The Brattle was one of Humphrey Bogart's favorite meeting places.

3. _____ Bogart Weeks have been common in many parts of the country.

4. _____ Bogart made 19 films.

5. _____ One student saw "Beat the Devil" so often he began to lisp.

6. _____ Mrs. John W. Pratt runs a movie theater in Cambridge, Mass.

7. _____ The Bogart Boom is said to have begun even before Bogart died.

8. _____ Students tend to identify with the great star.

9. _____ Bogart made very few "lousy" pictures.

10. _____ Television network ratings are unaffected by a Bogart presentation.

INFERENCES

1. _____ Which of the following statements is probably most accurate?
   (a) Most "art theaters" have to institute Bogart Weeks to stay in business.
   (b) Humphrey Bogart has become a more popular actor today than he was when he was alive.
   (c) Critic Leslie A. Fiedler takes Bogart films very seriously.

2. _____ Which of the following statements is probably inaccurate?
   (a) Bogart fans do not see only the good films, but also the bad ones.
   (b) Mrs. Pratt will not go near her theater on a Bogart night.
   (c) Students usually listen carefully to catch every word of dialogue.

COMPLETION Choose the best answer for each question.

1. _____ In college towns Bogart films are very popular: (a) because Bogart lisps so amusingly. (b) when Bogart plays a defender of the law. (c) around examination time. (d) during vacations.

2. _____ Bogart says, "Play it again, Tham," in: (a) "Beat the Devil." (b) "Casablanca." (c) "The Treasure of the Sierra Madre." (d) "African Queen."

3. _____ The author of this piece: (a) did not like Bogey. (b) must have known him well. (c) had never met him. (d) is Dooley Wilson.

4. _____ The Bogart Revival actually began: (a) before Bogart died. (b) in 1957 at the Brattle Theater. (c) on the West Coast. (d) on the third anniversary of Bogart's death.

5. _____ Leslie A. Fiedler is: (a) from Harvard. (b) an actor who knew Bogart. (c) a producer. (d) an eminent critic.

6. _____ In his films Bogart always: (a) played a gangster. (b) relied only on himself. (c) looked around challengingly. (d) shouted his lines.

DEFINITIONS Choose the definition from Column B that best matches each word in Column A.

Column A	Column B
1. incredible _____	a. famous
2. possibility _____	b. valued
	c. depend
3. eminent _____	d. representative
4. indulgence _____	e. therefore
5. treasured _____	f. unbelievable
	g. great
6. rely _____	h. a giving-in
7. revival _____	i. chance
	j. failed
8. symbolic _____	k. suspicion
9. thus _____	l. instead
10. tremendous _____	m. renewal of interest
	n. lost

5 · Sacco and Vanzetti

WILLIAM O. DOUGLAS

Was the trial of Sacco and Vanzetti fair? Did the mood of the nation rather than the evidence convict these two men? A Supreme Court Justice reviews the facts and gives his own opinion.

Nicola Sacco and Bartolomeo Vanzetti were Italians. Sacco worked in a shoe factory; Vanzetti was a fish peddler. Each was industrious; and neither had a criminal record prior to his arrest in 1920 for the murder of two men in a payroll robbery at Braintree, Massachusetts. The accused were pacifists and anarchists, but not communists. During World War I, they had "dodged" the draft. In 1920, they were active in "radical" circles in Massachusetts and on the suspect list of the Department of Justice.

In 1920, the federal government undertook the wholesale arrest and deportation of aliens who were suspected of being in sympathy with communist Russia. Hysteria seized many communities having a large proportion of foreign labor. Boston was as badly infused with fear as any city. It was in this atmosphere that Sacco and Vanzetti were tried.

They were convicted on the flimsiest of evidence. They were denied a new trial after an offer of proof which went far toward exonerating them by seriously implicating other men. Many disinterested observers felt the trial was infected with passion, prejudice, and unfairness. It seemed that the hysteria of the day had seized even the courts. A reading of the record years later leaves the impression that Sacco and Vanzetti, charged with murder, were convicted because they were pacifists, draft dodgers, and radicals. Perhaps they were guilty; perhaps not. That is not the question. What will always lie heavily on

SACCO AND VANZETTI From *An Almanac of Liberty* by William O. Douglas, copyright 1954 by William O. Douglas. Reprinted by permission of Doubleday & Company, Inc.

the conscience of America is that they went to their death on August 23, 1927, as a result of a trial which in retrospect seems not to have been a fair one.

LENGTH: 280 WORDS

VOCABULARY

pacifist   one who opposes war and the military
anarchist   one who believes government should be completely abolished
communist   one who believes all goods should be held in common, the system
   of government based on this theory
infused   affected by, soaked in
exonerate   clear of blame
implicating   involving others
hysteria   madness, overexcitement
disinterested   not prejudiced, unbiased, objective
retrospect   looking back in time

5 · Sacco and Vanzetti

SCORING: Reading time: _____ Rate from chart: _____ W.P.M.

RETENTION	number right _____ × 4 equals _____ points
INFERENCES	number right _____ × 3 equals _____ points
COMPLETION	number right _____ × 4 equals _____ points
DEFINITIONS	number right _____ × 3 equals _____ points

(Total points: 100)   **total** _____ points

RETENTION   Based on the passage, which of the following statements are True (T), False (F), or Not answerable (N)?

1. _____ Sacco and Vanzetti were born near Braintree, Massachusetts.

2. _____ Their trial seems to have been a fair one.

3. _____ In the 1920's Massachusetts was totally Republican.

4. _____ The evidence which convicted Sacco and Vanzetti was not very strong.

5. _____ Communist Russia seemed to threaten the United States even in 1920.

6. _____ Sacco and Vanzetti both were aliens.

7. _____ Both Sacco and Vanzetti were demonstrably in sympathy with Russia.

8. _____ Sacco and Vanzetti wanted to fight in World War I but could not.

9. _____ The author of the passage is certain Sacco and Vanzetti were innocent.

10. _____ In 1920 the government arrested and deported suspicious aliens.

INFERENCES

1. _____ Which of the following statements is probably most accurate?
   (a) People in Massachusetts were much more excitable in 1920 than now.
   (b) Sacco and Vanzetti were probably convicted for being radicals, not murderers.
   (c) The courts of 1920 found it necessary to shake off the hysteria of the times.

2. _____ Which of the following statements is probably inaccurate?
   (a) Sacco and Vanzetti were actually charged with murder.
   (b) Only Sacco and Vanzetti's war record spoke well for them.
   (c) Pacifists and anarchists were considered political radicals in 1920.

COMPLETION   Choose the best answer for each question.

1. _____ The author says the question is not whether Sacco and Vanzetti were guilty, but whether: (a) aliens have the right to be radicals.   (b) they were executed after due process of law.   (c) they were Russian spies.   (d) their trial was fair.

2. _____ The atmosphere of Boston during the trial was: (a) not healthy for anyone from Braintree.   (b) particularly bad for aliens and suspected radicals.   (c) quite calm and proper.   (d) the same as that of any other New England city.

3. _____ Hysteria seized many communities: (a) like Boston.   (b) with a large proportion of foreign labor.   (c) with records of frequent payroll robberies.   (d) with shoe stores and shoe factories.

4. _____ In 1920 Sacco and Vanzetti: (a) were active in radical circles in Massachusetts.   (b) were anarchists, but definitely not radicals.   (c) were associated with the Department of Justice.   (d) had a spotty criminal record prior to their arrest.

5. _____ The author of the passage: (a) is a radical pacifist himself.   (b) is certain that Sacco is guilty and Vanzetti innocent.   (c) has no opinion on the affair.   (d) is trying to be fair and objective.

6. _____ Apparently, Sacco and Vanzetti were: (a) unhappy at being American citizens.   (b) fronts for a subversive organization.   (c) industrious and hard-working.   (d) lazy and not ambitious.

DEFINITIONS   Choose the definition from Column B that best matches each word in Column A.

Column A		Column B
1. flimsy	_____	a. charged
2. prior	_____	b. bored
		c. previous to
3. infected	_____	d. grab
4. proportion	_____	e. weak and thin
		f. unprejudiced
5. seize	_____	g. contaminated
6. prejudiced	_____	h. carrying from one place to another
7. deportation	_____	i. having decided ahead of time
		j. ignorance
8. disinterested	_____	k. dull
9. hysteria	_____	l. being sent out of the country
10. accused	_____	m. excitement
		n. certain amount, relationship

6 · Paris

ERNIE PYLE

*America's most famous war correspondent tells what it was like
to be among the first Americans to liberate Paris at the end of
World War II.*

The other correspondents wrote thoroughly and well about the fantastic eruption of mass joy when Paris was liberated. I could not add much to what they reported in those first days. Actually the thing floored most of us. I felt totally incapable of reporting it. It was so big I felt inadequate to touch it. I didn't know where to start or what to say. The words you put down about it sounded feeble to the point of asininity. I was not alone in this feeling, for I heard a dozen other correspondents say the same thing. A good many of us feel we have failed to present adequately what was the loveliest, brightest story of our time. It may be that this was because we have been so unused, for so long, to anything bright.

At any rate, from two in the afternoon until darkness around ten, we few Americans in Paris on that first day were kissed and hauled and mauled by friendly mobs until we hardly knew where we were. Everybody kissed us—little children, old women, grown-up men, beautiful girls. They jumped and squealed and pushed in a literal frenzy. They pinned bright little flags and badges all over you. Amateur cameramen took pictures. They tossed flowers and friendly tomatoes into your jeep. One little girl even threw a bottle of cider into ours.

As we drove along, gigantic masses of waving and screaming humanity clapped their hands as though applauding a performance in a theater. We in the jeeps smiled back until we had set grins on our faces. We waved until our arms gave out, and then we just waggled our fingers. We shook hands until our hands were bruised and scratched. If the jeep stopped we were swamped instantly.

Those who couldn't reach us threw kisses at us, and we threw kisses back.

They sang songs. They sang wonderful French songs we had never heard. And they sang "Tipperary" and "Madelon" and "Over There" and the "Marseillaise." French policemen saluted formally but smilingly as we passed. The French tanks that went in ahead of us pulled over to the sidewalks and were immediately swarmed over.

And then some weird cell in the inscrutable human makeup caused people to start wanting autographs. It began the first evening, and by the next day had grown to unbelievable proportions. Everybody wanted every soldier's autograph. They shoved notebooks and papers at us to sign. It was just like Hollywood. One woman, on the second day, had a stack of neat little white slips, at least three hundred of them, for people to sign.

The weather was marvelous for liberation day, and for the next day too. For two days previously it had been gloomy and raining. But on the big day the sky was pure blue, the sun was bright and warm—a perfect day for a perfect occasion.

That first afternoon only the main streets into the city were open and used, and they were packed with humanity. The side streets were roped off and deserted, because the Germans had feeble fortifications and some snipers there.

Paris seemed to have all the beautiful girls we always heard it had. The women have an art of getting themselves up fascinatingly. Their hair is done crazily, their clothes are worn imaginatively. They dress in riotous colors in this lovely warm season, and when the flag-draped holiday streets are packed with Parisians the color makes everything else in the world seem gray. As one soldier remarked, the biggest thrill in getting to Paris is to see people in bright summer clothes again.

Like any city, Paris has its quota of dirty and ugly people. But dirty and ugly people have emotions too, and Hank Gorrell got roundly kissed by one of the dirtiest and ugliest women I have ever seen. I must add that since he's a handsome creature he also got more than his share of embraces from the beautiful young things.

There was one funny little old woman, so short she couldn't reach up to kiss men in military vehicles, who appeared on the second day carrying a stepladder. Whenever a car stopped she would climb her stepladder and let the boys have it with hugs, laughs and kisses.

LENGTH: 820 WORDS

VOCABULARY

inscrutable not understandable, mysterious
fortifications forts, protected positions
snipers hidden riflemen

6 · Paris

SCORING: Reading time: _____ Rate from chart: _____ W.P.M.

RETENTION	number right _____ × 4 equals _____ points	
INFERENCES	number right _____ × 3 equals _____ points	
COMPLETION	number right _____ × 4 equals _____ points	
DEFINITIONS	number right _____ × 3 equals _____ points	

(Total points: 100)   **total** _____ points

RETENTION   Based on the passage, which of the following statements are True (T), False (F), or Not answerable (N)?

1. _____ For two days before the liberation, the weather had been rainy.

2. _____ The French army entered Paris before the American army.

3. _____ The author was just an ordinary soldier in an army vehicle.

4. _____ The Germans changed command before the Americans arrived.

5. _____ All the songs the Parisians sang were old and familiar.

6. _____ The Parisians were dressed in bright colors.

7. _____ None of the Parisian girls kissed Hank Gorrell.

8. _____ Some people wanted autographs because they thought the author was from Hollywood.

9. _____ The author was riding in a French tank.

10. _____ The author entered the city at two in the afternoon of the first day.

INFERENCES

1. _____ Which of the following statements is probably most accurate?
   (a) The Parisians wanted to impress the American conquering army.
   (b) The Parisians knew liberation meant the end of the war.
   (c) Paris had never seen a military show like this one.

2. _____ Which of the following statements is probably inaccurate?
   (a) Ernie Pyle and the others had not known quite what to expect that first day.
   (b) The German army had received a similar welcome when it marched into the city.
   (c) Many correspondents tried to describe scenes Pyle observed.

COMPLETION   Choose the best answer for each question.

1. _____ Ernie Pyle says that when the jeep stopped: (a) people pinned little badges and flags on the Americans.   (b) everyone asked for autographs.   (c) it was swamped instantly.   (d) the French police waved formally.

2. _____ The little old woman got a stepladder the second day: (a) because she wanted to see what the men looked like.   (b) because she was too short to get autographs.   (c) because the military vehicles were dangerous.   (d) so she could stand on it to kiss the soldiers.

3. _____ One soldier said the best thing about getting to Paris: (a) was listening to people singing familiar songs again.   (b) was seeing people in bright summer clothes again.   (c) was having fresh tomatoes and flowers.   (d) was getting kissed by so many people.

4. _____ Some weird cell in the inscrutable human makeup caused people to want: (a) to ride in the jeep.   (b) to wave flags and take pictures.   (c) to kiss the soldiers.   (d) soldiers' autographs.

5. _____ Of the following songs, the article does not mention: (a) "Tipperary."   (b) "G. I. Joe."   (c) "Madelon."   (d) "Marseillaise."

6. _____ Paris seemed to have: (a) many French tanks.   (b) dirty and ugly people.   (c) all the beautiful girls it was said to have.   (d) flag-draped holiday streets packed with people.

DEFINITIONS   Choose the definition from Column B that best matches each word in Column A.

Column A		Column B
1. riotous	_____	a. foolishness
2. feeble	_____	b. tired
		c. praise
3. gloomy	_____	d. weak
4. swarmed over	_____	e. breaking out
5. applaud	_____	f. melancholy
		g. roughly handled
6. mauled	_____	h. wild
7. asininity	_____	i. before
8. eruption	_____	j. indecent
9. fortifications	_____	k. defenses
		l. overran
10. previously	_____	m. hurt
		n. clumsy

7 · Jívaro Headshrinking

HECTOR ACEBES

> *After an overnight stay in the jungles of Ecuador with the Jívaro Indians, Hector Acebes sees what few white men have ever seen. The Jívaros, head-hunters of the Orinoco, permit him to witness the process of shrinking a human head.*

We started off again just before dawn the following morning and days later had reached the jivaría of Chacallema, a broad-shouldered man in his late forties who had the face of an amiable pig and a voice like the croak of a laryngitic frog.

He was not happy to see us since we were now in the heart of the warring territory and his jivaría might at any moment be the scene of a battle. He did not want to have his tactics encumbered by the presence of an inexperienced *Apache* (white man). Thus we were permitted to stay overnight, but the first thing the next morning were urged to get on with our journey.

However, since we were all exhausted, Severo used a handful of my cigars as bribes, and Chacallema grudgingly agreed to let us stay several days in the area.

One evening the ten young warriors who had come to Paltazara's jivaría the night before we left arrived at Chacallema's. They were in high spirits, laughing and shouting at each other and explaining their exploits to Chacallema, who listened and occasionally nodded solemnly but never took his eyes off me.

Finally the young fighters seemed for the first time to notice me; they looked first at Chacallema, next at Severo, then, and for a much longer time, at me. After that I heard the word "Apache" repeated several times with a rising

JÍVARO HEADSHRINKING   From *Orinoco Adventure* by Hector Acebes, copyright 1954 by Hector R. Acebes. Reprinted by permission of Doubleday & Company, Inc.

crescendo of voices. For a time Severo said nothing; then he began talking loud and fast and, I hoped, convincingly.

There was a moment of silence, but when the laughing began again I realized I was safe.

A few minutes later Severo lumbered over to the darkened corner where I was sitting and explained that the young warriors had been suspicious of me, questioning whether it was safe to allow me to witness the highly secret head-shrinking process they were about to begin. He had done his best to persuade them, he said, and, oddly enough, at the last moment Chacallema had surprised him by agreeing.

As a result, said Severo, I was about to see what few white men have, the shrinking of a human head.

A few minutes later one of the warriors went outside and returned with a small, leaf-wrapped package. He seated himself on the ground, unfolded the leaves, and took out a blood-spattered head from which the skull had been removed.

It was the head of Yauri, the young son of Zacary.

Later I learned that Paltazara's party had arrived at Zacary's jivaría just before sunup two days earlier. Since they knew the territory and we had circled, they traveled much faster than we could. In the brief battle which followed Yauri had been the only casualty. The attackers had hurriedly cut off his head at the base, disappearing with it into the jungle.

As soon as they felt safe from counterattack, they made a cut from the top of the head to the base of the skull, skillfully separating the skin from the bones. Next they discarded the skull and carefully sewed shut the slit as well as the lips and the eye apertures.

Then they wrapped the skin in leaves and started for Chacallema's.

That evening, while I watched, Yauri's head became a *tsantsa*. First, the skin and hair were immersed in a clay pot filled with river water and some herbs; after that the pot was placed on a hot fire and left until the water boiled. At the same time sand and pebbles were being heated in other pots.

When the skin was removed from the now greasy yellow water, it had already shrunk a little, and it was allowed to dry partially overnight. The following day hot sand was poured in, left for some minutes, then poured out. This process was repeated three times. Each time the features of the face were painstakingly pressed into shape with a smooth, hot stone, and each time the skin became smaller.

Next, half a dozen smooth, hot stones were dropped in, shaken around, and the features again pressed into shape. By this time the skin was no larger than a good-sized apple or orange. Finally a single large stone was placed inside, rolled around, removed, and the skin placed over the fire and smoked until it was black and hardened into shape.

The prized trophy was taken outside and hidden, after which the warriors lay down and immediately fell asleep.

I went out into the fresh night air and vomited.

LENGTH: 980 WORDS

VOCABULARY

jivaría   village of the Jívaro Indians
laryngitic   husky-voiced
tactics   plans, strategy
encumbered   burdened, weighted down
exploits   adventures, activities
crescendo   rise in pitch or loudness
lumbered   walked with heavy, ungraceful footsteps
tsantsa   Indian word for shrunken head

7 · Jívaro Headshrinking

SCORING:	Reading time: _____ Rate from chart: _____ W.P.M.		
RETENTION	number right _____ × 4 equals _____ points		
INFERENCES	number right _____ × 3 equals _____ points		
COMPLETION	number right _____ × 4 equals _____ points		
DEFINITIONS	number right _____ × 3 equals _____ points		
	(Total points: 100) **total** _____ points		

RETENTION Based on the passage, which of the following statements are True (T), False (F), or Not answerable (N)?

1. _____ Chacallema had a face like a frog and a voice like a pig.

2. _____ Cigars were used as bribes by Severo.

3. _____ Chacallema was the man who gave permission for the author to stay.

4. _____ The author was deeply moved at the sight of Yauri's head.

5. _____ Many white men have seen the head-shrinking process in Ecuador.

6. _____ Zacary is the name of the author's guide through the jivaría.

7. _____ Smooth, hot stones are the principal tool used to shape the *tsantsa*.

8. _____ The new government is beginning a crackdown on headshrinking in the jivarías.

9. _____ Yauri's head had been taken after a battle at another jivaría.

10. _____ The author's reaction and the warriors' reaction to the scene were really quite similar.

INFERENCES

1. _____ Which of the following statements is probably most accurate?
   (a) Head-hunting is practiced only at times of great religious significance.
   (b) Chacallema took a genuine liking to the author.
   (c) Chacallema's young fighters think of head-hunting as adventure.

2. _____ Which of the following statements is probably inaccurate?
   (a) Severo had been in the jungle a number of times before.
   (b) Chacallema had great skill in arranging for peace between jivarías.
   (c) The Indians have suspicions about white men.

COMPLETION Choose the best answer for each question.

1. _____ The young warriors separated the skull from the skin of the head: (a) to avoid arousing suspicion. (b) when they felt safe from counterattack. (c) on the edge of the jivaría. (d) so Chacallema would not have to do it for them.

2. _____ Yauri was the young son of: (a) Paltazara. (b) Chacallema. (c) Severo. (d) Zacary.

3. _____ After the head was completely shrunken: (a) it was the size of a tennis ball. (b) it was taken outside and hidden. (c) it was left to dry partially. (d) it was wrapped in damp leaves.

4. _____ The process of pouring hot sand in the *tsantsa*: (a) was repeated three times. (b) was performed by Chacallema. (c) was only a preliminary one. (d) was one of the last processes.

5. _____ Chacallema did not want the *Apache* in his jivaría: (a) because of the secret nature of the ritual. (b) after nightfall. (c) because the *Apache* would be no help in case of attack. (d) because other jivarías would be resentful of Chacallema.

6. _____ When Chacallema said the author and his guide could stay: (a) everyone had a cigar. (b) the young warriors drew back into a corner. (c) there was a rising crescendo of voices. (d) the author was surprised.

DEFINITIONS Choose the definition from Column B that best matches each word in Column A.

Column A		Column B
1. grudgingly	_____	a. adventures
2. encumbered	_____	b. carefully
		c. dipped
3. exploits	_____	d. unhappily
4. solemnly	_____	e. burdened
		f. throw away
5. persuade	_____	g. reluctantly
6. casualty	_____	h. disturbed
7. discard	_____	i. stupidity
		j. convince
8. aperture	_____	k. opening
9. immersed	_____	l. seriously
10. painstakingly	_____	m. fatality
		n. hardened

8 · Organic Reading in New Zealand

SYLVIA ASHTON-WARNER

> *Sylvia Ashton-Warner, in her book* Teacher, *tells how Maori children, Indian natives of New Zealand, learn to read by working out stories about their own lives. Their vocabulary is organic— that is, it grows out of what the children are doing and thinking and feeling.*

It's a sad thing to say of the vocabulary of any set reading books for an infant room that it must necessarily be a dead vocabulary. Yet I say it. For although the first quality of life is change, these vocabularies never change. Winter and summer, for brown race or white, through loud mood or quiet, the next group of words, related or not to the current temper of the room, inexorably moves into place for the day's study.

I tried to meet this division between the climate of a room and an imposed reading book by making another set of books from the immediate material, but all I did was to compose another dead vocabulary. For although they are closer to the Maori children than the books of the English upper-middle class, their vocabulary is static too, and it is not the answer to the question I have asked myself for years: What is the organic reading vocabulary?

At last I know: Primer children write their own books.

Early in the morning this infant room gets under way on organic writing, and it is this writing that I use in relative proportions as the reading for the day; for the children just off the Key Vocabulary with their stories of two words up to those who can toss off a page or so. In this way we have a set of graded brand-new stories every morning, each sprung from the circumstances of their own lives and illustrated unmatchably in the mind.

The new words they have asked for during the morning's writing, and which have been entered in the back of their books, they put up on the blackboard each morning. The words range from one or two to ten or so. They reconsider these words after the morning interval when they come in for the intake hour. They read them and spell them for ten minutes. I don't require that they should all be learned and remembered. If they are important enough they will stay, all right, whatever the length. Neither is it for me to sort out which is important. I never say, "Spell 'pictures.'" I say, "Perri, spell one of your words." Then I get the real word and the right spelling. In fact, this is a thing that I hand to them: hearing each other spell. Sometimes, however, we run over these words before dispersing for lunch, and what they have picked up from the morning's writing and reading of the organic work, in terms of numbers of new words and their varying difficulties is sometimes a surprise.

Each afternoon, however, all the words, whether known or not, are rubbed from the board and each morning the new ones go up. It's exciting for us all. No one ever knows what's coming. Wonderful words appear: helicopter, lady's place, cowboy, sore ear, fish and chips, dirt, Captain Marble, mumps, Superman and King of the Rocket Men. Words following intimately from day to day the classroom mood; echoing the *tangi*° in the district, recounting the pictures in the hall the night before or revealing the drama behind the closed doors of the pa.

This is the main reading of the day. They master their own story first, then tackle someone else's. There is opportunity to read out their own story and it is from this reading that discussions arise. And since every background of every story is well known to all, the inner illustration flashes very brightly and the discussions are seldom sluggish.

In reading one another's stories, reference is continually made to the writer for the identification of new words. This hardly hurts the writer. Unwittingly, energetically and independently of me, they widen the intake.

How much easier and more pleasant all this is when the stories are followed with a personal interest, and with the whole of the background seen alive in the mind. The facts of suitable printing, length of line and intelligibility run nowhere in the race with meaning. As for word recurrence, there occurs a far more natural one here than anything we could work out. A word recurs as long as they want it and is then dropped cold: a word is picked up like a new friend and dropped when it becomes boring. Which is what I mean when I say it is a live vocabulary. Things happen in it.

Since I take this original writing as a basis for reading, a strict watch is kept on grammar and punctuation. And as for the writing itself, the handwriting I mean, it has to be at least the best that they can do, to save their

°*tangi:* Maori funeral

32   SYLVIA ASHTON-WARNER

own faces, when changing books. Which brings one more subject into the vent of creativity: handwriting.

This organic reading, however, is not meant to stand alone: it is essentially a lead up and out to all the other reading, and as a child rises through the infant room, reaching further and further out to the inorganic and standard reading, there is a comfortable movement from the inner man outward, from the known to the unknown, from the organic to the inorganic. The thing is to keep it a gracious movement, for it is to the extent that the activity in an infant room is creative that the growth of mind is good.

LENGTH: 1,000 WORDS

VOCABULARY

inexorably   inevitably, without control
static   constant, without change
organic   involved with life
disperse   spread out, scatter
varying   changing
unwitting   without knowing it
vent   area, category

8 · Organic Reading in New Zealand

SCORING: Reading time: _____ Rate from chart: _____ W.P.M.

RETENTION	number right _____ × 4 equals _____ points
INFERENCES	number right _____ × 3 equals _____ points
COMPLETION	number right _____ × 4 equals _____ points
DEFINITIONS	number right _____ × 3 equals _____ points

(Total points: 100)   **total** _____ points

RETENTION   Based on the passage, which of the following statements are True (T), False (F), or Not answerable (N)?

1. _____ The author says the vocabulary of graded readers is dead.

2. _____ The Key Vocabulary was developed by the author.

3. _____ The author skillfully separates the important and unimportant words.

4. _____ No words were ever actually written on the blackboard.

5. _____ The classroom mood is rarely disturbed by the words.

6. _____ The children make up their own stories and then read them aloud.

7. _____ No one can be certain of the backgrounds of another child's story.

8. _____ The author approves of word recurrence in the children's stories.

9. _____ When a word becomes boring, the children eliminate it from the vocabulary.

10. _____ Organic reading is meant to be the single reading process for the children.

INFERENCES

1. _____ Which of the following statements is probably most accurate?
   (a) The organic reading process proceeds from the known to the unknown.
   (b) The organic reading process never permits children to learn about each other.
   (c) Organic reading does not affect the children's interest level.

2. _____ Which of the following statements is probably inaccurate?
   (a) The children seem to approve of the organic reading method.
   (b) The success of the method lies in its roots in the children, not the teacher.
   (c) The teacher assembled a good vocabulary for the Maoris.

Choose the best answer for each question.

1. _____ The secret of the organic reading vocabulary is in: (a) ignoring the needs of the children. (b) having the children write their own books and stories. (c) letting the children develop in whatever way they can. (d) not pushing the children into anything unfamiliar.

2. _____ Instead of saying "Spell 'pictures,'" the teacher says: (a) "Spell whatever you can." (b) "Spell the idea you have." (c) "Spell something familiar." (d) "Spell one of your words."

3. _____ Having new words put on the board is exciting because: (a) nobody knows what is coming. (b) nobody is likely to have the same words. (c) everybody is involved in the learning process. (d) the children learn to love words.

4. _____ The stories children tell each other are bright and meaningful because: (a) the children talk about themselves. (b) the background of each one is well known to the children. (c) the teacher does not create the stories for them. (d) nobody tells the children what to say.

5. _____ The teacher watches grammar and punctuation closely since: (a) she likes to teach the children these important skills. (b) the children usually do not like them. (c) all future work is based on the first stories they write. (d) they must be the best the children can do.

6. _____ Another vent of creativity is: (a) handwriting. (b) grammar. (c) changing books. (d) self-identification.

DEFINITIONS Choose the definition from Column B that best matches each word in Column A.

Column A		Column B
1. suitable	_____	a. spread out
2. recurrences	_____	b. try again
		c. slow
3. intimate	_____	d. proper
4. sluggish	_____	e. personal
5. disperse	_____	f. repetitions
		g. mood
6. interval	_____	h. happenings
7. varying	_____	i. rarely
		j. irritation
8. temper	_____	k. fortunate
9. proportion	_____	l. pause, recess
		m. relationship
10. seldom	_____	n. changing

9 · Life on Skid Row

MICHAEL HARRINGTON

*The scene is the Bowery in New York City. The story is of life
there with drunks and down-and-outers, the people with no hope.*

Perhaps the bitterest, most physical and obvious poverty that can be
seen in an American city exists in skid row among the alcoholics.

During 1951 and 1952, I lived on Chrystie Street, one block from the Bowery in New York. I was a member of the Catholic Worker group that had a
house there. Beds were given out on a "first come, first serve" basis; we had
a bread line in the early morning that provided coffee and rich brown bread,
and a soup line at noon; and hand-me-down clothes that readers of the newspaper sent in were distributed. Those of us who came to live at the Worker
house accepted a philosophy of voluntary poverty. We had no money and
received no pay. We shared the living conditions of the people whom we were
helping: alcoholics and the mentally ill. We did not participate in the living
hell of that area, for we were not tortured by alcoholism and we had chosen
our lot. But we were close, very close, to that world. We could see its horror
every day.

The Bowery today does not look as it did then. The elevated tracks of the
Third Avenue El have been dismantled, and in time skid row may be driven
to some other part of the city, particularly if the Third Avenue property values keep going up. Thus, some of the places I describe no longer exist. Yet
that is mere detail, for the essential world of these impressions is still very
much with us.

The Third Avenue El gave the Bowery a sort of surrealist character. A
dirty, hulking structure, it was as derelict as the men who acted out their

misery beneath it. Along both sides of the street were flophouses where a man could get a bed for a night. Each morning, someone had to go through, checking to see if anyone had died during the night. The liquor stores were there, of course, specializing in cheap wine.

The men and women of the Bowery usually drank wine, or sometimes beer or shots of cheap whisky. For those in the direst straits, obsessed by the need for alcohol, there was always canned heat. It is liquid alcohol, and it can be drunk after it is strained through a handkerchief or a stale piece of bread. It has the reputation of knocking a man out before doing serious damage to his nervous system. It is, I am told, tasteless, a method of reaching oblivion and not much else.

There were other businesses around. The secondhand stores were there so that the men could sell whatever they could scavenge or steal (sometimes from one another). They preyed on the misery of the place, and they were indispensable to it. There were a couple of restaurants where at night the derelicts fought to keep their eyes open so that they would not be thrown out; these were most depressing, garishly lighted places. And there were missions, called by some "Three Sixteens" because they so often had the scriptural quotation from John 3:16 over the door: "For God so loved the world that He sent His only begotten Son . . . ." In warm weather the "Sallies"—Salvation Army lassies and men—would be out on the avenue.

Over the whole place there hung the smell of urine. The men lived out of doors when they didn't have money for a flop. Sometimes, in the winter, they passed out in the snow or crawled into a doorway. In the summer the stench from some of the favorite haunts was all but overpowering.

There is an almost typical face of the Bowery, or so it seemed to me. The men are dirty, and often their faces are caked with blood after a particularly terrible drunk. They wake up without knowing that they were hurt. Their clothes are ragged, ill-fitting, incongruous. Their trousers stink of the streets and of dried urine. And the human look is usually weak and afraid of direct contact with someone else's eyes.

In the summer the Bowery is at its best, if one can use such a word to describe a place of incredible physical and moral desolation. The men sit together and talk, or lounge along the walk in groups. They are capable of stripping the clothes from another alcoholic when he is passed out, but their drinking is hardly ever solitary. If one of them is lucky enough to panhandle his way to a bottle, he will seek out friends and share his good fortune.

Indeed, this is primarily a male society. There are a few women here, but the overwhelming impression is of standing, waiting, drunken men. Some psychologists have argued that there may be a link between homosexual tendencies and alcoholism. At the Catholic Worker, we occasionally ran into trouble in the house on this score. Whatever the eventual conclusions from scientific research, the Bowery has a locker-room camaraderie among some of the most broken and hurt of the society.

LENGTH: 980 WORDS

VOCABULARY

alcoholic   one addicted to alcohol and liquor
surrealist   real to a degree beyond actuality, dreamlike
derelict   lost or abandoned
direst   most terrible, most severe
straits   conditions
oblivion   forgetfulness, nowhere
scavenge   search for food or valuables
garish   gaudy, having a dazzling glare
incongruous   unlikely, out of place
camaraderie   good fellowship

9 · Life on Skid Row

SCORING: Reading time: _____ Rate from chart: _____ W.P.M.

RETENTION	number right _____ × 4 equals _____ points	
INFERENCES	number right _____ × 3 equals _____ points	
COMPLETION	number right _____ × 4 equals _____ points	
DEFINITIONS	number right _____ × 3 equals _____ points	

(Total points: 100)   **total** _____ points

RETENTION   Based on the passage, which of the following statements are True (T), False (F), or Not answerable (N)?

1. _____ "Sallie" is the nickname for a woman living on skid row.

2. _____ Skid Row is the official name of the main street of the Bowery.

3. _____ Canned heat knocked a man out, it was said, before it could kill him.

4. _____ The Third Avenue El was dismantled because it made the Bowery worse.

5. _____ The author was a voluntary worker in the Bowery.

6. _____ There is a distinct honor among the derelicts of skid row.

7. _____ The society of derelicts is almost exclusively a male society.

8. _____ The author refuses to believe there is a link between alcoholism and homosexuality.

9. _____ Skid row alcoholics are not usually solitary drinkers.

10. _____ The most common drink on the Bowery is wine.

INFERENCES

1. _____ Which of the following statements is probably most accurate?
   (a) Most of the larger cities in America have a skid row of alcoholics.
   (b) New York City can take no official recognition of the Bowery.
   (c) The Third Avenue El was designed to provide safe travel through the Bowery.

2. _____ Which of the following statements is probably inaccurate?
   (a) Missions and charities make life easier for some of the derelicts.
   (b) The derelicts live on the Bowery because they would rather not work.
   (c) The Bowery exhibits some of the most awful poverty in America.

COMPLETION   Choose the best answer for each question.

1. _____ From what the author says about it, the Catholic Worker is probably: (a) a training house for doctors. (b) a charitable organization. (c) a hotel. (d) a store serving alcoholics.

2. _____ Property values on Third Avenue are: (a) stable. (b) stagnant.
(c) rising. (d) falling.

3. _____ The human look of the derelicts is usually: (a) desperate. (b) weak.
(c) arrogant. (d) pathetic.

4. _____ Derelicts usually treat a passed-out comrade by: (a) taking his belongings. (b) comforting him. (c) sending for help. (d) pretending
he is not there.

5. _____ The Catholic Worker house set up: (a) beds for the derelicts. (b)
bread and soup lines. (c) a program of rehabilitation. (d) chapels
for prayer.

6. _____ The volunteers did not share the Bowery's "living hell" because:
(a) they lived around the corner on Chrystie Street. (b) they had
taken voluntary vows of poverty. (c) they were not tortured by
alcoholism. (d) they knew they could get out any time they wanted
to.

DEFINITIONS   Choose the definition from Column B that best matches each
word in Column A.

Column A		Column B
1. obvious	_____	a. abandoned
2. dismantle	_____	b. necessary
		c. apparent
3. participate	_____	d. serious
4. derelict	_____	e. take a part
5. straits	_____	f. solitariness
6. oblivion	_____	g. complete forgetfulness
7. indispensable	_____	h. destruction
		i. stupidity
8. dire	_____	j. conditions
9. stench	_____	k. odor
10. desolation	_____	l. take part in
		m. humorous
		n. impoverishment

10 · Democratic American Capitalism

ERNEST L. KLEIN

> *What kind of democracy did Thomas Jefferson imagine for America? Did industrial growth make democracy impossible? Here are some views about the effects of industrialization on the American way of life.*

Capitalism developed in America without the heart-rending pattern of social upheaval which accompanied the introduction of machine production and the factory system in England.

There was no occasion in the new United States as there was in England for a rash of factories to spring up to meet an established and an expanding domestic and export demand. When the time for factories did come here, their construction displaced no major economic group.

The somewhat belated development of capitalism in the United States was at once more gradual and more democratic than in England. Because it was gradual there was no need for it to be violent. Because it was democratic it was more humane.

It is necessary for us to review briefly the development of democratic capitalism in America.

If we realize the distance we have come in the past under the aegis of democratic American capitalism we will have greater confidence in our ability to go the remaining distance under the same banner. With this renewed confidence we will lose much of that confused haste which has characterized some of our recent efforts toward reform.

When history is hurried, it is called "revolution." When it is confused, revolution—always bloody—is futile and destructive of far more good than it can create.

DEMOCRATIC AMERICAN CAPITALISM Reprinted from *How to Stay Rich* by Ernest L. Klein by permission of Farrar, Straus & Giroux, Inc. Copyright 1950 by Ernest Klein.

The colonists had been industrious but not industrial. Their household industries differed from the domestic industrial system of England. They were conducted by members of the family, but the products were intended for consumption by the producers. Colonial families wove cloth, for example, but they wove it for themselves and not for the market, as did the domestic industries of England.

The continuation of this condition was encouraged and as far as possible was enforced by England. The King would not permit industrial development in the colonies. Under the mercantile system colonies were maintained as sources of raw materials, as markets for the industries of the mother countries.

The outline of capitalistic industrialism was fairly well defined when our Constitution was adopted. During the interval between independence and the Constitution, the United States had remained primarily an agricultural country, and it continued as such until after the dawn of the nineteenth century.

Neither of the two great statesmen of the early years of the Republic envisioned the United States as an industrial nation. Hamilton, with his aristocratic concepts, desired the government to be controlled by the wellborn, the better educated and more propertied classes. He endorsed an expansion of American industry on the assumption that it would increase the hold of his favored class on the reins of government. But he had no desire to industrialize America in the British manner.

Jefferson feared industrialism. His ideal was a democracy of small agriculturists. He much preferred that manufactured goods be imported in exchange for agricultural exports than that his rural economy be fouled with urban industry. He was so completely antagonistic to industrialism that it is ironic to find that it was during his two administrations that modern industry really began to develop here.

In the early years of the nineteenth century the Napoleonic Wars were ravaging Europe. The United States found her normal access to her customary sources of manufactured goods in Europe was about destroyed by the French and British sea blockades. To enforce these blockades the belligerents resorted to molestation of American ships on the high seas. Jefferson adopted a non-intercourse policy by which he hoped to preserve American neutrality and keep this nation out of the European conflict. This policy was capped by the Embargo Acts, which restricted American ships to coastwise shipping, and our isolation was completed and perfected. Under this condition agricultural America had no alternative other than the rapid development of her own industry.

In a democracy such as ours the surest indication of the major or minor status of any group is found in the election returns and in the measure of courteous consideration accorded the group by practical politicians.

There had been three traditionally important political groups in the United

States. They were the planters of the South, the small farmers, into whose hands Jefferson would have committed the country, and the mercantile and financial group along the middle and northern seaboard. The Age of Jackson had dawned before industrial employees had acquired the necessary numbers to gain recognition for their political importance.

From Jefferson to Jackson and from Jackson until the Civil War the factory system of capitalistic production expanded. It dotted the middle and northern coastal states and had penetrated the western states, where it shared an expanding economy with agriculture.

This development, as we have noted, was not accompanied by the distressing characteristics of early capitalism in England. American conditions provided no ready supply of factory labor comparable to the displaced craftsmen and their families who were found in England after the industrial revolution, destitute, bewildered and compelled to accept whatever terms and conditions of labor the employer might offer. The early American factory hands were drawn from the small towns and farms. They did not enter the factories because there was no other place to go. The great west was open and beckoning. Unless the factory owners had offered conditions more attractive than those in England, all their potential employees would have turned their faces westward.

LENGTH: 940 WORDS

VOCABULARY

capitalism economic system in which means of production are privately owned
aegis protecting influence
mercantile referring to business or trade
nonintercourse policy arrangement in which America refused to deal with Europe
belligerent one making war, a warrior

10 · Democratic American Capitalism

SCORING: Reading time: _____ Rate from chart: _____ W.P.M.

RETENTION	number right ____ × 4 equals ____ points
INFERENCES	number right ____ × 3 equals ____ points
COMPLETION	number right ____ × 4 equals ____ points
DEFINITIONS	number right ____ × 3 equals ____ points

(Total points: 100)   **total** ____ points

RETENTION   Based on the passage, which of the following statements are True (T), False (F), or Not answerable (N)?

1. ____ The colonists had been industrial, but not industrious.

2. ____ Colonial families wove cloth for themselves, but not for the market.

3. ____ Even after the revolution America was primarily agricultural.

4. ____ Jefferson's ideal was a democracy of small merchants.

5. ____ Ironically, the industrialization of America began during Jefferson's administration.

6. ____ President Madison sided with Hamilton on the farm issue.

7. ____ The Napoleonic Wars had no effect on the growth of American industry.

8. ____ Hamilton was in favor of industry because industry favors aristocracy.

9. ____ The English King wanted America to remain rural and agricultural.

10. ____ The English attitude toward Napoleon was similar to Jefferson's.

INFERENCES

1. ____ Which of the following statements is probably most accurate?
   (a) American progress toward industrialism was like England's.
   (b) Work in factories in the early nineteenth century must have been pleasant.
   (c) The development of industry in America was less painful and desperate than it was in England.

2. ____ Which of the following statements is probably inaccurate?
   (a) The author does not favor every kind of social change discussed in his essay.
   (b) The author believes the American system is almost perfect.
   (c) The author feels there is little wrong with the industrial system.

Choose the best answer for each question.

1. ____ When history is hurried, it is called: (a) mercantile. (b) bloody. (c) undemocratic. (d) revolution.

2. ____ The King of England wanted America to remain: (a) neutral. (b) poor. (c) a source of raw materials. (d) an industrial colony.

3. ____ Jefferson feared: (a) industrialization. (b) Alexander Hamilton. (c) Napoleonic aggression. (d) the small farmer.

4. ____ Which of the following is not mentioned as a traditionally important political group in the United States? (a) southern planters (b) northern loggers (c) small farmers (d) merchants and financiers of the eastern seaboard

5. ____ Early American factory hands could have gone: (a) to English factories. (b) to the expanding West. (c) to the beckoning farms. (d) into the army.

6. ____ The English factory worker: (a) was bewildered and forced to accept bad conditions. (b) was an anti-Napoleonic democrat. (c) had many alternatives in his choice of work. (d) was favored by British political conditions.

DEFINITIONS Choose the definition from Column B that best matches each word in Column A.

Column A		Column B
1. potential	____	a. parties at war
2. beckoning	____	b. unfriendly
3. penetrated	____	c. demonstrated
4. antagonistic	____	d. swift
5. ironic	____	e. calling
6. status	____	f. spread through
7. belligerents	____	g. condition, rank
8. rapid	____	h. unexpected
9. courteous	____	i. possible
10. envisioned	____	j. a beginning
		k. counting
		l. foreseen
		m. unseen
		n. polite

11 · Peking Man

JANNETTE M. LUCAS

*Long before history was written, the Peking Man was using fire
and making tools. This brief account gives us a glimpse of the
life of a prehistoric man, as reconstructed from his bones, found
near Peking, China.*

That Peking Man used fire there can be no doubt. In the cave where
his bones are found there are strata of blackened particles mixed with sand
and clay of different colors. Chemistry has proved that the particles are carbon
and the colors of sand and clay are due to firing. It seems unlikely that Peking
Man had progressed enough to have learned the invaluable knack of *making*
fire. His was rather the ability to use what he found—no mean method of
improvement. From brands ignited by volcanoes or dropping from forest fires
this Man of Peking managed to build a smaller but more permanent blaze in
a confined space.

Why Peking Man carried fire into his cave we may never know. It was not
for warmth alone. The climate did not demand a permanent shelter from cold
and there is abundant evidence that he did not live in the cave all the time.
This is proved by the many other bones of animals which must have used the
cave at the same period since their bones are fossilized in the same manner.
Some of these bones are those of bears and hyenas. Now there is little chance
that such different animals as this advanced primate and those flesh-eaters
could have lived in the same cave at the same time—at any rate for long.
There must have been various changes of inhabitants. Possibly the fire helped
drive away the owners whom the Man of Peking had temporarily dispossessed.

PEKING MAN   From *Man's First Million Years* by Jannette M. Lucas, copyright 1941 by Harcourt,
Brace & World, Inc., and reprinted with their permission.

We can picture a little group of the tribe sitting uneasily in the flickering light of flames they keep alive. They face a darkness irregularly broken by the gleam of eyes. Constantly one or the other of the tribe changes position as the soft sound of bodies in motion and the padding of feet in the darkness raise the fear that a flanking movement is being attempted by some evicted dweller seeking to regain his stronghold.

Against such attack Peking Man had another resource which proved he had advanced a long way on the road to the present. He had weapons. They were poor weapons but they showed a definite attempt to improve on the weapons bestowed by nature—hands and teeth. These artificial weapons were antlers of deer and roughly chipped flints largely made from chert (a poor grade of waxy, transparent quartz). Rough as these were in manufacture they must have added bite to their maker's blow. They also enabled him to strike from much greater distance for, judging from his brain, Peking Man was right-handed and could throw stones with, probably, considerable accuracy.

The antlers may have been tools as well as weapons. They may have helped to pry the bits of flint from the edge of the larger pieces—"flaking" is the technical term. The many jaws of deer which are found are pretty certain to have been tools and not weapons. They were probably scrapers used in separating flesh from bones. Certain of the flints might have been used in the same way.

Enough game was present to keep many weapons and tools busy: a small deer, a forerunner of our present Axis deer; a musk-ox of a type now extinct; a buffalo likewise vanished from our world. A rhinoceros, only slightly different from his European kin, was among the spoils of chase. There were various small rodents—some rabbits now extinct and a shrew whose descendants still scurry around the home of their ancestors. An elephant is represented among the bones found in the cave and this was the same kind as those which browsed in the forests of Pleistocene India. The animal whose bones are present in the greatest numbers is the deer whose antlers and jaws served as tools. This was not like any of our living deer. It must have looked as if suffering from an attack of mumps for the jaws show a thickening at the curve which must have given their owner the appearance of a swollen face. From this peculiarity this deer has been named the Deer with Thick Bones.

Evidently venison was used for food and Peking Man had acquired a taste for roast marrow. All the bones are split and many of them are charred with fire. But it must not be imagined that this early man had advanced to a stage of cooked food. That is a very advanced stage of culture and Peking Man was far from any state of civilization. Most of his meals were in a natural state and the marrow must have been just a treat roasted at some campfire.

LENGTH: 790 WORDS

VOCABULARY

strata   different levels of silt and rock
firing   heating to a high temperature to preserve the finish
invaluable   of great worth
knack   technique, trick
dispossessed   having possessions or belongings taken away
flanking movement   an attack from the side
evicted   thrown out, sent away from
bestowed   given, granted

11 · Peking Man

SCORING: Reading time: _____ Rate from chart: _____ W.P.M.

RETENTION	number right _____	× 4 equals _____	points
INFERENCES	number right _____	× 3 equals _____	points
COMPLETION	number right _____	× 4 equals _____	points
DEFINITIONS	number right _____	× 3 equals _____	points

(Total points: 100)   **total** _____ points

RETENTION   Based on the passage, which of the following statements are True (T), False (F), or Not answerable (N)?

1. _____ Peking Man was the first man able to control fire.

2. _____ Evidence shows Peking Man lived in his cave almost all the time.

3. _____ Cooked food was for all practical purposes unknown to Peking Man.

4. _____ Jaws of deer were used as tools by Peking Man.

5. _____ Chert is a form of stone.

6. _____ Peking Man's climate did not demand a permanent shelter.

7. _____ Peking Man's caves had a succession of different inhabitants.

8. _____ Pieces of arm bone show Peking Man was right-handed.

9. _____ Peking Man hunted game that was much like the game of our time.

10. _____ Peking Man seems to have acquired a taste for roast marrow.

INFERENCES

1. _____ Which of the following statements is probably most accurate?
   (a) Most of what we know about Peking Man was discovered in the last twenty years.
   (b) Fossils and bones have told us all we know about Peking Man.
   (c) Peking Man is our most important right-handed ancestor.

2. _____ Which of the following statements is probably inaccurate?
   (a) Peking Man is one of the earliest prehistoric men who brought fire into their caves.
   (b) Peking Man seems to have depended very strongly for support on a variety of deer.
   (c) Peking Man had difficulty in making use of the materials he found around him.

COMPLETION Choose the best answer for each question.

1. _____ Peking Man's source of fire probably was: (a) chipped flint. (b) sticks rubbed together. (c) brands from forest fires. (d) trees struck by lightning.

2. _____ A variety of bone representing an animal that probably lived in Peking Man's cave is that of the: (a) Axis deer. (b) musk-ox. (c) bear. (d) rabbit.

3. _____ An animal not mentioned by the passage is the: (a) shrew. (b) rabbit. (c) hyena. (d) mouse.

4. _____ Evidence does not show that the bones of deer were used for: (a) food. (b) weapons. (c) tools. (d) ornaments.

5. _____ Of the following animals, the species that definitely lived in Pleistocene India is the: (a) tiger. (b) rabbit. (c) elephant. (d) musk-ox.

6. _____ Peking Man was: (a) far from any state of civilization. (b) a roughly civilized human being. (c) actually surprisingly civilized for a cave dweller. (d) of a highly advanced civilization.

DEFINITIONS Choose the definition from Column B that best matches each word in Column A.

Column A		Column B
1. charred	_____	a. that which can be seen through
2. venison	_____	b. man-made
		c. a gift
3. peculiarity	_____	d. burnt
4. enable	_____	e. strangeness
5. transparent	_____	f. a way of preventing
		g. meat of the deer
6. artificial	_____	h. set on fire
7. abundant	_____	i. permit
		j. worthless
8. fossilized	_____	k. hardened to stone
9. invaluable	_____	l. very precious
		m. skull
10. ignited	_____	n. in great quantity

12 · Matthew Hopkins, Witch Finder General

RALPH AND ADELIN LINTON

> *In seventeenth-century England and America, witches were thought to be everywhere, and men like Matthew Hopkins were hired to seek them out. Often the witch was a person no one liked or one who had property that could be divided among greedy relatives. No one accused of being a witch ever could prove his innocence.*

In the superstition-ridden Middle Ages, it was understandable that there should be dread of witches. The witch huntings of the seventeenth century, however, had a different character. They had a religious excuse: the warnings of the Bible and the sanction of the church, but there was also a political and emotional character to the persecutions which was not found in the earlier day. At times of political tension or unrest, injustice and hysteria are likely to be present. And every bigot and zealous informer makes use of this atmosphere for his own purposes. We cannot be too scornful of the excesses of former times, for at times of fear and chaos we do our own witch hunting.

People were still ruled by superstition in the seventeenth century, but there were many who saw in witch persecutions an opportunity to advance themselves by battening on the public fantasies. Chief among these was a lawyer named Matthew Hopkins, who set himself up as "Witch Finder General," a self-conferred title. Professing to be an expert in the discovery of witches, he traveled through the counties of southern England, exacting a substantial sum from each town which he helped to rid of its witches. He claimed to be in possession of a notebook, which he had tricked the Devil into giving him, containing the names of many witches who had signed the Devil's pact. He also managed to standardize the various tests which were used to determine guilt at witch trials. Hopkins' tests continued to be used long after the outraged citizenry turned on him at last and gave him a taste of his own medicine.

In one of the Hopkins' tests the victim was taken to an old barn and forced to strip naked and sit cross-legged on a stool or table placed in the center of the building. Hopkins and his assistants would then go over the prisoner with long pins made especially "to find the mark." This mark was supposed to be the spot where the Devil had put his seal. It was insensible to all feeling and did not bleed. To find such a spot on the body was definite proof that the person was in league with the Devil.

As soon as the victims understood the meaning of this torture, they would of course cry out each time the pin went in. Hopkins took care of this by inventing a pricking instrument, made on the telescopic principle, which could be manipulated so that sometimes the pin went in and sometimes it did not. If the terrified victim screamed when the pin did not touch her body, it was almost as great a count against her as if she had not screamed when it did. It saved the victim some pain but increased the tension of the examination.

The mark having been found, as it usually was, it was believed that an imp, or succubus, would come to suck at it. A guard was assigned to watch through an aperture for the imp to come. The guard seldom failed to report such a phenomenon, since as soon as it was reported he could doze off comfortably.

Another of Hopkins' tests consisted of "swimming the witch." The idea was that water, being a pure element, will reject an evil, unbaptized person, so that witches do not sink. In this ordeal by water, the victim was taken to a pond. Here her two thumbs were tied with cord to her two great toes. She was then placed in a sheet which was loosely tied by the four corners by a cord with a long end. The bundle was placed at the edge of the pond. Someone at the other side of the pond would pull the bundle across by the cord. If it floated, as it usually did, being full of air as well as witch, the verdict was "guilty." If by some chance the bundle became soggy and sank before it reached the opposite edge of the pond but the witch failed to drown, her innocence was not necessarily proved. She was usually tortured into a confession. Few ever escaped the ban of Hopkins once he had made his charges.

At the end of three years of this cruelty, the people revolted against it. An obscure clergyman named Gaule, living in the town of Stoughton, in Huntingdon, began preaching and writing against the cruelties of witch hunting in general and Hopkins in particular. This was a courageous thing to do, for Hopkins was almost sure to bring charges of witchcraft against anyone who opposed him—a practice which was one of the secrets of his success. When Hopkins attempted to convince the dignitaries of Stoughton that they were in dire need of his services, these functionaries, to their everlasting credit, turned a cold shoulder and refused to let him and his assistants come to their town.

This broke Hopkins' power. Reluctant to lose such a profitable business, he began to advertise with leaflets distributed to one town after another. But the tide had turned. Hopkins was seized, accused of wizardry, and subjected to his own "ordeal by water." He failed to sink and was hanged on the gallows in 1677.

LENGTH: 910 WORDS

VOCABULARY

sanction approval
bigot a prejudiced person
zealous fanatical, over-excited
chaos disorder, uncertainty
battening on attaching to
succubus an evil spirit
aperture an opening, hole
phenomenon occurrence, event

12 · Matthew Hopkins, Witch Finder General

SCORING: Reading time: _____ Rate from chart: _____ W.P.M.

RETENTION	number right ____ × 4 equals ____ points	
INFERENCES	number right ____ × 3 equals ____ points	
COMPLETION	number right ____ × 4 equals ____ points	
DEFINITIONS	number right ____ × 3 equals ____ points	

(Total points: 100) **total** ____ points

RETENTION   Based on the passage, which of the following statements are True (T), False (F), or Not answerable (N)?

1. ____ Matthew Hopkins was a military man before he was a witch finder.

2. ____ People were still ruled by superstition in the seventeenth century.

3. ____ The people of New England named Hopkins "Witch Finder General."

4. ____ Hopkins' tests for witchcraft fell into disuse after he died.

5. ____ Hopkins himself did not believe in witches.

6. ____ Hopkins operated as a witch finder for three years.

7. ____ The "mark" was the point where the Devil entered the body.

8. ____ When tests failed, suspected witches were usually freed.

9. ____ Most of those suspected of being witches were women.

10. ____ Stoughton was a minister with enough courage to oppose Hopkins.

INFERENCES

1. ____ Which of the following statements is probably most accurate?
    (a) Hopkins believed too strongly in his Puritan religion.
    (b) People probably wanted to find witches even when there was no evidence.
    (c) Hopkins' basic holiness and love of man probably drove him to do what he did.

2. ____ Which of the following statements is probably inaccurate?
    (a) People of the seventeenth century did not believe as strongly in the Devil as we do.
    (b) Superstition in combination with religion can make people act in non-religious ways.
    (c) The officials gave Hopkins their sanction to test citizens for witchcraft.

COMPLETION   Choose the best answer for each question.

1. ____ People sometimes floated in the test called "swimming the witch" because: (a) they really were witches. (b) the bundle grew soggy. (c) the bundle contained air. (d) Hopkins tampered with the bundle.

2. ____ Witches were considered to be: (a) improperly baptized. (b) related to the succubus. (c) unbaptized. (d) imps.

3. ____ Hopkins made a practice of selling his services to: (a) towns. (b) counties. (c) local churches. (d) wealthy individuals.

4. ____ Hopkins invented a pricking instrument that: (a) was useful in torture. (b) sometimes pricked and sometimes did not. (c) could double as a telescope on dark nights. (d) was effective only in barns.

5. ____ The passage says that belief in witchcraft was: (a) necessary in the seventeenth century. (b) unpleasant but natural, given the religious beliefs of the day. (c) really a public fantasy. (d) localized and rare.

6. ____ Hopkins claimed to have a book belonging to the Devil in which: (a) all devilish devices were listed. (b) witches who had signed with the Devil were listed. (c) all the prescribed tests for witchcraft were given. (d) the Devil agreed to give up some of his power.

DEFINITIONS   Choose the definition from Column B that best matches each word in Column A.

Column A		Column B
1. persecution	____	a. incident, occurrence
2. zealous	____	b. decision
		c. genuinely exciting
3. pact	____	d. without feeling
4. insensible	____	e. oppression
		f. unknown
5. manipulated	____	g. used, handled
6. verdict	____	h. bargain
		i. phantom
7. phenomenon	____	j. fanatical
8. obscure	____	k. envious
		l. emerge
9. dignitary	____	m. terrible
10. dire	____	n. worthy man

13 · The Damned Human Race

MARK TWAIN

America's greatest humorist had no great love for the human race. This excerpt, published long after his death, shows Twain at his most sarcastic in his criticism of his fellow humans.

Cats are loose in their morals, but not consciously so. Man, in his descent from the cat, has brought the cat's looseness with him but has left the unconsciousness behind—the saving grace which excuses the cat. The cat is innocent, man is not.

Indecency, vulgarity, obscenity—these are strictly confined to man; he invented them. Among the higher animals there is no trace of them. They hide nothing; they are not ashamed. Man, with his soiled mind, covers himself. He will not even enter a drawing room with his breast and back naked, so alive are he and his mates to indecent suggestion. Man is "The Animal that Laughs." But so does the monkey, as Mr. Darwin pointed out; and so does the Australian bird that is called the laughing jackass. No—Man is the Animal that Blushes. He is the only one that does it—or has occasion to.

At the head of this article we see how "three monks were burnt to death" a few days ago, and a prior "put to death with atrocious cruelty." Do we inquire into the details? No; or we should find out that the prior was subjected to unprintable mutilations. Man—when he is a North American Indian—gouges out his prisoner's eyes; when he is King John, with a nephew to render untroublesome, he uses a red-hot iron; when he is a religious zealot dealing with heretics in the Middle Ages, he skins his captive alive and scatters salt on his back; in the first Richard's time he shuts up a multitude of Jew families in a

THE DAMNED HUMAN RACE   From *Letters from the Earth* by Mark Twain, edited by Bernard De Voto. Copyright © 1962 by The Mark Twain Co. Reprinted by permission of Harper & Row, Publishers.

Is man cruel by nature? Why do we have laws?
Compare to animals. What would happen if we didn't?

#3
Cruelty

tower and sets fire to it; in Columbus' time he captures a family of Spanish Jews and—but *that* is not printable; in our day in England a man is fined ten shillings for beating his mother nearly to death with a chair, and another man is fined forty shillings for having four pheasant eggs in his possession without being able to satisfactorily explain how he got them. Of all the animals, man is the only one that is cruel. He is the only one that inflicts pain for the pleasure of doing it. It is a trait that is not known to the higher animals. The cat plays with the frightened mouse; but she has this excuse, that she does not know that the mouse is suffering. The cat is moderate—unhumanly moderate: she only scares the mouse, she does not hurt it; she doesn't dig out its eyes, or tear off its skin, or drive splinters under its nails—man-fashion; when she is done playing with it she makes a sudden meal of it and puts it out of its trouble. Man is the Cruel Animal. He is alone in that distinction.

#3
destroys his own kind
Why do we suppose we go to war? Are there real reasons?

The higher animals engage in individual fights, but never in organized masses. Man is the only animal that deals in that atrocity of atrocities, War. He is the only one that gathers his brethren about him and goes forth in cold blood and with calm pulse to exterminate his kind. He is the only animal that for sordid wages will march out, as the Hessians did in our Revolution, and as the boyish Prince Napoleon did in the Zulu war, and help to slaughter strangers of his own species who have done him no harm and with whom he has no quarrel.

Man is the only animal that robs his helpless fellow of his country—takes possession of it and drives him out of it or destroys him. Man has done this in all the ages. There is not an acre of ground on the globe that is in possession of its rightful owner, or that has not been taken away from owner after owner, cycle after cycle, by force and bloodshed.

Read
means what? Could we exist not as slaves? What would life be like? Worth the trouble?

Man is the only Slave. And he is the only animal who enslaves. He has always been a slave in one form or another, and has always held other slaves in bondage under him in one way or another. In our day he is always some man's slave for wages, and does that man's work; and this slave has other slaves under him for minor wages, and they do *his* work. The higher animals are the only ones who exclusively do their own work and provide their own living.

#4 a slave & enslaves

#5
Patriot
Does Patriotism serve any positive function? How does Twain see it?

Man is the only Patriot. He sets himself apart in his own country, under his own flag, and sneers at the other nations, and keeps multitudinous uniformed assassins on hand at heavy expense to grab slices of other people's countries, and keep *them* from grabbing slices of *his*. And in the intervals between campaigns he washes the blood off his hands and works for "the universal brotherhood of man"—with his mouth.

Man is the Religious Animal. He is the only Religious Animal. He is the only animal that has the True Religion—several of them. He is the only animal that loves his neighbor as himself, and cuts his throat if his theology isn't

#6 What good does religion do?
What does Twain say about religion?
Which pt. do you agree c? Why?

62   MARK TWAIN

straight. He has made a graveyard of the globe in trying his honest best to smooth his brother's path to happiness and heaven. He was at it in the time of the Caesars, he was at it in Mahomet's time, he was at it in the time of the Inquisition, he was at it in France a couple of centuries, he was at it in England in Mary's day, he has been at it ever since he first saw the light, he is at it today in Crete—as per the telegrams quoted above—he will be at it somewhere else tomorrow. The higher animals have no religion. And we are told that they are going to be left out, in the Hereafter. I wonder why? It seems questionable taste.

Man is the Reasoning Animal. Such is the claim. I think it is open to dispute. Indeed, my experiments have proven to me that he is the Unreasoning Animal. Note his history, as sketched above. It seems plain to me that whatever he is he is *not* a reasoning animal. His record is the fantastic record of a maniac. I consider that the strongest count against his intelligence is the fact that with that record back of him he blandly sets himself up as the head animal of the lot: whereas by his own standards he is the bottom one.

In truth, man is incurably foolish. Simple things which the other animals easily learn, he is incapable of learning. Among my experiments was this. In an hour I taught a cat and a dog to be friends. I put them in a cage. In another hour I taught them to be friends with a rabbit. In the course of two days I was able to add a fox, a goose, a squirrel and some doves. Finally a monkey. They lived together in peace; even affectionately.

Next, in another cage I confined an Irish Catholic from Tipperary, and as soon as he seemed tame I added a Scotch Presbyterian from Aberdeen. Next a Turk from Constantinople; a Greek Christian from Crete; an Armenian; a Methodist from the wilds of Arkansas; a Buddhist from China; a Brahman from Benares. Finally, a Salvation Army Colonel from Wapping. Then I stayed away two whole days. When I came back to note results, the cage of Higher Animals was all right, but in the other there was but a chaos of gory odds and ends of turbans and fezzes and plaids and bones and flesh—not a specimen left alive. These Reasoning Animals had disagreed on a theological detail and carried the matter to a Higher Court.

LENGTH: 1,220 WORDS

VOCABULARY

indecency   vulgarity, grossness, impropriety
obscenity   lewdness, indecency
atrocious   outrageous, vile
mutilations   disfigurings, maimings
gouge   tear out, scoop out
zealot   one who is over-excited, a fanatic
heretics   those who do not believe in orthodox teachings
shillings   British coins worth 12½ cents
Hessians   German soldiers of fortune hired by the British
Zulu   member of warlike central African tribe
assassins   killers
theology   the study of religion and religious ideas
Caesars   the rulers of Rome around the time of Christ
Mahomet's time   the 6th century
inquisition   religious trials held by the Catholic church
England in Mary's day   from 1518 to 1558
Crete   small island in the Mediterranean Sea

13 · The Damned Human Race

SCORING: Reading time: _____   Rate from chart: _____ W.P.M.

RETENTION	number right _____ × 4 equals _____ points	
INFERENCES	number right _____ × 3 equals _____ points	
COMPLETION	number right _____ × 4 equals _____ points	
DEFINITIONS	number right _____ × 3 equals _____ points	

(Total points: 100)   **total** _____ points

RETENTION   Based on the passage, which of the following statements are True (T), False (F), or Not answerable (N)?

1. _____ By man's own standards he should be the lowest animal, not the highest.

2. _____ According to Mark Twain, man is the only animal that laughs.

3. _____ Napoleon's sortie against the North American Indians was thoughtlessly cruel.

4. _____ Mark Twain firmly believes in Darwin's Theory of Evolution.

5. _____ By comparison with man, the cat is innocent when it taunts a mouse.

6. _____ A man who beat his mother was not fined.

7. _____ According to Twain, the phrase "Higher Animals" includes man.

8. _____ The Hessians marched for wages.

9. _____ Twain's experiment with animals and men showed that animals are more peaceful.

10. _____ The Salvation Army Colonel was from Philadelphia.

INFERENCES

1. _____ Which of the following statements is probably most accurate?
   (a) Twain's experiment was a fictitious one.
   (b) The experiment was conducted impartially in England.
   (c) The experiment was devised by Twain or by one of his friends.

2. _____ Which of the following statements is probably inaccurate?
   (a) Man is more animalistic than animals themselves.
   (b) Man's pride disappears when he compares himself with the animals.
   (c) Twain's view of man as compared with animals is prejudiced.

COMPLETION   Choose the best answer for each question.

1. ____ The passage does not contain the remark that man is the: (a) Reasoning Animal. (b) Unreasoning Animal. (c) Possessive Animal. (d) Animal that Laughs.

2. ____ In an hour Mark Twain: (a) proved man is the Religious Animal. (b) taught a cat and a dog to be friends. (c) confined an Irish Catholic in Tipperary. (d) showed that man is incurably foolish.

3. ____ Man has the fantastic record of a: (a) slave. (b) monkey. (c) Caesar. (d) maniac.

4. ____ There is not an acre of ground on the globe: (a) that is in the possession of its rightful owner. (b) that is not worked by a slave of slaves. (c) that is peaceful for more than a generation. (d) that does not have its true religion.

5. ____ The Higher Animals have no religion, and Twain wonders why they: (a) do not blush when they are embarrassed. (b) are going to be left out of heaven. (c) constantly fight among each other. (d) think of themselves as superior to the monkey.

6. ____ Man will not walk into a drawing room with his back and chest naked: (a) because he is so alive to indecent suggestion. (b) because only animals hide nothing. (c) because he is "The Animal that Laughs." (d) because he is the only animal that has cause to blush.

DEFINITIONS   Choose the definition from Column B that best matches each word in Column A.

Column A		Column B
1. indecent	____	a. slowly
2. trait	____	b. limited
3. multitude	____	c. expensive
4. confined to	____	d. objectionable
5. bondage	____	e. not extreme
6. moderate	____	f. great number
7. blandly	____	g. slavery
8. incapable	____	h. chronic
9. fantastic	____	i. weird
10. incurable	____	j. subtly
		k. mildly
		l. attempted
		m. unable
		n. characteristic

14 · Beggars and Heroes in the Ghetto

EMMANUEL RINGELBLUM

> *This is an excerpt from a diary found after the Jewish Ghetto in
> Warsaw was completely wiped out by German troops. The author
> died fighting the Germans, but his diary survived to tell what it
> was like to live in terror and beggary.*

There have been cases of Germans dropping bread out of their cars
for beggars as they ride through the Ghetto, or stopping, calling a beggar boy
over, and giving him a loaf. But these are isolated instances of humanity. For
the most part, the beggar children stand near the hospital on Ogrodowa
Street, near the telephone building on Leszno Street, and wait for someone
to have pity and throw them a piece of bread.

A special class of beggars consists of those who beg after nine o'clock at
night. You stand at your window, and suddenly see new faces, beggars you
haven't seen all day. They walk out right into the middle of the street, begging for bread. Most of them are children. In the surrounding silence of night,
the cries of the hungry beggar children are terribly insistent, and, however
hard your heart, eventually you have to throw a piece of bread down to them
—or else leave the house. These beggars are completely unconcerned about
curfews, and you can hear their voices late at night, at eleven and even at
twelve. They are afraid of nothing and of no one. There has been no case of
the night patrol shooting at these beggars, although they move around the
streets after curfew without passes. It's a common thing for beggar children
like these to die on the sidewalk at night. I was told about one such horrible
scene that took place in front of 24 Muranowska Street where a six-year-old

1. State of mind
2 why no resistance
3 altered?

beggar boy lay gasping all night, too weak to roll over to the piece of bread that had been thrown down to him from the balcony.

Lately, whole families have been out begging, sometimes even well-dressed people. Musicians and singers take their children along with them to "work." The father plays an instrument, while his child or children put out their caps for a coin. There's one singer who stands outside with his young wife, who is dressed with real elegance. As he sings his wife collects alms. Near by, stands a cradle with a small child in it—the parents have no one to leave the child with. The child is being trained to be a beggar, literally in the cradle. Generally speaking, family begging has become the mode. Some parents do it because children attract attention, others because they can't leave the children alone at home. Incidentally, the beggars' practice of falling to the ground and lying there has stopped. Those who lay down because they were really too weak to stand have all died out; the simulators have apparently concluded that it's not a very profitable tactic. Some of the beggars have taken to singing in the courtyards. There are a number of songs, particularly popular being one about Bialystok.

They use horse-drawn wagons, pull handcarts, rubber-wheeled carriages, litters, etc. The horse-drawn wagons are loaded with bodies. The coffins of the poor are piled on top of one another. In some of the houses in the poorer section (e.g., in Wolynska Street), whole families die out. There are cases where the body of the last of the family to die lies untended for days until neighbors smell the odor of death. One mother hid her dead child so as to be able to enjoy his ration card as long as possible. There have been cases in some of the houses on Wolynska Street of rats gnawing at corpses that have been allowed to lie untended for several days. Ten houses are empty in 7 Wolynska Street. All the residents have died out. In general, this death of entire families in the course of one or two days is a very common occurrence. There has been an enormous increase in the number of orphans, since the grown-ups die first, particularly the men. [But] there are practically no children under two, simply because there's no milk at all, either for the infants or the nursing mothers. If things continue this way, the "Jewish question" will soon be resolved very quickly in Warsaw.

I heard about a social worker connected with YYGA [Jewish Social Self-Aid Society] who fasts once a week, and contributes his rations to the poor.

A very interesting question is that of the passivity of the Jewish masses, who expire with no more than a slight sigh. Why are they all so quiet? Why does the father die, and the mother, and each of the children, without a single protest? Why haven't we done the things we threatened the world with a year ago—robbery and theft—those things whose threat forced the House Committees to buy up food for the poorer tenants? There are a great many possible answers to these questions. One is that the [German] occupation forces have so terrorized the Jewish populace that people are afraid to raise their heads. The fear that mass reprisals would be the reply to any outbreak from the hungry masses has forced the more sensitive elements into a passivity designed not to provoke any commotion in the Ghetto. Still another reason is that the more active element among the poor has settled down one way or another. Smuggling offers a means of livelihood for thousands of porters, who, beside the portage fee, take another 10 zlotys per load smuggled in to keep quiet. The shops and the orders from the German jobbers give employment to a large number of other factory workers and artisans. Some enterprising workers have turned to street peddling (bread, for instance, on which they make 25 groschen a kilo). The result is that it is the inert, unenterprising poor people who are dying in silence. Another factor in keeping the populace in check is the Jewish police who have learned how to beat up people, how to "keep order," how to send folk to work camps. Significantly, it is the refugees from the provinces who are dying of hunger, those who feel lost, helpless, in these alien surroundings. Their protest is converted into a beggarly cry of woe, an energetic demand from the passerby for alms, a protest of sorts to their own *landsmannshaften*, a demand for a piece of bread—from a Jewish institution or House Committee. However, the aid given them is not sufficient, especially when whole neighborhoods consist of nothing but poor people. And, after a few cries, they turn quiet, resign themselves to their fate and wait—in fact ask—for Death, the Resolver of all evil, to hurry. I had a talk with one refugee who had been hungry for a long time. All his thoughts were occupied with food. Everywhere he went, he dreamed of nothing but bread. He stopped at every store window where food was on display. But at the same time, he had grown apathetic, nothing mattered to him any more. It was hard for him to bring himself to wash, and he did so only because of his childhood training. Perhaps this physical passiveness, a direct result of hunger, is a factor in the silent, unprotesting wasting away of the Jewish populace.

A few days ago, about the 25th or 26th of August, Engineer Luft was shot to death. His death was very characteristic of a certain kind of Jew. Luft had been an Austrian officer, and had been decorated with the Iron Cross. He was proud of his Jewishness. An argument arose between Luft and a uniformed Ukrainian over a ricksha. The Ukrainian ordered Luft to show his papers. Luft had a pass but categorically refused to show it. The Ukrainian prodded him with his bayonet; Luft still refused. Finally, the Ukrainian took out his revolver and shot Luft dead.

LENGTH: 1,230 WORDS

VOCABULARY

curfews   regulations requiring people to be at home during certain hours
simulators   those who make believe, pretenders
Bialystok   city in Poland
passivity   lack of fight, quietness
expire   die
reprisals   acts of punishment and revenge
zlotys   Polish coins worth about 25 cents
artisan   skilled worker
inert   not active, passive
alms   money, a gift for the poor
landsmannshaften   organizations of deported Germans
apathetic   unconcerned, indifferent
ricksha   a carriage drawn by hand
categorically   absolutely

14 · Beggars and Heroes in the Ghetto

SCORING:	Reading time: _____ Rate from chart: _____ W.P.M.		
RETENTION	number right _____	× 2 equals _____	points
INFERENCES	number right _____	× 2 equals _____	points
COMPLETION	number right _____	× 4 equals _____	points
DEFINITIONS	number right _____	× 2 equals _____	points
	(Total points: 100) **total** _____ points		

RETENTION   Based on the passage, which of the following statements are True (T), False (F), or Not answerable (N)?

1. _____ A principal occupation of ghetto life was smuggling.

2. _____ Generally speaking, family begging was uncommon.

3. _____ Most of the beggar boys were not Poles by nationality.

4. _____ Germans gave alms to the beggars.

5. _____ Whole families often died, but not on Wolynska Street.

6. _____ One mother killed her child in order to use his ration card.

7. _____ The horse-drawn wagons were loaded with beggars.

8. _____ Ten houses were empty on 7 Wolynska Street.

9. _____ The mothers usually died first in the family.

10. _____ A zloty is a Polish measure of weight.

11. _____ Jewish police helped the Germans keep order in the Ghetto.

12. _____ The unenterprising poor are not usually the ones to die first.

13. _____ All the people in the Ghetto were from Warsaw.

14. _____ Engineer Luft had been an Australian officer.

15. _____ There were whole neighborhoods consisting of poor people.

16. _____ The Germans engaged in the principal occupation, smuggling.

17. _____ A House Committee was a Jewish organization.

18. _____ Hunger forced many Jews to accept their fate passively.

19. _____ People were sent to work camps as punishment.

20. _____ The man who shot Luft was a Ukrainian.

Which three of the following statements, based on the passage, are probably justifiable? ____, ____ and ____

1. The Jews in Warsaw were being held in their homes.
2. Luft was killed because he was passive and inert.
3. Most of the Jews in the Ghetto expected to die.
4. The Germans did what they could to keep the Jews alive.
5. The Jews died primarily because they did not know how to survive in the city.
6. The Ukrainians were sympathetic to the Jewish cause.
7. Beggars worked during the day and after nine o'clock at night.
8. The Jews were optimistic about their fate.

COMPLETION Choose the best answer for each question.

1. ____ A special class of beggars are those who: (a) lock their doors when they go out. (b) beg only for milk. (c) beg after nine o'clock at night. (d) beg from Germans.

2. ____ The cases of Germans offering loaves of bread to beggars: (a) are limited to hours after curfew. (b) are isolated instances of humanity. (c) are becoming more and more common. (d) are fewer and fewer.

3. ____ Some families beg with their children because: (a) they cannot leave them home. (b) the Germans loved children. (c) the night patrol then would not shoot at them. (d) they wanted to train them to be good beggars.

4. ____ The hero in this passage was: (a) the German who gave the beggar boy bread. (b) the author, whose heart softened. (c) the Ukrainian who got the ricksha. (d) Luft, who had received the Iron Cross.

5. ____ The enormous increase in the number of orphans can be traced to: (a) the shortage of milk. (b) the fact that parents died first. (c) the Jewish Police. (d) the work of the YYGA.

6. ____ The Jews in the Ghetto once threatened: (a) to leave Warsaw entirely. (b) to rob and steal. (c) mass reprisals. (d) the lives of smugglers.

DEFINITIONS Choose the best meaning for each word.

1. ____ commotion: (a) frustration (b) noise (c) disturbance (d) despair

2. ____ fast: (a) speed up (b) do without food (c) ignore (d) cling to

3. ____ passivity: (a) tiredness (b) irritation (c) love (d) calmness

4. ____ populace: (a) citizenry (b) Ukrainians (c) well liked (d) policeman

5. ____ insistent: (a) demanding (b) noisy (c) tame (d) giving in

6. ____ isolated: (a) frequent (b) pleasant (c) crowded (d) rare

7. ____ elegance: (a) style (b) pleasantness (c) neatness (d) dullness

8. ____ simulator: (a) enemy (b) liar (c) masquerader (d) spy

9. ____ alien: (a) unpleasant (b) foreign (c) deserted (d) familiar

10. ____ resign oneself: (a) keep going (b) give in (c) quit (d) die

11. ____ scene: (a) saw (b) photograph (c) striking event (d) has been

12. ____ curfew: (a) specific hour (b) plan (c) short-sightedness (d) indifference

13. ____ eventually: (a) now (b) finally (c) immediately (d) sometimes

14. ____ untended: (a) unnoticed (b) unbelievable (c) unfettered (d) uncared for

15. ____ gnawing: (a) chewing (b) sulking (c) seeing (d) noticing

15 · Genesis

PETER FREUCHEN

*Life began in the sea, and exploring life in the sea today leads
to fantastic discoveries. This article tells of the search for and
discovery of the coelacanth, a fish thought to have been extinct
eighteen million years ago.*

Man is a conceited animal, and because he knew a little about the
land long before he had much more than a few fearful superstitions about the
sea, he likes to suppose that most of the life of this world is on terra firma.
Yet any way one looks at it, there is more in the sea.

Of all classes of animal life, 94 per cent can be found in the sea and 44
per cent only on the land; and the biggest animals and the longest-lived animals belong to the sea. Finally, life itself began in the sea, and had developed
to a fairly high order before a single living thing, animal or vegetable, appeared on the bare rocks of the land.

The basic mystery, of course, is how life started. All we really know is that
it happened in the sea. Somewhere, somehow, in the friendly shelter of salt
water, an organism, probably microscopic in size and composed of a single
cell, appeared with the ability to reproduce. It has been growing and changing ever since.

Scientists infer from their fossils and other data that life appeared about
two billion years ago. They know that half a billion years ago there was a
rich sea life, for fossils of all the principal groups of invertebrate animals have
been found dating that far back. Still there was no trace of life on land.

The scientists usually speak of the miracle of a one-celled living thing as taking place originally in a shallow sunlit pool. Their main reason for placing it there is that such a pool nowadays is more hospitable to these simple forms of life than cold, sunless water, and plants on which animal life depends need sunlight. But nowhere is the sea so cold or dark that it cannot find a tenant. In fact, by the time of which we have any exact knowledge through actual remains, there was a wide variety of plants, of animals which grew shells, of worms and jellyfish and sponges and those sea anemones which, living in great colonies, become coral. A little later, and still before the land had life, animals with backbones appeared in the sea. Only about three or four hundred million years ago, in about the middle of the Paleozoic era, did some of these plants and animals first discover how they could keep alive on shore.

The main divisions of life, then, were established in salt water. Some of the earliest microscopic organisms managed to use sunlight to turn water and chemicals into food for themselves. They became plants. Others discovered the device of taking into themselves the first type of organism. They became animals. Later on the animals learned how to eat each other instead of just plants—and some of the plants began to feed on animals. That is when life began to be confusing.

It grew more confusing, at least to simple land creatures like man, because in the sea life goes on in three dimensions, while we generally know about only two. Land life is limited to going to and fro, except for the birds and they do not go very high, but all sea life experiences the problems of up and down as well. This perhaps is why there is so much more variety. But of course there is much more room, too, and more varied environments, part of it stemming from the third dimension. The varieties of pressure are much greater, for example. Any land animal with lungs and warm blood would burst under pressures which a whale or a seal, using the same general mechanism, finds quite harmless. There is, of course, plenty of sea life which cannot stand a transfer from one pressure to another. There is, therefore, the life of the surface, which is what most people know. Then there is a less crowded life at intermediate levels; and finally the rather sparsely populated deeps.

It used to be believed that nothing could live more than a few hundred feet down. But a century ago men found living creatures on mud brought up from as much as a mile deep. Since then it has been established that some sort of life not only exists almost all over the ocean's floor, but that there are species which live and even thrive mightily in the middle layers of the sea, swimming or drifting at a depth too great for light to penetrate, and yet well above the bottom.

On the other hand, there are animals other than seals and whales which can shift from one to another level with an ease which is hard to understand. There are some small shrimps, for example, which go down below the level of light by day, apparently to escape being eaten, and return to near the surface at night. In the journey they experience a difference in pressure of about 500 pounds to the square inch. No land animal can come close to this, because on land there are no such pressure differences.

Scientists suppose that life emerged from the sea as the result of an accident—stranded by some sudden drop in the ocean's level or by a sudden rising of a stretch of land. They assume that the first successful switch from sea to land was made by plants, some species of seaweed which already had developed roots in order to cling to rocks, or some algaelike specimen which could get along in fresh water. It is argued that stranded animals with no plants to eat would have died unless they could reach the sea for food, and if they could have gotten back to the sea, they would have stayed there. Once plants had been acclimatized, stranded animals might be able to adapt themselves to the land, too.

Development of life in the sea did not stop with the departure of these emigrants, and in time the ocean even acquired some interesting repatriates from the land. Whales, for example, or their pioneer ancestors, originated on land. They roamed the earth not more than 150,000,000 years ago and probably less. They had legs, and the jaws and teeth of killers. It is presumed that their favorite hunting grounds eventually became the shallow waters at the mouths of rivers or off a level stretch of coast. Fish, both finny and shell, probably were more plentiful and easier to catch than meat, so these mammals spent more and more time in the water. Eventually they swam more easily than they walked. Millennia later they could do without legs altogether, and that was when they turned into whales. The forelegs became flippers used for steering. The hind legs shrank to mere traces, useless but still found in rudimentary form under the skin when a whale is cut up. In modern times, this has become not only the largest animal in the world but the almost undisputed king of the sea. Seals, porpoises and dolphins belong to the same family.

The strange, unpredictable forms which life took in the sea ran to fish with real legs, not just the remnants such as whales have. One of the oddest was a bluefish with four legs, known scientifically as coelacanth. Fossil remains show that they must have been extremely plentiful sixty million years ago, but then they began to slip in the race for survival. The last petrified specimen ever found had died an estimated eighteen million years ago.

Then, all of a sudden, in December, 1938, a fisherman netted one, alive and full grown, off Capetown, South Africa, in forty-five fathoms of water. That fish caused a sensation. It was five feet long, bright blue in color, and had a big head. The fisherman had never seen anything like it, which was not surprising because the species was supposed to have been extinct millions of years before human beings appeared in the world. Scientists gave it the name "Latimeria." They doubted that it could be the only one of its kind in existence, and a South African professor spent the next fourteen years trying to find another. He finally succeeded in 1952, near a little island northwest of Madagascar. Since then about twenty of these bluefish have been caught, and one was fed and kept alive in a tank for more than three months. Where had they been for nearly twenty million years? That is just one of the sea's unanswered riddles.

From the standpoint of elapsed time, it was not so mysterious a riddle as that of a mollusk which the *Galatea* expedition brought up from the deep Marianas Trench in 1956. The last previous specimen of this primitive mollusk was estimated to have been petrified four hundred million years ago.

While the oddities and realities of life down where life begins to fail have been studied only quite recently, the latest discoveries, including those of the strange bluefish and the mollusk, have led to a theory that in these regions we may find some new solutions to the riddles of evolution. One reasonable explanation I have heard, of why the bluefish never was seen in all these years, is that it had become a deep-sea dweller, living out of reach and out of sight of men. This, of course, does not tell us how the examples so recently found happened to stray up within our ken. But perhaps they were developing toward a form which would enable them to move into the realms of greater food supply nearer the surface.

At any rate, there is a theory now that studies of life at sea depths below those we have ever been able to reach before will turn up more animals known up to the present only by their fossils. It is true that most of the fish brought up from the deeps so far have not given much support to this theory. For the most part they resemble the species to be found at the surface, modified, of course, for life under great pressure and in total darkness or at best in deep gloom. It also is true that the greatest variety of forms has been found in the waters nearer the surface where basic plant foods grow.

Yet the exploration of deep water can hardly be said to have started—and the areas to be covered are enormous. Not only do they extend over most of the world horizontally, but they must be explored vertically as well, for distances down to five or six miles. And each level may present an environment quite different from the others.

Only in the last few years have we had the equipment for taking "cores" or samples from the deepest trenches, or cameras which can be used to photograph life under thousands of feet of water, or such devices as the bathysphere in which men have gone down a mile or more. So we are just at the beginning of the firsthand studies of deep-sea life.

LENGTH: 2,020 WORDS

VOCABULARY

genesis   the beginning
terra firma   land
infer   decide from evidence, understand
anemones   small sea animals that look like a flower
Paleozoic era   ancient geologic time
algaelike   like simple plant life
acclimatized   grown used to
repatriates   people who have returned to their own country
millennia   thousands of years
rudimentary   simple, crude
fossil   preserved skeleton
petrified   turned to stone
mollusk   shell fish
bathysphere   diving bell with windows that lowers men for deep-sea observations

15 · Genesis

RETENTION   Based on the passage, which of the following statements are True (T), False (F), or Not answerable (N)?

1. _____ Most of the fish brought up from great depths have resembled fossil life.

2. _____ The coelacanth was thought to have been extinct for eighteen million years.

3. _____ The whale probably was a land animal originally.

4. _____ Dolphins and coelacanths belong to the same family.

5. _____ The color of the coelacanth is a bright sea green.

6. _____ The coelacanth was first found off the coast of Madagascar.

7. _____ Scientists suppose life emerged from the sea by an accident.

8. _____ The first successful switch from sea to land probably was made by plant life.

9. _____ Some shrimp survive pressure changes of 500 pounds to the square inch.

10. _____ The lowest layers of the sea are impenetrable by light.

11. _____ The main divisions of life were established in fresh water pools.

12. _____ The first animals with backbones were land animals four hundred million years old.

13. _____ The earliest life probably was microscopic.

14. _____ There is more life near the intermediate levels of the sea than at the surface or the bottom.

15. _____ There is more life in the sea than on land.

16. _____ Life seems to have appeared one billion years ago.

17. ____ The basic mystery, of course, is where water came from.

18. ____ Coral is made by colonies of anemones.

19. ____ Life in the sea is lived in three dimensions of space.

20. ____ A century ago men found life on mud taken from a mile deep in the ocean.

INFERENCES Which three of the following statements, based on the passage, are probably justifiable? ____, ____ and ____

1. There is a strict division between land life and sea life.
2. More animals known now only as fossils will probably be discovered alive in the sea.
3. Animal life doubtless preceded plant life on land.
4. The whale, seal, and dolphin have lungs and warm blood.
5. The Marianas Trench is made primarily of coral.
6. The reasons for the coelacanth's reappearance are relatively simple.
7. The first life was probably neither plant nor animal by our terms today.
8. Certain land animals grow to sizes larger than the largest whale.

COMPLETION Choose the best answer for each question.

1. ____ When whales took to the sea: (a) dolphins became land animals. (b) their forelegs became flippers. (c) they learned to eat algae. (d) they learned to hold their breath.

2. ____ All we really know about the origin of life: (a) is that it began in the sea. (b) was learned by sea-hunters. (c) was learned a century ago. (d) relates to the coelacanth.

3. ____ The earliest life was probably: (a) plant. (b) animal. (c) large. (d) cellular.

4. ____ It is argued that life which emerged from the sea: (a) rooted in fertile soil. (b) was predatory. (c) needed plants to eat. (d) already had lungs.

5. ____ The fish said to have four legs is the: (a) mollusk. (b) shrimp. (c) dolphin. (d) coelacanth.

6. ____ The *Galatea* was: (a) a fossilized oyster. (b) an ancient mollusk. (c) an explorer. (d) a boat.

DEFINITIONS Choose the best meaning for each word.

1. _____ specimen: (a) example (b) tool (c) person (d) scientists

2. _____ extinct: (a) colored (b) alive (c) vanished (d) microscopic

3. _____ primitive: (a) early (b) ugly (c) permissible (d) late

4. _____ solution: (a) metallic (b) conclusion (c) answer (d) water

5. _____ petrified: (a) excellent (b) stony (c) pretty (d) concerned

6. _____ theory: (a) practice (b) fright (c) suspicion (d) explanation

7. _____ undisputed: (a) arguable (b) absolute (c) kindly (d) irritated

8. _____ shallow: (a) deep (b) profound (c) superficial (d) pale

9. _____ originate: (a) begin (b) organize (c) suffer (d) make

10. _____ stranded: (a) pleased (b) concerned (c) forsaken (d) destroyed

11. _____ ancestor: (a) reference (b) student (c) predecessor (d) relative

12. _____ estimate: (a) predict (b) count on (c) disturb (d) ignore

13. _____ explore: (a) discover (b) visit (c) differentiate (d) examine

14. _____ modified: (a) mild (b) unchanged (c) shaped (d) changed

15. _____ terra firma: (a) sky (b) sea (c) land (d) air

16 · Stalin, the Rise to Power

J. EDGAR HOOVER

The chief of the FBI tells about Stalin's struggle with Leon Trotsky, his arch-rival. After Stalin became the communist strongman in Russia, Trotsky retired to Mexico where he was assassinated in 1940.

In January, 1924, after a long illness, Lenin died, leaving open a struggle for power that was to last until the 1930's.

The Russian dictator sensed, some time before his death, the evil influence of the man who had squirmed his way to the position of the Party's General Secretary. Joseph Stalin, the son of a cobbler, had been an old-time Bolshevik. Born in 1879, he had attended a seminary at Tiflis, in the Caucasus, but in 1899 had been expelled. Already he was involved in revolutionary activities. From 1902 until 1913, according to the communists, he was arrested seven times, exiled six times, and escaped five times from exile.

Plodding by nature, Stalin lacked the brilliance of his chief rival, Leon Trotsky. However, his grasp of the Russian mentality was tremendous. Years as an agitator, prison inmate, and political schemer gave him an insight into communist intrigue that other Party leaders seemed to lack. Working silently but meticulously, he was quick to exploit any opportunity to increase his personal power.

Stalin liked to represent himself as the heir of Lenin, the man predestined to carry on the Bolshevik revolution. This claim is not borne out, however, by a "testament" prepared by Lenin shortly before his death. "Comrade Stalin," wrote Lenin, on Christmas Day, 1922, "having become General Secretary,

STALIN, THE RISE TO POWER   From *Masters of Deceit* by J. Edgar Hoover. Copyright © 1958 by J. Edgar Hoover. Reprinted by permission of Holt, Rinehart and Winston, Inc.

has concentrated an enormous power in his hands; and I am not sure that he always knows how to use that power with sufficient caution."

Then Lenin added a postscript dated January 4, 1923, a full year before he died:

> Stalin is too rude, and this fault, entirely supportable in relations among us Communists, becomes insupportable in the office of General Secretary. Therefore, I propose to the comrades to find a way to remove Stalin from that position. . . .

However, the time for action had passed. Lenin was too sick to implement his testament. The result: a terrific struggle between Stalin and Trotsky for power.

Trotsky (real name Bronstein) was born in 1879 (two months earlier than Stalin). Early a revolutionary, he spent many years as an exile from Russia. After the Bolshevik revolution he served as Lenin's Commissar of Foreign Affairs and later did much to organize the Red army.

Many differences separated Stalin and Trotsky, the chief one being Stalin's idea that Russia should concentrate on making itself powerful *first*, before undertaking extensive revolutionary action abroad. Trotsky, on the other hand, believed that the Russian revolution could survive only if communist revolutions were promoted in other countries. Both desired world conquest. Their dispute, clouded by a personal hunger for power, centered on how to achieve it. Stalin was the winner. Trotsky was exiled by Stalin in 1929, eventually finding refuge in Mexico. He was assassinated in 1940, reportedly by a secret communist agent.

Joseph Stalin was the fourth "top leader" of communism, claiming "divine" ancestry from Marx, Engels, and Lenin. Until his death in 1953, Stalin played a major role in the history of Russian and world communism, as a "continuer" of the work of Lenin. It was Stalin who, through murder, deceit, and brutality, gave communism *power*, firmly establishing Bolshevik control in Russia and spreading communism to other countries. However, he also was to become the first of the "Big Four" to be denounced by the communists and to have his name blackened by successors.

In carrying on the revolution Stalin became the interpreter of Marxism-Leninism. Under his rule the state, which Marx had visualized as "withering away," became even stronger, an agent of sheer oppression. The army, navy, secret police, and all political structures of the state grew ever more powerful and permanent. Slave labor camps multiplied. Soviet society became iron-clad, more rigid than under the most autocratic Czar. Army officials, Party henchmen, industrial managers, all emerged as classes, each jealous of the other. The "workingman," whom Marx had extolled, was now an inferior class, exploited and downtrodden.

Stalin carried to the extreme Lenin's concepts of the Party as a fanatical, disciplined group. To Stalin the Party was not only a tool to seize and maintain power but also a method of liquidating all personal opposition and a means of educating the masses in the communist way of life.

The Party, for this reason, was kept "pure," meaning completely loyal, disciplined, and blindly obedient. Party schools, cadre training, and regimented discipline were needed to saturate the members in communism. Weaklings were purged, expelled and exiled to Siberia, or executed. In Soviet Russia, and all her satellites, the Party was constantly "Bolshevized"—made "more perfect in communism."

One result of this insistent demand for discipline under Stalin was the increasing crystallization of Marxism-Leninism—already a harsh and regimented code—into an even more rigid, static, and often sterile body of doctrine. Like a shrinking garment, communist doctrine pressed ever more tightly on communists everywhere. Every action now had to be "justified" by theory. If the theory didn't fit, then it had to be reinterpreted. To deviate was to court disaster. Stalin, though not so good a theorist as Lenin, liked to pose as Marxism-Leninism's "expert" interpreter.

This ossification of communist doctrine, under which the individual was afraid to take any initiative, contributed largely to the violent reaction against Stalin after his death. His successors realized that *some* breathing room was absolutely essential, although during Stalin's reign they were content to serve, without protest so far as the record shows, as the executors of his policies.

Stalin also identified communism with nationalism and imperialism: *Russian* nationalism and *Russian* imperialism.

To him, communism seemed an ideal vehicle for Russian world conquest, and so, once communism was firmly entrenched in Russia, he embarked on a policy curiously similar to that of Czarist imperialists like Peter the Great and Catherine the Great.

Aided by disturbed world conditions between 1939 and 1953, Stalin started the Soviet chariot of conquest. He directly annexed a number of areas, such as eastern Poland, Estonia, Latvia, Lithuania, part of Finland, eastern Czechoslovakia, part of Roumania. Then, using communism as an ideological adhesive, Stalin created a Soviet orbit: Yugoslavia, China, Poland, Hungary, Bulgaria, North Korea, Czechoslovakia, Roumania, East Germany, Albania, Tibet, Outer Mongolia, and North Indochina (where bloody fighting was in progress at the time of his death). No wonder William Z. Foster in February, 1956, could boast that seventeen countries were "actually building Socialism or are definitely orientating in that direction," having a total population of 900,000,000! He adds: "They constitute the beginning of the new Socialist world." Note the use of the word "beginning."

Native communist parties, aided by Moscow, were often the instruments of subjugation, Trojan horses of the twentieth century. At other times Russian military power paved the way. Peoples with long traditions of freedom were betrayed into slavery. Significantly, no entire country has ever gone communist and become a satellite by the free choice of election.

This grandiose conquest was abetted by Stalin's inheritance of the tools of Marxism-Leninism, a way of life that is imperialistic, overbearing, and dictatorial. Some individuals may accuse Stalin, alone of the communist "Big Four," of being responsible for the terror of modern-day communism. Marx, Engels, and Lenin, however, are also fully accountable, and so are Stalin's henchmen, who still rule in the Soviet Union. Stalin may have been the active agent of conquest in our generation, but his knives were sharpened on the diabolical teachings of his communist predecessors.

LENGTH: 1,620 WORDS

VOCABULARY

Bolshevik   a member of the Communist Party
plodding   dull, slow but persevering
mentality   intellectual capacity
meticulously   paying close attention to details
exploit   to take unfair advantage of
predestined   determined by fate
testament   evidence, document, written will
implement   to put into effect
extensive   widespread, great
exiled   sent out of the country
denounced   spoken against forcefully
autocratic   tyrannical, dictatorial
emerge   to come forth
extolled   praised highly
liquidating   getting out of the way, killing
cadre training   training of officers who can train others
saturate   to soak thoroughly, indoctrinate
purge   to purify, remove undesirable elements
ossification   stiffening, turning to bone
ideological   having to do with a political belief
subjugation   being forced to follow orders, subservience
grandiose   over-large, high-flown
abetted   helped
diabolical   devilish

16 · Stalin, the Rise to Power

SCORING: Reading time: _____ Rate from chart: _____ W.P.M.

RETENTION	number right _____ × 2 equals _____ points	
INFERENCES	number right _____ × 2 equals _____ points	
COMPLETION	number right _____ × 4 equals _____ points	
DEFINITIONS	number right _____ × 2 equals _____ points	

(Total points: 100)   **total** _____ points

RETENTION   Based on the passage, which of the following statements are True (T), False (F), or Not answerable (N)?

1. _____ Lenin was born the son of a cobbler from Tiflis.

2. _____ Leon Trotsky was a principal organizer of the Red army.

3. _____ Lenin's brilliance was extensive and remarkable.

4. _____ Trotsky believed that revolution abroad was necessary for Russian survival.

5. _____ Under Stalin the state "withered away" as Marx had predicted it would.

6. _____ Stalin used the Party as a means of education.

7. _____ Lenin developed the concept of the Party.

8. _____ Trotsky agreed with Lenin's attitude toward Africa and Asia.

9. _____ Trotsky was exiled by Stalin.

10. _____ The Communist code is only a sterile body of doctrine.

11. _____ Hoover says that only Stalin is responsible for the "terror of modern-day communism."

12. _____ The purges of 1939 weighed heavily on Stalin's conscience.

13. _____ Stalin's policy was, of course, quite unlike that of the Czar.

14. _____ Only one country has ever chosen communism by open election.

15. _____ When Stalin died, no communist countries were actually at war.

16. _____ Stalin made communist doctrine flexible and easy-going.

17. _____ Annexation was a method used by Trotsky to extend communist influence.

18. _____ Stalin was not as good a theorist of communism as Lenin.

19. _____ Stalin did not believe that each of his actions had to be justified by theory.

20. _____ Trotsky was plodding by nature.

INFERENCES   Which three of the following statements, based on the passage, are probably justifiable?   _____, _____ and _____

1. Stalin was not ambitious for Russia and communism, but merely for himself.
2. Trotsky expected to found a new communist country in Mexico.
3. Stalin and Trotsky, though not in agreement, were both communists.
4. Marx and Engels had a power struggle similar to the one between Stalin and Trotsky.
5. Marx was responsible for the spread of communism to "satellite" countries.
6. Almost half of the world's population is communist.
7. Yugoslavia could be considered a modern-day Trojan horse.
8. Stalin's concept of government was to favor repression.

COMPLETION   Choose the best answer for each question.

1. _____ When the party was "Bolshevized" it was: (a) made more universal.   (b) made more strict and severe.   (c) made more perfect in communism.   (d) made more in line with Lenin's statement of 1922.

2. _____ The following was not specifically mentioned as a class: (a) secret police.   (b) party henchmen.   (c) workingmen.   (d) army officials.

3. _____ Lenin's main objection to Stalin was: (a) that he was too swift and sudden.   (b) that he was once a seminary student.   (c) that he was too rude.   (d) that he disagreed so violently about basic doctrine.

4. _____ The first "top leader" of communism was: (a) Stalin.   (b) Trotsky.   (c) Lenin.   (d) Marx.

5. _____ Trotsky was murdered in   (a) 1902.   (b) 1913.   (c) 1929.   (d) 1940.

6. _____ Stalin liked to represent himself as: (a) a world conqueror.   (b) the heir to Lenin.   (c) a Bolshevik expert.   (d) Comrade Stalin.

DEFINITIONS   Choose the best meaning for each word.

1. _____ rival: (a) friend   (b) beginning   (c) enemy   (d) leader

2. _____ struggle: (a) pacify   (b) conflict   (c) swim   (d) paralyze

3. _____ exploit: (a) use (b) fend off (c) suggest (d) desire

4. _____ agitator: (a) dictator (b) beginner (c) stooge (d) revolutionary

5. _____ influence: (a) love (b) success (c) observe (d) power

6. _____ promote: (a) encourage (b) stifle (c) lose (d) destroy

7. _____ assassination: (a) foolishness (b) surprise (c) thievery (d) murder

8. _____ sufficient: (a) nuisance (b) plenty (c) enough (d) dearth

9. _____ ironclad: (a) flexible (b) metallic (c) unbending (d) nonferrous

10. _____ harsh: (a) cruel (b) personal (c) loud (d) shove

11. _____ inferior: (a) better (b) worse (c) neutral (d) inside

12. _____ extreme: (a) sudden (b) cold (c) outside (d) excessive

13. _____ regimented: (a) begun (b) organized (c) militarized (d) touched

14. _____ liquidate: (a) eliminate (b) aggravate (c) stimulate (d) correlate

15. _____ embarked: (a) begun (b) slowed down (c) shortened (d) approved

17 · Manhattan and the Blizzard of '88

IRVING WERSTEIN

In the blizzard of 1888, which is still a legend, the entire northeast of the nation suffered incredible winds and snowfalls. This is an account of several persons' experiences in Manhattan during the storm.

Neither the Hudson River nor the East River ferries were running. An effort had been made to keep the Brooklyn ferries in operation, but at 1:00 P.M., when a boat loaded with commuters set out from Fulton Street for Brooklyn and nearly capsized in midstream, all ferry service between Brooklyn and New York was immediately canceled. The strong winds had made the East River as choppy as the English Channel.

On the west side of town, the side-wheeler Jersey City ferryboat *Communipaw* bucked the turbulent Hudson River until she was nearly swept out to sea in a cross current. Her captain promptly turned around and fled back to Jersey City where he stayed put for the duration of the storm.

And only a madman would have attempted to sail a Staten Island ferryboat on the heaving waters between Manhattan and Staten Island. It was a perilous passage for a big ocean steamer, let alone a clumsy, slow-moving ferry. So it went. Not a single ferry line was operating, from the Battery to East 59th Street.

With no public transportation operating (all four elevated roads were out; horsecars had long since stopped; the Broadway omnibus stages and the big Fifth Avenue coaches gave up about noon), only a single route to Brooklyn was still open—the Brooklyn Bridge. There, a cable car crossed the span and continued to make infrequent trips all morning. However, it could carry only a handful of people at a time and when a winch on the Manhattan side of the bridge froze up, that shuttle run ended as well.

Crowds waiting to board the car filed onto the pedestrian path and started the long and dangerous trek across the bridge. High over the river, men inched forward cautiously. They clung to the railings and dragged themselves ahead, hand-over-hand, cursing the snow and the wind. Hundreds of hats went skimming into the river. Although nobody was hurt, and nobody fell into the water, the police finally closed the bridge. They feared the weight of the snow added to that of the many people on it, would send the structure crashing down.

Soon everyone knew there was no way off Manhattan Island. Anyone living across the Bay or on the opposite side of one of the rivers was trapped. This realization sparked a spate of rumors. Dreadful (and unauthenticated) tales of disaster skipped through saloons, restaurants, bars and hotel lobbies. Anywhere anxious crowds gathered, the rumors came alive: a fire had destroyed a Brooklyn school and a hundred children had died; a ferryboat had gone down in the East River with great loss of life; the roof of the Jersey City Terminal had caved in under a mountain of piled-up snow, crushing many; an El train had been blown off the tracks as it rounded the long curve between 105th and 110th streets. The rumors became wilder and more farfetched; nobody knew the truth.

Even worse than being cut off from home was the impossibility of sending any word. Those stranded in town worried about the safety of wives, children and friends. The city was like a void where each individual struggled alone with his fears and anxieties. At last a feeling of resignation took hold; the folks left behind in New Jersey or Brooklyn, Staten Island or uptown simply had to shift for themselves. One could only hope they had sense enough to stay indoors.

Obviously, no one could remain out in the streets all night. Suburbanites took whatever shelter they could while anyone living within walking distance plodded home from downtown Manhattan. This resulted in some grueling experiences. Even a few blocks was a grim trial of strength and endurance.

A man named Henry Tochs, who lived at First Avenue and 15th Street, took two hours to walk there from Second Avenue and 5th Street. Cross winds, whipping through the open spaces around Stuyvesant Square Park, were so strong that they knocked him down every time he tried to pass that exposed area and he was forced to crawl almost all the way on his hands and knees.

The prospects grew dim that anyone living uptown would see his family that night. A wealthy man could hire a hack; early in the day, cabbies were willing to risk their vehicles, horses and lives at fees ranging between $20.00 and $50.00 for destinations up to 59th Street from City Hall Park. These profiteers did not lack for customers, but even they had to give up by midafternoon. No horse could pull a hack a hundred yards, even on Broadway.

The adventures of James Algeo were typical of all who sought to go home the only way left—on foot. About 1:00 P.M., Algeo and the 39 other American Bank Note Company workers on the job at Trinity Square were advised they could leave at any time. After vainly searching for a place to spend the night, Algeo decided to walk back to East 84th Street. He commenced his five-mile hike up Broadway, planning to follow that main thoroughfare to 14th Street, turn east there and then take First Avenue all the way. He was a strong, athletic young man, and in fair weather that distance would have been a mere stroll for him. Now, those miles stretched on like an interminable hell.

Northbound, with the wind at his back, he plodded on, nearly stupefied by the cold. He moved like a robot, lurching, falling, picking himself up, gaining a few yards, slipping on icy patches. Most of the time he could not tell exactly where he was. The snow had blanketed or altered every landmark; every street sign was covered. He stumbled past stores and hotels; theaters and offices—a stranger in an alien land. Even when he reached 14th Street, Algeo had trouble recognizing his surroundings. Union Square was deserted.

He struggled on his painful journey for more than five hours. His cheeks cracked in the frozen air; his frostbitten nose swelled grotesquely. His hands and feet were numbed. His coat was glazed in solid ice. At East 84th Street, which he identified by instinct rather than some tangible sign, he turned eastward. The south side of the street was still comparatively free of snow, but on the north side, the wind-blown drifts towered to thirty feet, burying lampposts and piling against houses to the second floor and beyond.

Nearly blinded and half-dazed, he still tottered on. For a while, he became hysterical, shouting meaningless words, railing at the blizzard and the darkness (not a single gas street light could be turned on in the entire city). When finally he reached his own block, all he could see of his house were the third-story windows and the rooftop. He ran frantically in circles, screaming his wife's name until he could barely whisper; he wept in frustration and the tears froze to his cheeks. He tried to climb the monstrous drift that hid his house; it might as well have been the Matterhorn. Scrabbling, he dragged himself to the top and pounded with his fists on the closed shutters.

After a long while, his wife opened the window and pushed back the shutters. With a startled cry she set down the lamp that she was carrying and dragged him inside. He collapsed on the floor. Sobbing, she cradled him in her arms. Miraculously he recovered completely.

LENGTH: 1,310 WORDS

VOCABULARY

ferry   a boat designed to carry passengers and merchandise across a river
trek   difficult journey
spate   flurry, sudden outpouring
grueling   laborious, difficult
interminable   without end
stupefied   speechless, shocked
grotesquely   hideously, in a distorted way
tangible   real, actual
Matterhorn   snow-covered mountain in the Alps on the Swiss-Italian border
scrabbling   scratching, scraping with the hands

17 · Manhattan and the Blizzard of '88

SCORING: Reading time: _____ Rate from chart: _____ W.P.M.
RETENTION number right _____ × 2 equals _____ points
INFERENCES number right _____ × 2 equals _____ points
COMPLETION number right _____ × 4 equals _____ points
DEFINITIONS number right _____ × 2 equals _____ points
(Total points: 100) **total** _____ points

RETENTION Based on the passage, which of the following statements are True (T), False (F), or Not answerable (N)?

1. _____ The only route to Brooklyn left open was the Fulton Street ferry.

2. _____ The *Communipaw* set out from Fulton Street to Brooklyn.

3. _____ A winch froze up on the Brooklyn side of the Brooklyn Bridge shuttle.

4. _____ Police closed down the Brooklyn Bridge because two men fell into the river.

5. _____ A Brooklyn school was destroyed by fire during the blizzard.

6. _____ Submarines still could negotiate the route to Staten Island.

7. _____ Henry Tochs took two hours to walk ten blocks.

8. _____ Early in the day the cab drivers could not start their engines.

9. _____ Forty employees of the American Bank Note Company were on the job in Trinity Square.

10. _____ James Algeo was old, but strong and athletic.

11. _____ Algeo tried to walk five miles in the blizzard.

12. _____ Algeo identified East 84th Street by instinct.

13. _____ The drifts on Algeo's street were almost fifteen feet high.

14. _____ Mrs. Algeo lived in Union Square.

15. _____ When they could operate, taxicabs charged up to $50.00 for a trip.

16. _____ The Staten Island ferryboat operated until a winch froze solid.

17. _____ People threw their hats off the Brooklyn Bridge early in the day.

18. _____ The captain of the *Communipaw* was a madman.

19. _____ Rumors of great disaster circulated in saloons and hotels during the storm.

20. _____ Henry Tochs used the ferry to get home.

INFERENCES   Which three of the following statements, based on the passage, are probably justifiable?   _____, _____ and _____

1. New York City was not prepared for the fury of the storm.
2. The cab drivers were the only ones who charged excessively for services.
3. Those stranded in the city suffered anxious hours worrying about their families.
4. An elevated train had been blown off the tracks by cross winds.
5. Tochs and Algeo were typical cases of New Yorkers anxious to try their strength.
6. After five hours of struggling toward home, Algeo operated on instinct.
7. The drift in front of Algeo's home reminded him of the Matterhorn.
8. The author remembers the storm well.

COMPLETION   Choose the best answer for each question.

1. _____ Algeo had trouble recognizing his surroundings at: (a) 14th Street.   (b) 62nd Street.   (c) Stuyvesant Square.   (d) Trinity Square.

2. _____ Strong winds had made the East River as choppy as: (a) the Hudson.   (b) the North Atlantic.   (c) the English Channel.   (d) the Labrador Straits.

3. _____ Algeo's wife did not answer his calls because: (a) the gas lamps were out.   (b) she went to sleep at 9:30.   (c) she thought he was at work.   (d) his voice was no louder than a whisper.

4. _____ Algeo probably reached his home at: (a) 10 P.M.   (b) 6 P.M.   (c) 1 P.M.   (d) 5 A.M.

5. _____ Both Algeo and Tochs travelled by: (a) cab.   (b) ferry.   (c) foot.   (d) cab and foot.

6. _____ The author begins his discussion with ferry boats because: (a) everyone in New York knows them well.   (b) they are huge and reliable even in storms.   (c) there was a strike against the ferries.   (d) when they have trouble, the storm must be really serious.

DEFINITIONS   Choose the best meaning for each word.

1. _____ destination: (a) home   (b) city   (c) goal   (d) height

2. _____ commence: (a) search   (b) begin   (c) establish   (d) graduate

3. _____ mere: (a) only   (b) all   (c) none   (d) half

4. _____ rumor: (a) news story   (b) uncertain story   (c) lie   (d) true story

5. _____ plod: (a) walk heavily   (b) rig   (c) run lightly   (d) trip

6. _____ farfetched: (a) plausible   (b) impossible   (c) improbable   (d) distant

7. _____ anxieties: (a) irritants   (b) worries   (c) beginnings   (d) efforts

8. _____ grueling: (a) intimidating   (b) soupy   (c) tiring   (d) durable

9. _____ capsize: (a) overturn   (b) disappear   (c) head out   (d) overwhelm

10. _____ clumsy: (a) skillful   (b) delicate   (c) awkward   (d) dull

11. _____ infrequent: (a) rare   (b) slow   (c) without end   (d) interminable

12. _____ heaving: (a) swelling   (b) turning   (c) stopping   (d) learning

13. _____ attempt: (a) lure   (b) begin   (c) indict   (d) try

14. _____ perilous: (a) dangerous   (b) fortuitous   (c) lecherous   (d) pleasant

15. _____ hysterical: (a) silly   (b) uncontrolled   (c) thoughtful   (d) unkind

18 · The End of Quantrill's Raiders

PAUL I. WELLMAN

Late in the Civil War and in the years immediately after, raiders plagued the American Middle West. This account tells how one of the most ruthless killers the country has ever known met his end.

With Quantrill at the time were, apparently, only eleven guerrillas: John Ross, William Hulse, Payne Jones, Clark Hockensmith, Isaac Hall, Dick Glasscock, Bob Hall, Bud Spence, Allen Parmer, Dave Helton, and Lee McMurtry.

A heavy rain was falling, and Quantrill was napping in the hayloft of the barn. Wakefield, the farmer, stood idly talking with Dick Glasscock, sheltered by the wide eaves of the stable, while others of the men held a sham battle inside, choosing up sides and using corncobs for ammunition.

Suddenly Glasscock uttered a wild yell:

"Here they come!"

He saw, galloping over the rise through the pelting downpour, a body of horsemen in blue uniforms.

The surprise was complete. Quantrill had not dreamed that an enemy was within twenty-five miles of him.

Shots began thudding out. Some of the guerrillas scrambled for their horses and rode away, others plunged into a nearby pond and hid under the bushes on its border.

Quantrill slid down from the loft and tried to mount his horse, but the animal, frightened by the shooting, yelling, and confusion, became unmanageable, reared, and broke away from him.

THE END OF QUANTRILL'S RAIDERS From *A Dynasty of Western Outlaws* by Paul I. Wellman, copyright © 1961 by Paul I. Wellman. Reprinted by permission of Doubleday & Company, Inc.

In that moment, alone in the barnyard with the blue cavalry roaring toward him, all the strangeness and terror of his life must have passed before him. Where now was that column of lean, terrible hunters he once led? Dead, many of them. Following other leaders, most of the rest.

Horseless, he turned and sprinted from the barnyard for the woods, but the oncomers were close now, shooting at him.

Then Glasscock, seeing his peril, bravely turned back to rescue him. His horse was hit by a bullet and began to rear and plunge, making it impossible for Quantrill to mount behind. A moment later Glasscock was knocked out of his saddle by a lead slug, dead.

Quantrill whirled as if to fire at the charging foe, but at that instant Clark Hockensmith came galloping back. Quantrill did not shoot, but tried to get up behind his man.

A level sheet of flame seemed to blaze from the blue line, ranged behind the farmyard fence. Hockensmith was stretched dead by the volley. And Quantrill was down, struck by a ball in the back, his spine shattered so that he was paralyzed below the shoulders, while another bullet took off a finger of his right hand.

There, on the wet ground, with the rain pelting his face, Quantrill lay near the bodies of the two men who had given their lives for him, fully knowing that his wound was mortal. Blue-clad soldiers gathered about him.

"Are you Quantrill?" he was asked.

"No," answered the pallid lips. "I'm Captain Clarke, Fourth Colorado Cavalry, U.S. Volunteers."

There was no such regiment.

Someone took off his boots, and a blanket was fetched, in which he was carried to the house. He asked that Hockensmith and Glasscock be given soldier's burials. Then, knowing there was no use longer to deny it, he admitted his identity. By that time the rest of his band had made good their escape.

Ironically, Quantrill suffered his death stroke at the hands of "Federal" guerrillas no better than himself. The leader of the company called himself Captain Edwin Terrill. He was a deserter from the Confederate Army, who became a guerrilla and announced his "loyalty" to the Union cause when he saw the way the tide of war was turning.

Quantrill was left at the Wakefield house that night. He was helpless, able only to move his arms and head. In the dark hours some of his men, including Frank James, came to the house and begged him to let them carry him away. He refused. He told them he knew he was going to die and had pledged his word to stay. Furthermore, if he broke his parole and allowed them to take him with them, Wakefield's house would be burned down in reprisal. The guerrillas stole away and left him.

Next day Terrill returned and took Quantrill to Louisville in a farm wagon filled with straw to ease the jolting. He was placed in a military hospital, where he lingered in pain until June 6, when he died.

Quantrill was a Catholic. Before his death he was visited by two old priests, and to one of them he made a complete confession of his life's sins. It must have curled the hair of the aged clergyman to listen to that lengthy and unexpurgated catalogue. But in the end Quantrill received the Church's blessing.

As one of the last acts of his life, he entrusted two thousand dollars in gold to the priest who confessed him, asking him to deliver it to Kate Clarke, whose address in St. Louis he gave. The good father later faithfully carried out the errand, but he must have been taken aback somewhat by the use she made of the money.

She established what the times euphemistically called a "fancy house," and for years was a well-known figure in the red-light district of St. Louis.

There is one especially unpleasant aftermath of the Quantrill story.

He was buried in a Catholic cemetery in Louisville. His mother, Mrs. Caroline Clarke Quantrill, living in a strongly pro-Union community at Canal Dover, Ohio, had throughout the war expressed great surprise and horrified disapproval whenever she heard of her son's deeds. After the war, however, when feeling had somewhat cooled, she began to profess grief and affection for the memory of Quantrill, and eventually induced W. W. Scott, a neighbor at Canal Dover, to try and find his grave. This was in 1887. Scott succeeded in his mission, and Mrs. Quantrill then visited the place with him.

Next she requested that the dead man's bones be exhumed so that she could take them "to the family burial ground in Ohio." Scott at first refused, but she pleaded so strongly that at length he did as she asked.

With the connivance of the custodian of the cemetery and an employee, to both of whom Scott gave a few dollars, Quantrill's bones were disinterred, placed in a box, and turned over to Mrs. Quantrill.

Scott's written account of the episode ends with these words:

"Mrs. Q. [Quantrill] afterwards had the lot sold and received the money."

Quantrill was no good. But the ghoulish mother, who sold her son's bones as curios, could hardly have been much better.

LENGTH: 1,110 WORDS

VOCABULARY

guerrillas irregular soldiers
sham something false, deception
ironically contrary to expectations
unexpurgated uncensored
euphemistically using a pleasant or mild word for an unpleasant action, thing, or idea
exhumed dug out of the ground
connivance secret cooperation
disinterred exhumed
ghoulish fiendish, horrible

18 · The End of Quantrill's Raiders

RETENTION   Based on the passage, which of the following statements are True (T), False (F), or Not answerable (N)?

1. ____ Quantrill once led a column of lean, terrible hunters.

2. ____ Probably Quantrill had more in common with his attackers than he knew.

3. ____ During the attack, the cornfields were covered with snow.

4. ____ Quantrill probably thought he was facing a detachment of Union cavalry.

5. ____ Quantrill knew that enemy men were very close at hand.

6. ____ In normal times, Quantrill would have had many more than eleven men.

7. ____ At the critical moment, all Quantrill's men turned coward.

8. ____ When the attack began, Quantrill was playing "war games" in the barn.

9. ____ Quantrill lied about his identity after he was wounded.

10. ____ Hockensmith and Glasscock died trying to save Quantrill's life.

11. ____ Not one of Quantrill's men escaped.

12. ____ The man who captured Quantrill was a deserter from the Union Army.

13. ____ Quantrill died in an army hospital near the place where he was buried.

14. ____ Before he died, Quantrill confessed to a priest and received a blessing.

15. ____ One of Quantrill's men delivered $2,000 to Quantrill's mistress, Kate.

16. ____ With Quantrill's money Kate opened a restaurant.

17. ____ W. W. Scott helped Mrs. Quantrill recover her son's bones.

18. ____ Officials of the cemetery permitted the bones to be taken.

19. ____ Mrs. Quantrill sold the bones as curios.

20. ____ Mrs. Quantrill probably only pretended disapproval of her son's behavior.

INFERENCES   Which three of the following statements, based on the passage, are probably justifiable?   ____, ____ and ____

1. The old priest was happy to hear Quantrill's confession.
2. Quantrill was as desperate and worthless as the man who ran him down.
3. Quantrill's grave had no marker on it.
4. W. W. Scott was in love with Mrs. Quantrill.
5. Terrill was avenging poor Kate Clarke.
6. All this happened during or after the Civil War.
7. Quantrill had been a soldier in the Confederate Army.
8. Quantrill and his mother were probably more alike than people knew.

COMPLETION   Choose the best answer for each question.

1. ____ When the attack came, Quantrill was: (a) in mock battle with his men.   (b) planning a new attack.   (c) sleeping in a barn.   (d) telling Wakefield about his exploits.

2. ____ The guerrilla Terrill was loyal to the Union side because: (a) he had been born in Louisville.   (b) he saw that the Union would win.   (c) it gave him a chance to track down Quantrill.   (d) the Confederates had killed a friend of his.

3. ____ A man not with Quantrill during the attack was: (a) Frank James.   (b) Clark Hockensmith.   (c) Allen Parmer.   (d) Dick Glasscock.

4. ____ Quantrill probably lied about his name at first: (a) to save his mother embarrassment.   (b) to confuse the attackers.   (c) to help Wakefield save his house.   (d) to let his men escape.

5. ____ Quantrill was removed from Wakefield's farm in: (a) a hay-filled wagon.   (b) a blanket.   (c) a remarkable hurry.   (d) order to burn the place to the ground.

6. ____ The bullet that hit Quantrill: (a) killed him instantly.   (b) was a special slug.   (c) paralyzed him.   (d) was sold later in Ohio.

DEFINITIONS Choose the best meaning for each word.

1. ____ idle: (a) figurine (b) occupied (c) disturbed (d) unemployed

2. ____ utter: (a) speak (b) shrill (c) storm (d) flow

3. ____ pelt: (a) clever (b) hit (c) feel (d) touch

4. ____ sprint: (a) amble (b) stride (c) run (d) race

5. ____ plunge: (a) call (b) swim (c) dive (d) pull

6. ____ whirl: (a) kill (b) twirl (c) shove (d) unfurl

7. ____ mortal: (a) fatal (b) good (c) inevitable (d) weak

8. ____ ironically: (a) surprisingly (b) coincidentally (c) happily (d) stiffly

9. ____ guerrilla: (a) deserter (b) soldier (c) irregular (d) officer

10. ____ identity: (a) name (b) face (c) subject matter (d) sermon

11. ____ parole: (a) imprisonment (b) freedom (c) word of honor (d) success

12. ____ errand: (a) wandering (b) mistake (c) short trip (d) boy

13. ____ linger: (a) slow down (b) remain (c) run (d) slink

14. ____ aftermath: (a) later happening (b) recent occurrence (c) now (d) later

15. ____ mission: (a) accomplish (b) job (c) not hit (d) explanation

19 · Medicine and the Civil War

JACK COGGINS

The incredible number of deaths among soldiers on both sides in the Civil War was caused by poor medical care as much as by bullets.

No one will ever know how many men died in the Civil War. It was probably over 600,000, and of these more than twice as many died of disease as from enemy bullets. These are shocking figures, but too often the blame is laid solely on the medical profession. Actually they did the best that could be done with imperfect knowledge, equipment, and techniques, at a time when stethoscopes were a novelty, when there were probably not more than twenty clinical thermometers in the whole Union army, and when such diseases as lockjaw, septicemia, malaria, and gangrene were attributed, among other things, to the "evening dews and damps."

In studying statistics on sickness and death from wounds it must be remembered that, to begin with, facts relating to personal hygiene and public health were all but unknown. The unsanitary and unhealthful conditions of normal civilian life of the period were multiplied by the gathering together in close quarters of huge numbers of men, many of whom looked on army life as an escape from the restrictions of society and "either from apathy or from laziness neither washed their persons nor the clothes they carried with them."

Cold, damp, unsuitable or inadequate clothing, atrocious food, and contaminated water all took their toll. Also, many recruits were young boys from isolated areas, particularly susceptible to such common ailments as mumps, measles, and scarlet fever. Men unaccustomed to wet and exposure were subject to bad colds, which in turn often led to bronchitis and pneumonia. That ever-present scourge of all armies, dysentery, laid many low, and under the necessarily crowded conditions, communicable diseases of all kinds spread like wildfire.

To make matters worse, the physical examinations given recruits were, in most cases, a joke, and the rolls included a high percentage of those with pre-service disabilities: epileptics, syphilitics, and so forth.

However, attempts were rapidly made to better conditions, at least as far as hygiene and public health were concerned. Booklets on hygiene were distributed and efforts made to clean up the camps and provide proper latrines and toilet facilities.

The better the discipline of the unit, the better the health was likely to be, and in those regiments where the officers were intelligent enough to issue and enforce orders relating to sanitation, drinking water, etc., the sickness rate was much lower than in those units in which the officers were too ignorant or too lazy to care.

As the war progressed the men became better able to take care of themselves, and a veteran regiment in the field would show a far smaller sick list than a "green" regiment under canvas.

A major problem during the first part of the war was the collection and transportation of the wounded. There was no system and no central control. The collection was bad enough—the men detailed for this job were usually the ones the company commanders could best spare—that is, the skulkers and shirkers, and the bandsmen, who were expected to "double in brass"—or blood, when the occasion arose. In consequence, many men were left lying on the battlefields unattended—sometimes for days.

But even more unnecessary death and suffering were caused by the failure of the medical service to provide for moving the wounded from the regimental aid stations to the large general hospitals in the rear. (It is stated that after the First Battle of Bull Run, no casualties reached Washington in ambulances—although some wounded walked the twenty-seven miles.)

Transport was largely in the hands of the Quartermaster Corps. The ambulances, what there were of them, were usually driven by civilians—a drunken, good-for-nothing lot, by all accounts, who were likely to take off for the rear at the shriek of the first shell. At Ball's Bluff it was reported that one surgeon had to fire on the ambulance attendants to make them do their job.

Care of the wounded was far down the priority list, and there were cases where the ambulance horses were taken for mounts by the cavalry. The Government—or at least the War Department—seems to have turned a blind eye to these appalling conditions, while the Medical Department, which at the outbreak of the war was geared to meet the needs of an army of some 16,000 regulars, was utterly unable to cope, physically or mentally, with its sudden expansion into a vast and completely untrained citizen army.

Meantime, in August 1862, McClellan had issued an order setting up a much-improved system, which later became standard with all Union armies. Among other things, this insured that ambulances and hospital supply wagons, etc., were no longer operated at the convenience of the Quartermaster Corps. Eventually the Federal Ambulance Corps became a model organization.

The original system of regimental hospitals, both Federal and Confederate, was cumbersome and inefficient. One criticism was that one regimental surgical staff might be overwhelmed by a rush of casualties, while another nearby might be inactive. There also seems to have been a reluctance on the part of some regimental surgeons to treat the wounded of other regiments. In addition, when brigaded with other regiments, there was duplication of equipment, and unnecessary enlargement of the hospital train.

In the system as finally adopted, the wounded first walked, or were carried to a forward dressing station, established by the regimental medical officers as close to the firing line as possible. After hasty first aid they were loaded on ambulances and sent to the divisional field hospital, which was usually set up just out of artillery range. There the worst cases were operated on, and from there all who could be moved were sent to the base or general hospitals, of which there were, at one time, two hundred and five on the Federal side alone.

The average Federal divisional hospital train consisted of fourteen army wagons and four medical wagons, carrying twenty-two hospital tents and medical and surgical supplies and equipment sufficient to care for seven thousand to eight thousand men.

LENGTH: 1,200 WORDS

VOCABULARY

stethoscope   device that a doctor uses to listen to the heart beat
apathy   lack of concern
atrocious   awful
susceptible   prone to
dysentery   intestinal inflammation that causes diarrhea
under canvas   in tents in the field
skulker   someone who is sneaky
shirker   someone who is lazy
double in brass   to do double duty as bandsman and soldier
priority list   order of importance of jobs or duties
appalling   shocking
cumbersome   difficult, clumsy

19 · Medicine and the Civil War

```
SCORING:     Reading time: _____ Rate from chart: _____ W.P.M.

        RETENTION      number right _____ × 2 equals _____ points

        INFERENCES     number right _____ × 2 equals _____ points

        COMPLETION     number right _____ × 4 equals _____ points

        DEFINITIONS    number right _____ × 2 equals _____ points

                       (Total points: 100)   total _____ points
```

RETENTION   Based on the passage, which of the following statements are True (T), False (F), or Not answerable (N)?

1. _____ One in three deaths during the Civil War was due to disease, not to bullets.

2. _____ Washington has accurate figures on the death totals for the Union side.

3. _____ There were not more than twenty stethoscopes in the entire Union army.

4. _____ Many men actually entered the armed service with communicable diseases.

5. _____ More "green" troops fell ill than did seasoned troops.

6. _____ The discipline of the group had nothing to do with their health.

7. _____ Often the wounded lay on the battlefield for days.

8. _____ The problem of transportation of the wounded was solved relatively quickly.

9. _____ Some wounded men walked the twenty-seven miles from Bull Run to Washington.

10. _____ At the war's outbreak, the Medical Department was geared for an army of 16,000 men.

11. _____ The War Department always gave priority to the needs of the Medical Department.

12. _____ Regimental medical outfits often worked independently of one another.

13. _____ The average Federal divisional hospital eventually consisted of seven or eight tents.

14. _____ Regimental medical outfits were very efficient.

15. ____ Lack of sanitation was a principal fact of life both in and out of the army.

16. ____ McClellan set up the first effective ambulance system.

17. ____ Lincoln empowered all regiments to mobilize a medical corps.

18. ____ Public opinion was marshalled on the side of more medical support.

19. ____ No casualties reached Washington in ambulances after the First Battle of Bull Run.

20. ____ Bandsmen were expected to fight or to help with the wounded.

INFERENCES Which three of the following statements, based on the passage, are probably justifiable? ____, ____ and ____

1. The government was not prepared for a large-scale war.
2. The Confederacy took better care of its wounded than the North did.
3. When a man was shot, his chances of dying from the wound were great.
4. Concern for the wounded was uppermost in the minds of the military.
5. Conditions of life in general had little or no bearing on life in the army.
6. Concern for human life and for human suffering was probably high in 1865.
7. The Medical Department did not know so many men would need immediate attention.
8. Septicemia was the disease that surprised everyone with its destructiveness.

COMPLETION Choose the best answer for each question.

1. ____ Transport was mostly in the hands of: (a) the War Department. (b) the Medical Department. (c) individuals. (d) the Quartermaster Corps.

2. ____ The First Battle of Bull Run took place about: (a) 100 miles from Atlanta. (b) 75 miles from Vicksburg. (c) 50 miles from Boston. (d) 25 miles from Washington.

3. ____ A reason why the men rarely washed themselves might be: (a) ignorance. (b) psychological problems. (c) laziness. (d) restrictions of society.

4. ____ The ambulances were usually driven by: (a) skulkers. (b) civilians. (c) officers. (d) the wounded.

5. ____ Ambulance drivers had a reputation for: (a) genuine bravery. (b) cowardice. (c) drunkenness. (d) diligence.

6. ____ One innovation of the system of army-wide medical treatment was: (a) the use of ambulances. (b) the use of thermometers. (c) hospitals in protected areas. (d) first aid on the battlefield.

DEFINITIONS   Choose the best meaning for each word.

1. ____ technique: (a) device (b) method (c) machinery (d) skill

2. ____ restrictions: (a) abilities (b) evidences (c) summaries (d) limitations

3. ____ contaminated: (a) polluted (b) pure (c) muddy (d) transparent

4. ____ recruits: (a) nurses (b) soldiers (c) enemies (d) officers

5. ____ "green": (a) weak (b) inexperienced (c) cowardly (d) wounded

6. ____ system: (a) organization (b) regiment (c) body (d) plan

7. ____ issue: (a) to dismiss (b) to afford (c) to become (d) to give out

8. ____ casualties: (a) sick (b) wounded (c) missing (d) nurses

9. ____ in consequence: (a) therefore (b) however (c) as a result (d) nevertheless

10. ____ cope with: (a) defend (b) deal with (c) stay with (d) attack

11. ____ overwhelmed: (a) overrun (b) overturned (c) overlooked (d) overseen

12. ____ cumbersome: (a) unwieldy (b) unnecessary (c) inefficient (d) false

13. ____ adopt: (a) borrow (b) use (c) ignore (d) skill

14. ____ consist: (a) desist (b) comprise (c) insist (d) resist

15. ____ hasty: (a) incomplete (b) slow (c) subtle (d) quick

20 · The Cost of Discrimination

JACOB JAVITS

*A United States Senator tells how discrimination hurts our coun-
try. Statistics tell one story—loss in terms of educated citizens
and loss in dollars—but statistics do not tell about the grave loss
of political prestige Americans suffer by not practicing the freedom they preach.*

Outside the South, the antidiscrimination forces can count on a
hard reality of modern American life: prejudice has proved to be ineffective
politics. In the past, bigotry and hate may have had some success, but today
they simply do not work. In my own career in politics, I have had no little experience with religious smear campaigns. In the late part of the senatorial campaign of 1956, literature appeared in New York City—which has a large Jewish
population—carrying the innuendo that I had forsaken the Jewish faith. The
matter was brought out into the open during a television interview when
viewers telephoned in the question: "Is it true that you changed your Jewish
faith?" Questions such as this, as every public figure knows, are like that old
verbal trap which calls for a yes or no answer to the question: "Have you
stopped beating your wife yet?" Air time ran out before I could reply that I
had not changed my religion. Yet, according to my analysis of the 1956 results,
the question had little or no effect on the voters of New York State.

Equally clearly, other attempts to use bigotry did not pay off. In Connecti-
cut, Abraham Ribicoff won election for governor despite the injection of anti-
Semitism into the campaign. The late Senator Richard L. Neuberger of Oregon
scored an upset victory in a campaign marred by many expressions of bigotry,
one of which openly urged voters to elect candidates who were "Christian."

THE COST OF DISCRIMINATION From *Discrimination—U.S.A.* © 1960, by Jacob K. Javits. Reprinted by permission of Harcourt, Brace & World, Inc.

117

Senators Paul Douglas of Illinois and Hubert Humphrey of Minnesota won despite strenuous efforts to label them as recipients of special support from Communist sympathizers and Jews.

The most spectacular proof that appeals to religious prejudice do not work in modern American politics came in the West Virginia presidential primary battle of 1960 between Senator John Kennedy, a Catholic, and Senator Hubert Humphrey, a Protestant. Although Senator Humphrey made it ringingly plain that he wanted no votes gained from religious bias, anti-Catholicism was a blatant part of the campaign. Seasoned observers thought the prejudice might well have a decisive effect: West Virginia is 95 per cent Protestant and was supposed to have a strong anti-Catholic tradition. But when the votes were counted, Kennedy had won a thumping three-to-two victory. He was hurt little or not at all by the anti-Catholic campaign. On the contrary, apparently he was actually helped by it. Heavily Protestant West Virginia seemed the more determined to give the Senator, a Catholic, a victory as a way of showing that it wanted no part of elections determined by irrelevant questions of religion.

The antidiscrimination forces can count on still another fact—that there are, after all, such things as facts. The simple truth is that prejudice and discrimination grow out of men's primitive fear of the strange and the unknown. They are nourished on the tensions and uncertainties of modern civilization. They affect every home and institution, undermining respect for law and order, weakening our defenses, and corrupting the moral fiber of our nation. The moral and material costs of discrimination to our country are so enormous that they can only be approximated. The money damage alone has been estimated by a former cabinet official to be as high as thirty billion dollars a year. A recent project at Columbia University reported that denial of equal educational opportunities deprived America each year of about 158,000 Negro high school graduates and 14,000 Negro college graduates. These are totally needless losses, and we cannot afford them.

There are approximately 18,000,000 Negroes in the United States, one-half of whom live in the South, and another third in five urban centers in the North. Statistics offer a dramatic picture of how meagerly they share in our expanding economy. In 1939, the median income for white workers was $1,112 a year; for nonwhite workers, it was $460. In 1955, white workers had a median income of $3,986, contrasted with $2,342 for nonwhite workers. These figures make plain that while the nonwhite population has shared in our general prosperity and reduced the difference between incomes, the Negro nevertheless continues to pay a severe price solely because of the color of his skin. Today, two out of every five Negro families earn less than $2,000 a year. Average Negro incomes are still only 52 per cent as large as white incomes.

There is a final fact about the results of discrimination, the most important of all. The future of our nation—indeed, its very existence—may well depend upon whether nonwhites living in the underdeveloped countries choose Communism or freedom. The great contest revolves around the one billion two hundred million people—largely Negro and Oriental—who live in the Far East, the Middle East, and Africa. This global picture is crucially related to our domestic struggle over civil rights and the ending of discrimination. It is so importantly related because the nonwhites are watching closely to see whether we practice what we preach about equality and justice.

This truth was brought home to me forcibly on my trip around the world in 1956. In India, I talked with Prime Minister Jawaharlal Nehru, and he could not have been more emphatic in his point that our handling of the color question could be a serious handicap—or a great asset—to the United States among the people of Asia, the Middle East, and Africa. In Taipei, the Nationalist Chinese leader, Chiang Kai-shek, expressed the same opinion.

No American domestic situation gives the Soviet Union and the international Communist party more fuel for their propaganda machines than America's two faces on civil rights. In terms of world prestige, Little Rock cost us more in one day of violent prejudice than the launching of all the Russian space satellites. The Soviet press had a field day with statements like: "The United States monopolies train the murderers of tomorrow in such barbarous actions as the recent outbreaks of racism in the United States. Racial discrimination is an integral part of the United States policy, and the white people in the United States want to annihilate the Negroes." A Russian picture magazine could play up the Little Rock story, featuring one particularly ghastly four-color photograph, showing a group of white-hooded figures beating one Negro while another Negro hung naked from a tree. In the background a Klansman held aloft a large American flag.

Even more damaging to our prestige was the reaction of the press in the uncommitted areas of Asia, the Middle East, and Africa. Typically, the *Times of Indonesia* declared: "It is hard to realize that this is taking place in a country proclaiming its democratic liberties for all to hear." We simply cannot hope to win the nonwhite peoples of the world conclusively to our side if they doubt that we will consider them equals. They will continue to doubt just as long as we wave our Constitution at them with one hand, and with the other tolerate the denial to a substantial part of our citizens in a broad region of our own country of their rights under that Constitution.

The disastrous effects of American racism on American policy abroad, the price we pay for it at home, the naked injustice of barring 10 per cent of our population from full participation in the national life—all of these things are tragic facts, and the people of the United States are daily becoming more aware of them. In 1943, when Wendell Willkie proclaimed "one world" and warned against "our imperialisms at home," he was striking a note that was new and strange to many in the United States. Today, the thought is becoming commonplace, and the more commonplace it is, the more powerful a weapon is placed in the hands of the antidiscrimination forces. The growing knowledgeability and maturity of the American people are another strong indication that the onrushing decades will be an era of rapidly expanding rights and opportunities for those who have had to wait so very long.

As the United States hurries along the road toward genuine democracy, all kinds of efforts will help. The agitations of organizations will have their importance; so, too, will the labors of dedicated individuals and the studies of psychologists, sociologists, economists, and historians. But the prime need is law—more firm, carefully formulated legislation on the federal, state, and municipal levels directed toward making equal rights and equal opportunities ultimate realities. Law is the indispensable advance guard of social change. It gives well-intentioned men a standard to which they can repair. It nudges the indifferent and it tames the hostile.

LENGTH: 1,480 WORDS

VOCABULARY

innuendo   hint, insinuation
blatant   outright, brazen
irrelevant   beside the point, not pertinent
meagerly   slightly, poorly
crucially   very importantly
annihilate   do away with, destroy
ghastly   awful, terrifying
agitations   activities, disturbances

20 · The Cost of Discrimination

SCORING: Reading time: _____ Rate from chart: _____ W.P.M.

RETENTION	number right ____ × 2 equals ____ points	
INFERENCES	number right ____ × 2 equals ____ points	
COMPLETION	number right ____ × 4 equals ____ points	
DEFINITIONS	number right ____ × 2 equals ____ points	

(Total points: 100)   **total** ____ points

RETENTION   Based on the passage, which of the following statements are True (T), False (F), or Not answerable (N)?

1. ____ Prejudice is politically effective in the South today.

2. ____ Javits himself was once accused of having left the Jewish faith.

3. ____ West Virginia has a predominantly Catholic population.

4. ____ No one knows the moral and material cost of discrimination in America.

5. ____ A project at Columbia estimates that 14,000 Negroes are deprived of a college education each year.

6. ____ Approximately 6,000,000 Negroes live in five urban centers in the North.

7. ____ White workers have a median income almost twice that of Negro workers.

8. ____ There is no connection between Communism abroad and Negro opportunity at home.

9. ____ Nehru was uninterested in the color question when Javits spoke with him.

10. ____ The Russians like to think that racism is integral to the American way of life.

11. ____ Wendell Willkie proclaimed "one world" in 1943.

12. ____ Nonwhites represent about 20 percent of the total population of the U.S.A.

13. ____ Nonwhites represent more than 50 percent of the total population of the world.

14. _____ "Our imperialisms at home" could be such things as social security and taxes.

15. _____ Americans are becoming more knowledgeable and mature about prejudice.

16. _____ Genuine democracy is what the *Times of Indonesia* respects.

17. _____ Problems of prejudice have not harmed Javits' political career.

18. _____ The law is not quick enough to keep apace of social change.

19. _____ Equal rights is an ideal that cannot be achieved, though we should try.

20. _____ Law nudges the indifferent and tames the hostile.

INFERENCES Which three of the following statements, based on the passage, are probably justifiable? _____, _____ and _____

1. No one in America wants to be prejudiced.
2. Prejudice often accompanies poverty, backwardness, and hard times.
3. Javits probably stayed out of politics because of prejudice.
4. The Russians are fortunate not to have prejudice in their country.
5. Javits favors legal reform of prejudicial conditions.
6. Other countries stay silent on the issue of prejudice.
7. Our prestige in the Far East is directly linked to our handling of prejudice at home.
8. In 1960, Hubert Humphrey completely ignored the issue of prejudice.

COMPLETION Choose the best answer for each question.

1. _____ The money damage of discrimination has been estimated to be: (a) thirty billion dollars a year. (b) eighteen million dollars a year. (c) one hundred fifty-eight million dollars a year. (d) three billion dollars a year.

2. _____ West Virginia is: (a) 95 percent Catholic. (b) 50 percent Catholic. (c) 35 percent Catholic. (d) 5 percent Catholic.

3. _____ Today two out of five Negro families earn less than: (a) $2,000 a year. (b) $1,700 a year. (c) $1,500 a year. (d) $466 a year.

4. _____ Little Rock cost more in one day of prejudice than the: (a) total of all other racial outrages. (b) battles of World War II. (c) cabinet was able to estimate. (d) launching of all Russian space satellites.

5. ____ The fact that we are hurrying "along the road toward genuine democracy" means: (a) nothing. (b) that we are not now a genuine democracy. (c) that we have good intentions. (d) that democracy is a good thing.

6. ____ The great contest between Russia and America revolves around: (a) racial understanding and good will. (b) Chiang Kai-shek and Nehru. (c) Jacob Javits and the New York legislature. (d) 1.2 billion Asians and Africans.

DEFINITIONS   Choose the best meaning for each word.

1. ____ ineffective: (a) useful (b) harsh (c) useless (d) undesirable

2. ____ reply: (a) answer (b) differ (c) pretend (d) repair

3. ____ analysis: (a) differentiation (b) examination (c) systems (d) aid

4. ____ marred: (a) defaced (b) moved (c) hurled (d) bent

5. ____ despite: (a) rest (b) with anger (c) instead (d) in spite of

6. ____ primary: (a) last (b) first (c) important (d) unimportant

7. ____ bias: (a) suit-fabric (b) two by two (c) stubborn (d) prejudice

8. ____ seasoned: (a) out-of-doors (b) experienced (c) new (d) worn-out

9. ____ irrelevant: (a) unimportant (b) necessary (c) frilly (d) pleasant

10. ____ nourish: (a) feed (b) relish (c) curry (d) give assistance

11. ____ apparently: (a) obviously (b) surely (c) probably (d) doubtfully

12. ____ deprive: (a) resent (b) destroy (c) shove (d) dispossess

13. ____ severe price: (a) little (b) small price (c) heavy price (d) no price

14. ____ emphatic: (a) forceful (b) weak (c) middling (d) serious

15. ____ hostile: (a) irritated (b) sensible (c) unfriendly (d) perplexed

21 · John Logie Baird:
Inventor of Television

HENRY and DANA LEE THOMAS

John Baird failed at everything he tried until, thrown back on a hobby because he had no work, he single-handedly solved the most difficult technical problems of television.

Even during his business activity Baird had speculated with the possibility of developing an apparatus for sending an image of the human face through the ether. Television.

The word television is a hybrid derived from the Latin *video*, "I see," and the Greek *tele*, "at a distance." For years scientists had been certain of the theoretical possibility of television. Just as the human voice had been translated successfully into electric current variations and transmitted over long distances, so it was believed that the rays of light reflected from a human face could be changed into electrical impulses, amplified and radiated from a broadcasting station to a receiving post.

The problem was to devise an instrument which would perform in television the role of the microphone in radio; to perfect an "electric eye" sensitive enough to "pick up" the image to be signaled along the wave lengths.

In 1888 the German professor, Heinrich Hertz, had embarked on a project of research which led eventually to the development of a kind of photoelectric cell. It seemed at first as if this would perform the trick of changing light into electric signals. But further investigation revealed that the cells were too insensitive to respond sufficiently to available quantities of light. Several years before Hertz, a scientist had explored selenium cells. But research indicated that these cells also were too sluggish to react efficiently to the tremendous speeds of signaling.

When Baird began his independent research in 1924, no one had as yet succeeded in televising an image in half-tones on a screen.

Setting up his laboratory in a narrow attic above an artificial flower shop, he used the equipment of the rank amateur. He based his motor on an old tea chest, rotating a disc of cardboard by means of a bicycle chain he had purchased second-hand. He fitted a projection lamp into a biscuit box, and he fashioned mountings from darning needles and discarded lumber. The entire apparatus was held together by glue, string and sealing wax. To develop the high voltage needed for his experiments, he bought ordinary pocket flashlight batteries and clipped them together in rows. Whenever his technical knowledge failed him in his work, he went out to the public library and thumbed through books to "sweat out" the answer.

What Baird hoped to accomplish with his jerry-built apparatus was simple enough in theory. When a human face is televised, the variations of light from the features are transformed by photoelectric cells into variations of electric current. These currents modulate a radio wave which passes through space and is retranslated at the receiving end into electric signals. These, in turn, direct the light that builds up the original image.

According to Baird's plan, by a process of scanning, a powerful beam of light would examine the face and transmit the image point by point. At the receiving post the image would be reassembled by an exactly reverse process, recreated as a painter builds his picture, stroke by stroke.

The key to the success of the system lay in the perfecting of a sufficiently responsive photoelectric cell. For months Baird worked perseveringly in his little studio. And one afternoon he obtained tentative results. His improvised heap of batteries, darning needles and hat boxes actually transmitted the tiny, unsteady image of a Maltese cross over a distance of a couple of yards.

In 1925 he moved up to London, and he continued his experiments in a two-room attic near Soho. The proprietor of Selfridge's London Department Store became sufficiently interested in Baird's investigations at this stage to invite him to give demonstrations of his "shadowgraphs" for customers. The circular sent out by Selfridge's to advertise the demonstrations reminded its clientele that although Baird's pictures were as yet primitive, "Edison's first phonograph announced 'Mary had a little lamb' in a way that only hearers who were 'in the secret' could understand."

The visitors at the exhibition displayed little understanding of the possibilities of Baird's apparatus. One old lady asked him if television became general whether she would be able to preserve her privacy by pulling down the blinds when she took a bath.

The greatest struggles were still ahead of the inventor. His transmission of simple shadows was not yet true television. He was still unable to send anything in the way of a living human face; no light, no shade, no actual detail.

He had not bridged the gulf between the shadow and substance. In an effort to find the secret of true television, he experimented with all varieties of light-sensitive cells. He even obtained a human eye from a surgical friend and constructed a cell out of the visual purple. But the sum of his investigations was meager. The human face that appeared at the receiving end of his apparatus remained merely an oval of white. The mouth was indicated by a flickering spot of black. Nothing more.

Early backers who had put money into his apparatus in the hope that they could quickly profit on the commercial potentialities became impatient with Baird's negative results. The public itself was convinced that Baird's machine would never transmit the image of a recognizable human face.

The young Scotchman went bankrupt. He actually denied himself the necessities of life to purchase equipment for his experiments. He was compelled to sell vital parts of his apparatus to pay his rent. Hitherto he had refused to ask his relatives in Scotland for financial assistance. But now he swallowed his pride. Several members of his family were people of means, and they contributed handsomely. They helped him form a company, Television Incorporated, and bought several thousand dollars' worth of shares.

Freed from financial headaches, Baird continued to perfect his photoelectric cell. And then on October 2, 1926, the miracle of true television occurred.

He had been using for a subject in his experiments a doll that once belonged to a ventriloquist. Hitherto "Bill's" head had been telecast upon the screen as a white blob with three black circles vaguely indicating the position of the eyes and nose. But on the above-mentioned date the unbelievable happened. Bill's face appeared as a recognizable image with shading and detail. The nose, the eyes and even the round top of the head could be clearly distinguished.

Flushed with excitement, Baird determined to try his "electric eye" on a human being. He dashed down the stairs, grabbed hold of an office boy who worked on the floor below and dragged him into his laboratory. Placing him before a battery of blinding lights he told him to sit still as he rushed over to the receiving screen. Undeniably, a lifelike face looked out at the inventor. The problem was solved.

Baird changed places with the lad and directed him to cast an eye upon the screen. And the office boy became the second living person to witness the wonder of television.

LENGTH: 1,230 WORDS

VOCABULARY

ether   the atmosphere

hybrid   something made by combining different or incongruous things

photoelectric cell   a cell for changing light into electricity

half-tones   a picture whose lights and shadows are composed of minute dots
obtained by photographing the original through a finely lined screen

jerry-built   badly made

modulate   change or alter

improvised   constructed from whatever was available

21 · John Logie Baird: Inventor of Television

SCORING:	Reading time: _4.25_ Rate from chart: _345_ W.P.M.
RETENTION	number right _____ × 2 equals _____ points
INFERENCES	number right _____ × 2 equals _____ points
COMPLETION	number right _____ × 4 equals _____ points
DEFINITIONS	number right _____ × 2 equals _____ points
	(Total points: 100) **total** _____ points

RETENTION Based on the passage, which of the following statements are True (T), False (F), or Not answerable (N)?

1. _____ Baird probably was a businessman before he became an inventor.

2. _____ *Television* is a hybrid word meaning, "I see through the ether."

3. _____ The problem was to devise a "visual" microphone.

4. _____ Hertz, of course, was the real inventor of the photoelectric cell.

5. _____ Baird began independent research in 1888.

6. _____ Baird wanted to change variations of light into variations of electric current.

7. _____ Baird's original apparatus was professional enough for his purposes.

8. _____ The process of scanning the image to be transmitted was all Baird's idea.

9. _____ The first image Baird successfully sent was that of a Maltese cat.

10. _____ People were quick to see the great possibilities of television.

11. _____ Baird began by transmitting what were essentially mere shadows.

12. _____ Once Baird used a cow's eye as a photoelectric cell.

13. _____ Even with his early success, the problem of getting half-tones remained.

14. _____ Baird was actually a Welshman, not an Englishman.

15. _____ When the going got rough, Baird's early backers stood behind him.

16. _____ An office boy was the first person to witness the wonders of TV.

17. _____ Television Incorporated was established with the help of Baird's family.

18. _____ "Bill's" head was the head of a friend of Baird's.

19. _____ It was not until the end of 1926 that television was really achieved.

20. _____ Selfridge's London Department Store specialized in hardware and radios.

INFERENCES Which three of the following statements, based on the passage, are probably justifiable? _____, _____ and _____

1. Baird probably had a sound theoretical knowledge of radio.
2. Selfridge was a shrewd man who saw the possibilities of television early.
3. Baird's method might be described as "cut and try."
4. People thought television would change the world more than it did.
5. Baird's resourcefulness was a key factor in his eventual success.
6. Nobody, not even Selfridge, thought the inventor would succeed.
7. Baird was a man of large, but not great, wealth.
8. Baird succeeded because he gave all his energy and time to his invention.

COMPLETION Choose the best answer for each question.

1. _____ Baird and others thought they could transmit visual images through space because: (a) it had been done long before. (b) no one told them otherwise. (c) sound had been sent through space. (d) light reflected from the human face.

2. _____ In order to get high voltages Baird: (a) experimented with biscuit boxes. (b) used rows of ordinary flashlight batteries. (c) rigged up the house current. (d) asked the help of a ventriloquist.

3. _____ To achieve success took Baird approximately: (a) six months. (b) one year. (c) two years. (d) four years.

4. _____ The image was to have been transmitted: (a) point by point. (b) as quickly as the apparatus would allow. (c) through the wall. (d) for Selfridge.

5. _____ Even without television transmission, the radio wave is: (a) a little television signal. (b) not there. (c) doing its regular job. (d) traveling through space anyway.

6. _____ Most of Baird's experiments were conducted in London in: (a) a department store. (b) a friend's offices. (c) his family's rented flat. (d) a two-room attic.

DEFINITIONS Choose the best meaning for each word.

1. _____ speculate: (a) look at (b) consider (c) regard (d) permit

2. _____ activity: (a) passivity (b) pretending (c) action (d) occurrence

3. _____ devise: (a) invent (b) permit (c) struggle (d) proclaim

4. _____ perform: (a) revise (b) do (c) have (d) let

5. _____ perfect: (a) revise (b) distort (c) make do (d) make final improvements

6. _____ embark: (a) send out (b) set out upon (c) yelp (d) begin again

7. _____ revealed: (a) shown (b) reported (c) given (d) played

8. _____ sluggish: (a) energetic (b) worn out (c) slow moving (d) preposterous

9. _____ transmit: (a) send forth (b) have done (c) stop now (d) caution

10. _____ responsive: (a) irritable (b) well-said (c) asleep (d) alert

11. _____ proprietor: (a) beginner (b) owner (c) buyer (d) seller

12. _____ primitive: (a) crude (b) jungle-like (c) stony (d) unsuccessful

13. _____ varieties: (a) supplies (b) shows (c) kinds (d) orders

14. _____ meager: (a) insane (b) egotistical (c) bother (d) inadequate

15. _____ compelled: (a) forced (b) permitted (c) requested (d) left

22 · Where the Wheel Hasn't Been Invented

ANONYMOUS

> *It is hard to believe, but some people live today just as their ancestors lived 30,000 years ago. In the jungles of Venezuela, the wheel literally has not been invented. The Makiritare Indians, cheerful, friendly, and witty, have just discovered and been discovered by the outside world.*

You won't find Canaracuni on most maps. All it amounts to is half a dozen little huts of fiber and some dried clay, a half mile from a river of the same name, a name that in the language of the Makiritare Indians means River of the Bananas.

Here, in the basin of the Southern Orinoco, where the jungles of Venezuela and Brazil join to form a single lost world, there are several scattered villages like Canaracuni, belonging to the Makiritare, the Waika, the Chirisana and several other nomadic groups that still live in the Stone Age.

For them, the wheel does not exist. Agriculture has not been developed. Metal instruments are unknown. Fire is a great miracle obtained by rubbing two sticks together. Clothing, except for a loin cloth for men and women, is not used.

These people speak no Spanish. Nor can one tribe communicate vocally with another, though they may live only a mile apart. Their individual languages consist of a few words with several meanings each. For example, the Makiritare, whose name means "People of trees and river," use a word that sounds like "adua" to signify "now," "that's enough," "goodby," "thank you" and several other things.

Although they are considered Venezuelans, they had—until a few months ago—been entirely cut off from the country, a country they do not know exists.

Their only communication with the world beyond their jungle was by dug-out canoe along the Canaracuni River, into the Caura River, and finally into the Orinoco. There are no land roads to anywhere.

Through the ages, the tribes—believed to be descendants of Mongoloid peoples who migrated here thousands of years ago—have survived in their isolation.

The river and rain forest have kept them alive. The men paddle up river and dip the roots of a tree into the water. The roots absorb the water's oxygen and the fish die. Little ones, the size of a sardine, that they call curata, and big ones they know as amayra then float down river where the womenfolk scoop them up.

The Makiritare also fish with arrows they shoot into the air. Their marksmanship is so amazingly good that the arrows fall into the river at the exact point where a fish has been sighted.

Arrows and the darts used in the blow guns of these people, are tipped with curare, the paralyzing poison of a plant the Indians obtain in the highlands, 15-days' journey away, and are employed for hunting birds, wild boar, deer, tapir, jaguar and other animals.

The Makiritare's principal sustenance, however, is a paste derived from the yucca plant. This is to them what the tortilla is to Indians farther north.

But, because of the lack of proper nourishment and because of the increasing toll of tuberculosis, malaria, parasites and other diseases, the tribes of the region are dying off.

For the last few years, a couple of missionaries from the French order of the Little Brothers of Jesus, the first strangers ever to visit the area, have been trying to help them, providing rudimentary medical care and teaching them the art of communicating with each other.

Cut off from the world, except for the river, the missionaries found their task hopeless. They appealed for help by radio to the Venezuelan armed forces.

Today, that appeal is being heeded by the Venezuelan Air Force, as part of the military's civic action program originated by the United States to help Latin armies improve their image among people long accustomed to the military as an oppressive power. The Air Force is flying in food and medical supplies, as well as "magical" gifts, like the little yellow birds that lay eggs that can be eaten, and the thin metal things that make light when there is no sun.

I came along on one of the mercy flights and was surprised on the one hand, to see people living as their ancestors did perhaps a million years ago, and on the other to see how friendly, though timid, they are.

I was able to mix freely with the Makiritare and the Waika who live near the river, after gaining their confidence with presents of hard candies, matches and cigarettes (a great improvement over the tobacco wrapped in pieces of bark that they smoke).

These copper-colored Indians are not pygmies, but they are extremely short. The men are about 4 feet 5 inches tall, and the women much shorter.

Although my communication with them was by means of sign language, I found they had an excellent, though extremely simple, sense of humor, laughing innocently at the same slapstick comedy we supposedly sophisticated beings laugh at in the civilized world.

Several children were especially delighted with the movement of the carriage on my typewriter and how I would let it snap back at their waiting fingers. They laughed uproariously at this and, if they had had their way, would have kept me at it all day.

Men and boys alike were taken with the garments we wore. One man insisted on trading his bow and arrow for my sports shirt. He did not want money: other than making personal adornments out of silver coins, these people have no use for it.

The tribes of this particular area are not cannibals. They do, however, keep the bodies of their deceased relatives for three months, burn them and then eat the ashes. The idea, a strangely devout concept if you can see it their way, is to maintain within themselves the spirit of their departed ones.

There are no beauty parlors or barber shops in Canaracuni. So the women, and the men and children too, paint themselves with a native seed—long streaks of red all over the body. The men are shaved with the help of their women and of the powder from a root. The woman applies the powder, which softens the beard, and then yanks the hairs out.

Whatever they are doing when the Air Force C-47 comes into sight, flying through a narrow canyon toward the makeshift landing strip, the Indians stop their activities and run to meet their new friends. They realize that the "guaranyate," the giant bird, is bringing them friendship and, more important, gifts to help them stay alive.

LENGTH: 1,380 WORDS

VOCABULARY

Orinoco   large river rising in Brazil and flowing through central Venezuela
Mongoloid   a race of Asiatic origin
migrated   moved from one place to another
isolation   being alone, separated from other peoples
absorb   soak up
yucca   lily-like plant
malaria   tropical disease
parasites   plants or animals that live on or in other organisms, including human beings
rudimentary   crude, elementary
oppressive   burdensome, cruel
sophisticated   well educated, knowledgeable

22 · Where the Wheel Hasn't Been Invented

SCORING: Reading time: ___4-25___ Rate from chart: ___345___ W.P.M.

RETENTION	number right _____ × 2 equals _____ points	
INFERENCES	number right _____ × 2 equals _____ points	
COMPLETION	number right _____ × 4 equals _____ points	
DEFINITIONS	number right _____ × 2 equals _____ points	

(Total points: 100)   **total** _____ points

RETENTION   Based on the passage, which of the following statements are True (T), False (F), or Not answerable (N)?

1. _____ The Makiritare Indians are actually Venezuelans.

2. _____ The Indians of the Canaracuni cannot communicate vocally with other tribes.

3. _____ *Adua* means "water" in the language of the Makiritare.

4. _____ Many of these Indians have been in the smaller Venezuelan cities.

5. _____ According to speculation, these people once migrated from Asia.

6. _____ Facts suggest that the Indians migrated by means of dugout canoes.

7. _____ The river and rain forest both isolate the Indians and give them life.

8. _____ To catch fish, the men of the Canaracuni hit them with the roots of trees.

9. _____ *Curata* and *amayra* are names of arrows and darts, among other things.

10. _____ The Makiritare fish only with arrows.

11. _____ Because of the nourishment provided by the yucca plant, the tribes are increasing.

12. _____ The Air Force were the first strangers ever to visit these people.

13. _____ The Makiritare assume that modern technical devices like flashlights are magic.

14. _____ The Makiritare are distantly related to the American Indian.

15. _____ Although these people live as they did a million years ago, they are warlike.

16. _____ The author is a missionary with the Little Brothers of Jesus.

17. _____ The author introduced smoking to the tribes in the area.

18. _____ There seems to be a relationship between the sense of humor of the tribal Makiritare and that of the modern American.

19. _____ The tribes of this area are basically cannibalistic.

20. _____ Makeup for these people is restricted, as with Americans, to the face.

INFERENCES Which three of the following statements, based on the passage, are probably justifiable? _____, _____ and _____

1. The Venezuelan government is helping the Makiritare to stay alive.
2. As a missionary, the author has been effective and helpful.
3. No one knows why the Makiritare want to stay on the Canaracuni River.
4. Money is of no importance to the Makiritare.
5. The Air Force uses the tribal landing strip for training purposes.
6. The curiosity of the Makiritare is quite as lively as that of any people.
7. The Makiritare and other tribal groups have been continually killing each other.
8. Most of the diseases known to the white man are unknown to these people.

COMPLETION Choose the best answer for each question.

1. _____ Eating the ashes of the dead is: (a) an ordeal of faith. (b) rather ghastly. (c) a strangely devout concept. (d) permitted under the law.

2. _____ Women soften the men's beards by applying: (a) hot water. (b) red from a native seed. (c) ashes from the fire. (d) powder from a root.

3. _____ The important things the Air Force is carrying in are: (a) "magical" gifts. (b) Bibles and prayerbooks. (c) chickens and eggs. (d) food and medicine.

4. _____ The military's civic action program was started by: (a) the United States. (b) the United Nations. (c) Venezuela. (d) the Council of Latin Armies.

5. _____ The people who appealed for help for these tribes were: (a) the Makiritare themselves. (b) the Little Brothers of Jesus. (c) the author and some friends. (d) the Venezuelan Air Force.

6. _____ The Makiritare's principal food is: (a) large and small fish. (b) the yucca plant. (c) tapir and jaguar. (d) tree roots.

DEFINITIONS   Choose the best meaning for each word.

1. _____ sustenance: (a) food   (b) substance   (c) energy   (d) maintain

2. _____ scoop: (a) hurt   (b) catch   (c) begin   (d) run

3. _____ obtain: (a) get   (b) prevent   (c) disturb   (d) eliminate

4. _____ toll: (a) bell   (b) sounds   (c) payments   (d) irritation

5. _____ curare: (a) fish   (b) poison   (c) ashes   (d) medicine

6. _____ descendants: (a) relatives   (b) peoples   (c) nourishments   (d) containers

7. _____ survive: (a) die off   (b) pretend   (c) come back to life   (d) live

8. _____ isolation: (a) like others   (b) solitude   (c) quiet   (d) whispers

9. _____ rudimentary: (a) excellent   (b) hopeless   (c) friendly   (d) crude

10. _____ appeal: (a) cry   (b) ask   (c) call down   (d) affront

11. _____ heed: (a) beg   (b) considerate   (c) masculine   (d) listen to

12. _____ timid: (a) angry   (b) shy   (c) retentive   (d) learned

13. _____ innocent: (a) resistant   (b) stubborn   (c) unsophisticated   (d) quiet

14. _____ adornment: (a) jewelry   (b) earnings   (c) foods   (d) support

15. _____ devout: (a) perspicacious   (b) intelligent   (c) considered   (d) religious

23 · English in Finland

CHESTER G. ANDERSON

> *What is it like to teach English in a foreign country like Finland? Does a teacher honestly enjoy having his students so polite that they never ask a question? Professor Anderson describes his experiences as a Fulbright Scholar teaching in Helsinki.*

What is it like for an American to teach English to university students in Finland?

Finland is a culturally affluent nation. There is no illiteracy in Finland. It is bilingual (Finnish and Swedish), and about half of the younger people have studied English for six or seven years. Bookstores and booksales are in overwhelming larger proportion to population than in the United States. Finland leads all of the nations in the world in proportion of its national income (6.5%) spent on education. Its national and municipal governments subsidize professional theaters, and its creative workers in literature, sculpture, architecture are its main national heroes.

One would think, then, that teaching in the greatest Finnish university, Helsinki, in a hotbed of readers of high intelligence, would be more rewarding and stimulating for an American than teaching at home. Not so. And I wonder why.

It should be said first of all that teaching in Finland does have its rewards. The university professor there is a much more highly honored member of the community than he is in the United States, and a great deal of this social distinction rubs off on the foreign visitor. The hours are good—five 45-minute periods a week. Time-consuming and academically unprofitable extra-curricular

ENGLISH IN FINLAND From *Teacher Education Quarterly*, fall 1964. Reprinted by permission of the author and *Teacher Education Quarterly*.

assignments, administrative chores, committee meetings and department meetings are all but unknown. (Students run their own outside activities; registration and course credit are handled by the simple procedure of having the professor sign the students' registration books during the first and last class period of each term; there are few committees; the English department met twice last year, but I did not have to attend.)

Classrooms are adequate, though most of them are designed for lecturing, so that they tend to be somewhat formal and austere. The library holdings in English books and periodicals are very good in philology, Old English, Middle English and Early Modern English, but leave something to be desired for more recent centuries.

The students are very deferential, rising to their feet when the professor enters and leaves the classroom, listening in an attitude of the utmost non-committal respect to all professorial opinions no matter how foolish or footling they may be, never asking an embarrassing question or pointing out an error or offering a contrary opinion. Curiously enough, this deference does not lead the teacher to put forth his least effort. It makes him realize that he himself will have to approve his lectures, and he burns the midnight oil trying to gain such reluctantly-tendered approbation.

Secondly, the ability of Finnish university students of English to read and write the language (though not to speak it) is in several respects higher, on the average, than that of American students. In spelling, punctuation and grammar, mistakes in written work are rarities. This virtual perfection is partly due, no doubt, to general standards of excellence which pervade the society. From waitresses and bus-drivers to skiers and musicians, sloppiness of performance is almost unknown. But it also seems to be partly due to the students' having learned English word-by-word and grammatical form by grammatical form. Because Finnish is not an Indo-European language, its differences from English in structure and vocabulary are almost absolute. While this makes the learning of English more difficult in one sense, it gives the advantage of keeping the languages distinct, preventing false analogies and the inaccurate substitution of meanings from one language to cognate words in the other. Also, the Finnish students have not formed the kinds of bad habits in the use of English during their childhoods and schooldays which are so difficult to correct later on, when the substandard pattern has been reinforced by years of practice. Since Finnish is spelled phonetically and Swedish nearly so, the Finnish child is not so frustrated at an early age about learning to spell that he adopts a despairing vagueness about it. Because he is already acquainted with the relatively difficult grammar of Finnish and the somewhat easier grammar of Swedish by the time he begins to study English, he accepts the grammatical approach as a matter of course and is undaunted by apparent grammatical inconsistencies. Once he has mastered the grammar, of course, punctuation presents no problems whatsoever and can be done correctly in a mechanical fashion.

This "correctness" of the Finns' English extends in certain ways to the expression of meaning. Instances of confused syntax, faulty references of pronouns, ambiguous meanings, cliché-filled sentences, jargon, verbosity, incomplete grammar and mixed-up idioms, which abound in almost any set of American student papers, are almost absent in Finnish papers. I have never heard from a Finn the most common defense of the American student against the charge that his statements are unclear: "But you get what I mean, don't you, Prof?" Although the Finnish student may be at a loss for words in conversation, wrinkling his brow and asking, "Oh, how do you say . . .?" his lack of a half-learned vocabulary—the very lack of fluency works to his advantage in the precise quality of his written work, where the dictionary and thesaurus fill the holes in his vocabulary. He does not load his papers with clichés and jargon-words, partly because he does not know them. His sentences are related mainly to his reading and his grammatical knowledge rather than to the conversational patterns that ring—often with such false notes—in the ears of native speakers of English. He does not confuse his idioms because he either understands them or, more frequently, avoids them.

The spoken English of the Finnish student, though more halting, is equally correct, for he does not learn from ungrammatical contemporaries or family members, but primarily from his teachers. On the English faculty of the University of Helsinki there are six Englishmen, a Scotsman and five Americans (including the Fulbright lecturers); and the Finns who teach English speak it impeccably and idiomatically. Candidates for the *laudatur* degree in English (about like a master's degree) are required to spend three months in England or America; many spend six months or more.

The Finnish student also learns spoken English from American motion pictures, television programs and popular songs. About a dozen American films play each night in Helsinki. Regular television fare includes "Doctor Kildare," "Ben Casey," "Wagon Train," "Father Knows Best," "Leave It to Beaver," "The Dick Powell Show," "87th Precinct," "Mr. Novak," "East Side, West Side," and old Shirley Temple movies. American popular songs of a decade or so ago are played for several hours daily on Finnish radio stations; more recent musical concoctions can be heard on jukeboxes and private phonographs. Stories in English, keyed to graded readers, are read regularly on the state radio station. On short-wave radio (more generally listened to than in America) American English can be heard on the Voice of America, and British English can be heard even more easily from London, Peiping and Moscow. The British Council, the Finnish-British Society and the Finnish-American Society provide conversational opportunities at regular meetings and in conversation classes. And Berlitz-like commercial schools teaching English do a thriving business.

But when all this is said, we come to two of the reasons why the teaching of English by an American in Finland is less rewarding than in America. First, through no fault of the students, their English has a sterile quality in its correctness, a lack of colloquial and idiomatic turns of phrase, an absence of sensitiveness to rhythmical qualities which rob the teacher of one of his great joys in teaching in America—the chance to help the potentially good writers to learn to write beautiful English. Or at least to look on as they learn. This "tin ear" reception of the English language also limits the critical appreciation which the students can have of English poetry and prose. They can appreciate fully the plot, character and thought, but not the diction. This accounts in part for the high critical estimate in Finland of a ponderous, verbose and clumsy writer like Theodore Dreiser and of a windbag like Somerset Maugham. Finnish students are little more able to distinguish between the mellifluous beauty of the speech of John Synge's Irish peasants and the hoked-up staginess of the speech of Eugene O'Neill's Irish sailors than an American who "knows German" can evaluate the diction of Georg Buchner as opposed to that of Friedrich Durrenmatt.

Another reason—again it is caused by circumstance and not by any fault of the Finns—lies in the very different characters of American and Finnish students. Unlike their American counterparts, Finnish students seem to take little delight in controversy. Their combination of shyness and politeness prevents enthusiastic or heated discussions. While their ideals of excellence are indeed high, they do not manifest themselves in intellectual aggressiveness or the spirit of attack on the opinions of others. Their extreme individualism, together with the homogeneity of their ethnic and religious backgrounds and of their educations, seems to reduce the intensity of their ideological commitments. For example, in the graduate seminar which I conducted last year there were no Freudians, no Marxists (in a country where more than one-fourth of the population is Communist!), no Thomists, no disciples of Maimonides, no Kierkegaardians, no Cassirer-ites—all of whom might well be found in a comparable seminar in an American urban university. The students are intelligent, reserved, tender-hearted, judicious and to an American, if I may say so, somewhat dull. Their best work is distinguished more for its industrious competence than for its novel insight or individualistic brilliance.

Finally, the American professor in Finland feels like an idiot. He knows only enough Finnish and Swedish to buy coffee and a hamburger, and his graduate-school French and German hardly match the French and German of his students, much less of his Finnish colleagues. Shopgirls, secretaries and schoolboys daily put him to shame (without ever meaning to) by remarkable displays of conversation in many tongues. He is aware that if he were only more familiar with Continental literatures (or, of course, if his students were more familiar with literature in English—but why put it that way?) he could make many points clear which he has left obscure. He loves the Finns—that's what he thinks of them!—and wishes that in some respects both he and his American students were more like them and that some of the Finnish respect for learning and the Finnish passion for culture could be infused into the mainstream of American life. He is under no illusion that John O'Hara and J. D. Salinger can provide valuable "new goals of enlightenment, freedom, and decency" among Finns. He may even pray to Ukko daily that the Finns hang on to their old ones.

LENGTH: 1,760 WORDS

VOCABULARY

affluent   wealthy
austere   severe, plain
philology   study of language, linguistics
deferential   polite
approbation   approval
pervade   spread through
Indo-European   basic family of languages
cognate words   words derived from a common original form
verbosity   wordiness
thesaurus   book of synonyms and antonyms
impeccably   without mistake
ponderous   heavy, unskillful
mellifluous   flowing sweetly
homogeneity   sameness
ethnic   of a racial or national group
ideological   having to do with a philosophical or political belief
Maimonides   (1135–1204) Spanish rabbi, theologian, and philosopher
Kierkegaard   (1813–1855) Danish theologian and philosopher
Cassirer · (1874–1945) German philosopher

23 · English in Finland

```
SCORING:    Reading time: _____ Rate from chart: _____ W.P.M.

      RETENTION     number right _____ × 2 equals _____ points

      INFERENCES    number right _____ × 2 equals _____ points

      COMPLETION    number right _____ × 4 equals _____ points

      DEFINITIONS   number right _____ × 2 equals _____ points

                    (Total points: 100)  total _____ points
```

RETENTION   Based on the passage, which of the following statements are True (T), False (F), or Not answerable (N)?

1. _____ Finland is a culturally undernourished country.

2. _____ The author taught English at the university in Helsinki, Finland.

3. _____ Teaching English in Finland, the author says, is less rewarding than he expected it to be.

4. _____ On the whole, Finnish students are less polite than American students.

5. _____ Finland leads all the countries in the world in the proportion of its income spent on education.

6. _____ The classroom atmosphere in Finland is informal and casual.

7. _____ The Finns make remarkably few mistakes in English grammar and punctuation.

8. _____ The author suggests that a teacher is much happier if his students accept everything he has to say without question.

9. _____ One reason for the Finns' speaking English correctly is that, unlike most Americans, they have never heard sloppy or incorrect English.

10. _____ There is a remarkable difference between the correctness of the Finns' spoken and written English.

11. _____ One thing the Finnish student never says is, "But you get what I mean."

12. _____ What the student says is likely to sound more like written English than conversational English.

13. _____ Candidates for an advanced degree in English must spend three months or more in England or America.

14. _____ Popular songs do not help the Finns learn conversational English.

15. _____ The Finnish radio often programs stories in English.

16. _____ Finland does not have American TV programming.

17. _____ The author was surprised that Finnish students do not get excited about their ideological commitments.

18. _____ One fourth of the population of Finland is Communist.

19. _____ Ukko is probably an ancient Finnish god.

20. _____ Finnish students are not so bright as Americans, but they are more exciting.

INFERENCES Which three of the following statements, based on the passage, are probably justifiable? _____, _____ and _____

1. The quality of teaching in Finland is not up to that of the teaching in America.
2. The teacher's responsibilities in a Finnish university are primarily teaching, not committee work and other extra-curricular chores.
3. The author is not basically an English teacher.
4. Finnish universities have no extra-curricular activities for their students.
5. People in Finland are extremely conscious of language.
6. Sometimes the American professor in Finland feels like an idiot.
7. The Russians pressure the Finns to include Russian in their courses.
8. Finns appreciate the best and most important parts of any literary works written in English.

COMPLETION Choose the best answer for each question.

1. _____ As far as Finnish culture is concerned, the author is: (a) completely disinterested. (b) very favorably impressed. (c) not very well informed. (d) impressed, but not very favorably.

2. _____ In spelling, punctuation, and grammar, Finnish students make mistakes: (a) rarely. (b) frequently. (c) never. (d) but always apologize.

3. _____ In Finland, as compared with America, the university professor is: (a) overpaid. (b) underworked. (c) no one special. (d) more highly respected.

4. _____ Curiously enough, the main national heroes of Finland are: (a) professors. (b) writers and artists. (c) soldiers and statesmen. (d) students.

5. ____ One English language writer mentioned as being very popular in Finland is: (a) Hemingway. (b) Dreiser. (c) Sholokov. (d) Berlitz.

6. ____ Often the shopgirls an English-speaking professor meets: (a) know more about his subject than he does. (b) snub him. (c) laugh at his ignorance. (d) speak more languages than he does.

DEFINITIONS Choose the best meaning for each word.

1. ____ reserved: (a) ignorant (b) detailed (c) shy (d) arrogant

2. ____ competence: (a) capability (b) politeness (c) quiet (d) disturbance

3. ____ urban: (a) country (b) village (c) suburb (d) metropolitan

4. ____ concoction: (a) bad song (b) mixture (c) fixture (d) poison

5. ____ idiom: (a) linguistic (b) Finnish (c) language oddity (d) normal language pattern

6. ____ ponderous: (a) weighty (b) lithe (c) sly (d) ignorant

7. ____ mellifluous: (a) harsh sounding (b) loud (c) soft (d) sweetly flowing

8. ____ thriving: (a) successful (b) unsuccessful (c) mediocre (d) dull

9. ____ absolute: (a) approximate (b) cautious (c) perfect (d) sluggish

10. ____ cliché: (a) fresh (b) impolite (c) sustained (d) trite

11. ____ frustrated: (a) becalmed (b) baffled (c) prepared (d) impressed

12. ____ approbation: (a) approval (b) disdain (c) concern (d) displeasure

13. ____ subsidize: (a) consider (b) discern (c) support (d) ignore

14. ____ procedure: (a) opportunity (b) plan (c) arrange (d) limitation

15. ____ pervade: (a) spread through (b) invade (c) submit (d) include

24 · Polaris

RALPH E. LAPP

> *One of the realities of life in our time is the presence of armed missiles ready to strike. Polaris missiles, based in highly mobile submarines, differ from fixed missiles in hardened silos. Lapp tells about the fire power and the advantages of the deadly underwater atomic weapon.*

In 1956 the Navy had set up a Special Projects Office and assigned Rear Admiral William F. Raborn to lead it in the development of a solid-fuel rocket which could be launched from a submarine. Within two years this missile, named Polaris, and a program for arming a fleet of nuclear-powered submarines with it were well underway. The Navy thus came into competition with the Air Force in the role of providing the strategic force for deterrence against attack. But it had an appealing slogan which disarmed overt opposition in the Pentagon or in Congress:

> *Move deterrence out to sea,*
> *Where real estate is free,*
> *And where it's far away from me.*

In effect, the Polaris submarine is the first stage of a missile. Powered by nuclear engines which can take it on very long journeys under water, it roams the world's oceans in concealment and can fire its missiles from within comparatively short range of the enemy. Because it does not need to be fired as far as an ICBM, the Polaris rocket can be much smaller. The missile is 26 feet long. It is fitted with a 600-pound warhead yielding nearly two-thirds of a megaton of explosive power—more than 30 times that of the Hiroshima bomb.

POLARIS From *Kill and Overkill* © 1962, by Ralph E. Lapp, Basic Books, Inc., Publishers, New York.

The submarine locker in which the Polaris is housed first pops the missile up out of the water by compressed air. The rocket then is ignited, and its two stages throw the warhead into a ballistic trajectory. An inertial guidance system of gyroscopes and accelerometers, coupled to computers, keeps the missile on course during the powered part of its flight; the computers signal the cut-off of the second-stage engine and the release of the warhead at the proper time. For accurate aiming at the target, it is essential that the submarine know its precise position with respect to the target when the Polaris is released. In the broad ocean, this is a very tricky problem. It was solved by the development of an elaborate device called SINS (ship's inertial navigation system) which automatically tells the submarine's exact position on the globe at all times. The Polaris submarine carries three of these devices.

Each submarine has 16 Polaris missiles, adding up to a total fire power of about ten megatons. The range of the missile started at 1,200 to 1,500 miles but has been extended to 2,500 miles. The Navy has authorized construction of 41 Polaris submarines, carrying a total of 656 missiles. Counting the cost of the submarines (about $110 million apiece), each Polaris missile will represent an investment of more than $10 million—about one-fourth the cost of an Atlas or a Titan in its hardened silo.

The Air Force, not to be outdone, also set out to acquire a "cheap," solid-fuel, instant-firing missile like the Polaris. The weapon it developed was a three-stage ICBM called the Minuteman, capable of carrying a warhead of about the same size as the Polaris for a distance of some 6,000 miles. The Minuteman is a slim, 54-foot projectile, shaped like a bullet but weighing 65,000 pounds. It fits into a concrete silo some 80 feet deep and only ten feet in diameter. A reinforced-concrete sliding door four feet thick covers its hole. The missile can be readied for firing from its silo within 30 seconds. It is a case of one silo, one shot—for the exhaust gases destroy the launcher so that the silo cannot be used again. Surrounded by three acres of ground enclosed with barbed-wire fencing, the Minuteman has no attendants at its silo; it is fired by remote control by officers in underground shelters some distance away. The nuclear warhead cannot explode in its silo, because the switch that arms it for firing is not turned on until after the missile has been launched.

A total of 800 Minutemen has been authorized. In squadrons of 50 and flights of ten, they will be based at Air Force centers in Montana, North and South Dakota, Missouri, and other central states.

What has the Soviet Union been doing, meanwhile, in missilry? Whatever information the United States may have on this vital question is known only to our intelligence agencies. But some reasonable guesses can be made. The Russians' reaction to our U-2 flights over their country provides illuminating clues.

The giant Soviet rockets probably could carry warheads of 20 megatons or more. Yet the very size of the huge boosters is their Achilles heel. One high United States official has said: "Russia does not bother to harden—that is, to put her ICBMs under the ground. Some of their launching pads look like so many huge asparagus beds." The monstrous missiles would be most difficult to conceal or bury in hardened silos. They would be easy targets for destruction. As long as the U.S.S.R. was able to conceal its rocket activities and its missile sites behind the Iron Curtain, it was not urgently concerned about this problem. But our U-2 overflights destroyed that security. It is now generally known that the U-2s made revealing photographs of the Soviet rocket locations. As a result, the Soviet planners no doubt felt that they must speed up the development of less vulnerable ICBMs.

On this line of reasoning, it becomes easier to understand why Premier Khrushchev broke the moratorium and resumed the testing of nuclear weapons in the fall of 1961. His multimegaton explosions in that series of tests were stunts for psychological and political purposes, but along with these the Soviet tested many smaller weapons. Professor Hans Bethe told a Congressional committee that many of them were "in the range from one to five megatons." What could this mean? It suggests that in all likelihood the Soviet weaponeers were testing more efficient new bombs as warheads for modest-sized ICBMs that could be placed in hardened and concealed silos. The Soviet Union, then, must have its own counterparts of the Minuteman, the Polaris, the Titan, and so on.

Without doubt the intercontinental ballistic missiles of the nuclear powers will advance rapidly in power, ease of firing, and accuracy. By 1965 their accuracy is expected to be one mile or less—good enough to pinpoint any target. They are already highly automatic—especially the Minuteman—and capable of being fired in salvos. They compress the time-scale of war to a point that allows no time for hesitation or deliberate thought and opens the door wide to global destruction by accident. The era of push-button warfare is already here.

Tartaglia, the great ballistics expert of the sixteenth century, had a guilty premonition of the shape of things to come. In the preface to his *The Art of Projecting Bombs*, he wrote:

"One day meditating to myself, it seemed to me that it was a thing blameworthy, shameful, and barbarous, worthy of severe punishment before God and man, to wish to bring to perfection an art damageable to one's neighbor and destruction to the human race. . . ."

LENGTH: 1,210 WORDS

VOCABULARY

deterrence   prevention, discouraging the opposition
ballistic   pertaining to the path of a missile
trajectory   the path of a missile
inertial   referring to the uniform motion of a projectile
gyroscope   device to keep a moving object balanced
accelerometers   devices to measure rates of acceleration
Achilles heel   a fatal weakness
salvos   simultaneous firings of several missiles

24 · Polaris

SCORING: Reading time: _____ Rate from chart: _____ W.P.M.

MAIN SENTENCE	number right _____ × 4 equals _____ points	
GENERALITIES	number right _____ × 4 equals _____ points	
RETENTION	number right _____ × 2 equals _____ points	
COMPLETION	number right _____ × 3 equals _____ points	
DEFINITIONS	number right _____ × 2 equals _____ points	

(Total points: 100)   **total** _____ points

MAIN SENTENCE   Each of these sentences appears in the text. Which one best describes the contents of the passage?   _____

1. The giant Soviet rockets probably could carry warheads of 20 megatons or more.
2. Without doubt the intercontinental ballistic missiles of the nuclear powers will advance rapidly in power, ease of firing, and accuracy.
3. The era of push-button warfare is already here.

GENERALITIES   Based on the passage, which of the following generalities seem justifiable?   _____, _____

1. No one wants a war that involves missiles like the Polaris.
2. Concealment is the principal reason for hardened, silo missiles.
3. Polaris missiles are especially mobile.
4. America's attitude toward missile development is considerably different from Russia's.

RETENTION   Based on the passage, which of the following statements are True (T), False (F), or Not answerable (N)?

1. _____ Tartaglia is the genius of Russian ballistics.

2. _____ America's U-2 flights revealed Russian missile sites.

3. _____ The Soviet Union probably has counterparts of American hardened missiles.

4. _____ American hardened missiles are based in seaboard states.

5. _____ Russia's huge boosters are called the Achilles.

6. _____ Until now Russia has not bothered to "harden" her missiles.

7. ____ Polaris submarines cost about $10 million apiece.

8. ____ The Minuteman launching pad can be used only once.

9. ____ The Polaris launcher can be used up to 20 times.

10. ____ William F. Raborn was the developer of the Minuteman missile.

11. ____ The Polaris missile has 30 times the power of the Hiroshima bomb.

12. ____ The SINS guidance system keeps the submarine informed of its position with respect to the target.

13. ____ The Polaris missile can be small because it does not have to go far.

14. ____ Each submarine has 656 Polaris missiles.

15. ____ Minuteman was designed by the Navy.

16. ____ The silos which harden missiles are constructed from steel tubing.

17. ____ The nuclear device is armed in the silo just before launching.

18. ____ The U-2 flights probably scared Russia into making new atomic tests.

19. ____ The accuracy of ICBMs is probably close to 1,750 yards or less.

20. ____ Lapp is not worried about accidental triggering of these weapons.

COMPLETION   Choose the best answer for each question.

1. ____ The Minuteman missile is capable of being fired in: (a) time.   (b) turn.   (c) salvos.   (d) tune.

2. ____ All missiles are: (a) hardened.   (b) deadly accurate.   (c) either Russian or American.   (d) unpleasant to think of.

3. ____ Russia did not bother to harden her early missiles because: (a) there were no U-2 planes.   (b) the Russian people would not stand for it. (c) no one had ever suggested she do so.   (d) they were too large.

4. ____ The number of Polaris submarines authorized for construction by the Navy was: (a) 10.   (b) 16.   (c) 41.   (d) 110.

5. ____ The Minuteman silos are surrounded by: (a) elaborate guard systems.   (b) three acres of ground.   (c) smaller silos.   (d) Marines and servicemen.

6. ____ One of the points made in the article is that no matter what the United States does in its missile program: (a) Russia will know about it in detail.   (b) the Russians will not like it.   (c) the U.S. Navy will take issue with the U.S. Air Force.   (d) the Russians will do nearly the same.

DEFINITIONS   In the following passage, each underlined word has a number. In the columns below, match the number of each underlined word with the letter of the word that is closest to it in meaning.

1   2

The submarine locker in which the Polaris is housed first pops the missile up

3   4

out of the water by compressed air. The rocket is then ignited, and its two

5   6   7   8

stages throw the warhead into a ballistic trajectory. An inertial guidance system

9   10

of gyroscopes and accelerometers, coupled to computers, keeps the missile on

11   12   13

course during the powered part of its flight; the computers signal the cut-off

14   15

of the second-stage engine and release of the warhead at the proper time.

Column A	Column B
1. ____	a. notify
2. ____	b. compartment
	c. identification
3. ____	d. is maintained
4. ____	e. pressurized
5. ____	f. path
	g. exact
6. ____	h. notification
7. ____	i. organization
8. ____	j. calculators
	k. parts
9. ____	l. joined
10. ____	m. segment
	n. driven
11. ____	o. fired
12. ____	p. letting go
13. ____	q. control
	r. tested
14. ____	s. beginning
15. ____	

25 · A Moon Is Born

HEINZ HABER

> *The Earth's atmosphere and its field of gravity present the biggest problems in sending aloft a man-made satellite. They make it possible for Earth to collect meteoroids from outer space, but difficult for us to send our own moons back out there.*

A meteoroid floats through space. It is about the size of a fist—an irregular chunk of metal with a rough surface, weighing perhaps 20 pounds. The blinding rays of the Sun hit it like a spotlight, and it glitters against black space like a dust mote in a darkened theater. Slowly it tumbles about its own axis, and an ever-changing pattern of sharp lights and deep shadows plays over its surface.

Were it not for the slow rotation, one would think the meteoroid was suspended in space, motionless. Actually, it hurtles forward with a speed of many miles in every second, sweeping along a tremendous orbit that leads all the way around the Sun. Since the beginning of our solar system this meteoroid has swung around the Sun billions of times, like the planets in their own serene orbits. Its vast trajectory crosses the orbits of Venus, Earth, and Mars. During the long journey of the meteoroid there may have been thousands of near misses between it and these three planets.

Now the meteoroid is approaching Earth. If an observer were moving beside it, he would see the disk of the planet slowly growing larger, brighter against the blackness of space. The meteoroid is on a collision course, approaching the planet from the rear with its superior speed.

The pull of Earth's gravity now adds to the speed of the meteoroid. Earth's disk grows still larger and larger—now it spans half the sky. A few atoms of air begin to impinge on the leading face of the meteoroid and tear away the

A MOON IS BORN   Reprinted by permission from *Stars, Men and Atoms* by Heinz Haber. Copyright © 1962 by Heinz Haber and Golden Press, Inc.

fine cosmic dust accumulated there during the eons of the past. Seconds later the object—now a visible meteor—begins to glow as it rams down into the denser air below. The terrific friction produces a heat of thousands of degrees, and the meteor becomes a streak of luminous metallic vapors and incandescent air. Minutes later a softly glowing band still marks the path where the meteor met its end. Earth, with its atmosphere, has gained about 20 pounds in mass.

Every hour Earth's air engulfs uncounted millions of meteoroids, most of them microscopically small. Their number is so great that the planet grows by about 1,000 tons every day. Many scientists believe Earth and the other planets originally formed from billions of small particles—meteoritic material —that filled the space around the Sun and gradually accumulated to form larger masses. The formation of Earth is not yet fully completed, and the fall of our meteor was just one more event among billions that once brought Earth into existence.

Whatever comes in from outer space Earth holds fast with the mighty grip of her gravity. All meteoritic material that has ever come within this grip is still part of Earth today. Except for a few forlorn atoms that escape into space from the topmost layer of air, the planet has never given up a single piece of matter once gained. Gravity is a jealous, efficient guard.

Just as our meteor plunges to its flaming death, a celestial body of another kind enters the scene. As it emerges from the shadow of our planet, it reflects the sunlight sharply. Like the meteoroid, it hurtles through space and it consists of metal; but in other respects it is strikingly different. It is regular in shape—a perfect sphere with a highly polished metallic surface that mirrors the Sun in a blinding highlight. It also weighs about 20 pounds. But this 20 pounds makes up one of the most remarkable pieces of matter in the physical history of the planet: the artificial satellites. This one was, like the others, once part of Earth's mass, but it has just left Earth to begin its existence as a celestial body equal in rank to the Moon.

From the beginning of Earth's history, the traffic of matter near it has been one-way. Now, for the very first time, pieces of solid matter are traveling in the opposite direction—*away* from Earth.

This reversal of traffic in the vicinity of Earth could only happen through man's technical ingenuity. He found a way of overcoming the force of gravity that normally keeps everything chained to Earth. The thrust of rocket engines sends satellites away from the planet and lifts them into an orbit around it. The satellites are moons of man's own making.

Unlike the natural Moon that lovers have gazed at through the ages, the artificial satellites are intricate, highly sophisticated tools of science. Even as an inert shell of metal rounding Earth, a satellite becomes a revolutionary tool that can solve many problems for which there was no answer before. But scientists are more ambitious: they are making satellites that function as alert, accurate observers. In many ways satellites act as though alive. They are equipped to "see," "hear," and "feel" what is going on in the fringe area between atmosphere and space. They have an electronic "memory" to remember their "sensations," and a radio voice capable of giving answers to questions radioed from the ground.

For a satellite there is a lot to see, hear, and feel that can never be observed by an Earth-bound instrument. Some of its artificial eyes keep watch on the Sun and scan the solar ultraviolet rays. Others are trained on Earth below, observing the ever-changing cloud cover. Artificial ears listen to the fine clicks caused by the impacts of tiny meteoroids upon the satellite's metal surface, and other "sense organs" keep a record of larger meteoroids big enough to punch a hole through the hull. Heat-sensitive elements measure temperatures. A "magnetic" sense traces the magnetic field of Earth, and there are devices to detect charged particles given off by the Sun and to record cosmic rays.

Whatever the satellite learns is stored in its electronic memory—a tiny set of magnetic cores or, in some models, a miniature tape recorder taken aloft. Once during each round trip, when the satellite is at the right spot, a radio signal from the ground commands it to spill its stored information. The satellite then speaks through its radio voice, transmitting to the ground all the data picked up during the last revolution.

Satellite-borne instrumentation is a marvel of scientific and engineering design. Each instrument is almost unbelievably light in weight, because an ounce saved in construction may spell the difference between success and failure in getting the satellite into the desired orbit. If a special instrument cannot be built within a strict weight limit, it cannot go along for the ride. Scientists have worked out a highly sophisticated program for these "inboard" experiments that will give the most information for the least weight. Army, Navy, Air Force, several universities, and industries are involved in these experiments.

In the first satellites the batteries for the power supply claimed the lion's share of weight—about one third of the entire weight of the satellite. The rest of the weight went into the electronic gear: receivers, transmitters, relays, multi-channel telemeter, and memory units. These items are so tiny that they put the two-way wrist radios of comic-strip supermen to shame. All the miniature marvels of the modern electronic art go into these sets: transistors, printed circuits, tiny condensers, magnetic cores—so tiny and light that everything can be crammed into a package no larger than a stack of half a dozen saucers. Each of these electronic units has more individual parts than a big color television set, yet it fits into the palm of one's hand. The electronic equipment of a satellite can perform the most intricate tasks of sensing, measuring, storing and transmitting at a minimum of power expense. Small batteries can run the equipment for one to two weeks.

Some of the more recent satellites are equipped with solar batteries. These promising instruments of the modern electronic age are able to convert an appreciable percentage of solar energy into useful electrical power. Solar batteries are most ideal for satellites, since there is an abundance of free sunshine in space. Unless a meteoroid hits a satellite and destroys the delicate circuitry, space-borne radio and TV equipment powered by solar batteries can virtually run forever.

Since the first Sputnik started on its lonely trip into space, the population of satellites has been steadily increasing even though some of them orbited only for a few weeks or months. At one time—in January of 1962—a total of 35 man-made vehicles were coasting through space, many of them still busy relaying their scientific measurements back to their creators on Earth. Not all of these vehicles are true satellites. Russian engineers have made two successful attacks on the Moon. On September 14, 1959, at 5 p.m. New York time, the first object originating from Earth reached the Moon. A spherical instrument package with a total weight of 858 pounds crashed on the lunar surface with a speed of 7,500 miles per hour after a trip of about 35 hours. On October 6, 1959, a Soviet rocket, launched three days earlier, coasted around the Moon and upon radio command from Earth pointed its two cameras at the back of the Moon. An intricate mechanism developed the pictures inside the rocket, scanned them, and radioed them to Earth, affording a glimpse of lunar landscapes that have so far been hidden from the searching eye of man. The photographs revealed about 70 percent of the invisible part of the Moon's surface. The Soviet scientists exercised the classic right of a discoverer by naming several conspicuous craters, mountain ranges, and plains.

LENGTH: 1,750 WORDS

VOCABULARY

meteoroid small particle of matter moving through space
impinge touch, hit
cosmic dust fine particles of matter collected by the earth from outer space
eons great spans of time
luminous glowing
incandescent bright, filled with light
engulf swallow up
inert without movement or action
telemeter apparatus for determining distances
intricate complicated, delicate
circuitry electronic elements which function together, electronic circuits
scanned examined, measured

25 · A Moon Is Born

<table>
<tr><td colspan="2">SCORING: Reading time: _____ Rate from chart: _____ W.P.M.</td></tr>
<tr><td>MAIN SENTENCE</td><td>number right _____ × 4 equals _____ points</td></tr>
<tr><td>GENERALITIES</td><td>number right _____ × 4 equals _____ points</td></tr>
<tr><td>RETENTION</td><td>number right _____ × 2 equals _____ points</td></tr>
<tr><td>COMPLETION</td><td>number right _____ × 3 equals _____ points</td></tr>
<tr><td>DEFINITIONS</td><td>number right _____ × 2 equals _____ points</td></tr>
<tr><td colspan="2" align="center">(Total points: 100) total _____ points</td></tr>
</table>

MAIN SENTENCE   Each of these sentences appears in the text. Which one best describes the contents of the passage? _____

1. Whatever comes in from outer space Earth holds fast with the mighty grip of her gravity.
2. Every hour Earth's air engulfs uncounted millions of meteoroids, most of them microscopically small.
3. Satellite-borne instrumentation is a marvel of scientific and engineering design.

GENERALITIES   Based on the passage, which of the following generalities seem justifiable? _____, _____

1. The weight of a satellite is highly critical.
2. Gravity is probably less important than solar energy to a satellite.
3. A meteoroid is exactly like a satellite in most important respects.
4. Gravity and batteries have in common the fact that each represents energy.

RETENTION   Based on the passage, which of the following statements are True (T), False (F), or Not answerable (N)?

1. _____ Space is more critical than weight in the construction of a satellite.

2. _____ Satellites have electronic memories that store and report their "experiences."

3. _____ In the first satellites, the batteries weighed about as much as a lion.

4. _____ Satellites use electronic "sense organs" to examine space.

5. _____ The Navy is not involved with the space experiments.

6. _____ Before Sputnik, all space traffic had been one way—to Earth.

7. ____ Meteoroids glow brightly even before they reach the atmosphere of the Earth.

8. ____ Satellites are more similar to the moon than to meteoroids.

9. ____ Normally, gravity keeps on Earth everything that arrives from space.

10. ____ The satellite keeps watch on the cloud cover of the Earth.

11. ____ When a meteoroid falls to Earth, the Earth gains half the weight of the object.

12. ____ Every day the Earth gains 1,000 tons in weight.

13. ____ No meteoroids that hit Earth now could have existed since the beginning of the solar system.

14. ____ The color of space is blue.

15. ____ Ordinarily, meteoroids actually hit artificial satellites.

16. ____ A sphere that lands on the moon is not a true satellite.

17. ____ Soviet rockets were the first to photograph the dark side of the moon.

18. ____ Certain lunar landmarks now bear Russian names.

19. ____ Some tiny electronic devices for satellites have more parts than a Ford.

20. ____ Two-way wrist radios are more advanced than devices in a satellite.

COMPLETION   Choose the best answer for each question.

1. ____ If an artificial satellite were just a round metal ball with nothing inside it: (a) it would not work.   (b) we could stop testing right now.   (c) it would solve many problems.   (d) no one would know.

2. ____ The reversal of space traffic could happen only: (a) in Russia.   (b) through man's technical ingenuity.   (c) because of an integrated national effort.   (d) after gravity had been thoroughly understood.

3. ____ An artificial satellite is equal in rank to the: (a) meteoroids in space.   (b) moon.   (c) sun.   (d) Russian rockets.

4. ____ All meteoritic material that has come within the grip of Earth's gravity: (a) has been seen in the sky.   (b) came from the moon.   (c) has been kept by the earth.   (d) was recorded by little clicks of sound.

5. ____ A meteorite becomes visible from Earth when: (a) the scanning camera picks it up.   (b) it reaches the atmosphere of the Earth.   (c) gravity takes command of it.   (d) it loses half its weight.

6. _____ A meteoroid's trajectory might cross the path of: (a) Venus, Earth, and Mars. (b) other meteoroids. (c) Russian rockets. (d) itself.

DEFINITIONS In the following passage, each underlined word has a number. In the columns below, match the number of each underlined word with the letter of the word that is closest to it in meaning.

　　　　　1
The pull of Earth's gravity now adds to the speed of the meteoroid. Earth's

　2　　　　　　　　　　　　　　　　　　3
disk grows still larger and larger—now it spans half the sky. A few atoms of

　　　　　　　4　　　　5　　6　　　　　　　　　　　7
air begin to impinge on the leading face of the meteoroid and tear away the

　8　　9　　　　　　10　　　　　　　　　　　11
fine cosmic dust accumulated there during the eons of the past. Seconds later

　　　　　　　　12　　　　　　　13　　　14
the object—now a visible meteor—begins to glow as it rams down into the

　　15
denser air below.

Column A	Column B
1. _____	a. exceptional
2. _____	b. gathered
3. _____	c. shine
4. _____	d. hit
5. _____	e. ages
6. _____	f. forward
7. _____	g. pertaining to space
8. _____	h. remove
9. _____	i. tiny
10. _____	j. attraction
11. _____	k. surface
12. _____	l. spreads over
13. _____	m. circular form
14. _____	n. thicker
15. _____	o. hurt
	p. spins
	q. shoves
	r. gripping
	s. apparent

26 · Educating Computers

EDMUND BERKELEY

> *Today we can program a computer so that it can begin thinking for itself. Edmund Berkeley tells us what terms like "think" and "educate" mean in connection with computers.*

The word "program" has come into use to refer to the sequence of instructions which the machine carries out. It is more useful than the words "routine" or "schedule" or "sequence" and enables more linguistic compounds to be made, such as the verbal form "programming" and the noun "programmer." A *program* for a computer is an exact sequence of instructions that it uses to solve a problem. Many programs are composed in such a way that portions of them, called subprograms or subroutines, can be selected and copied from a library of machine programs (probably on punched paper tape or magnetic tape). This re-use saves the human labor of looking up the previous subprogram and copying it. An example is the program for finding the square root of a number. (A *square root* of a number N is a number x such that x times x equals the number N; for example, 5 is a square root of 25, since 5 times 5 equals 25.) The solutions of many mathematical problems require the finding of square roots; and clearly the most efficient sequence of computer commands to find square root needs to be determined only once.

Programming for automatic computers has become an important occupation in the computer field. A good deal of knowledge, common sense, and training is needed to program well, for it requires: (1) understanding the operations of a business or the steps of a scientific calculation; (2) understanding the best ways for having a computer carry out these operations and steps; (3) arriving

EDUCATING COMPUTERS From *The Computer Revolution* by Edmund C. Berkeley, copyright © 1962 by Edmund C. Berkeley. Reprinted by permission of Doubleday & Company, Inc.

at a good sequence of commands for the computer to solve the problem; and (4) adequately translating these commands into computer language. In fact, programming has proved a serious bottleneck in many applications of computers, and so a good deal of effort among computer manufacturers has gone into methods of automatic programming. This has taken several forms.

One form is the construction of *compiling programs* or compilers, which use the computer to take subprograms out of a library and hitch them together appropriately so as to solve a new problem. A second form is the construction of programs called *interpreters*, which accept instructions in certain standard words and translate these words into machine language, so that the machine "knows" what the words "mean." A third form is the development of common languages for automatic programming for problems, so that any problem when expressed in such a language can be given to an automatic computer, and the computer will solve it. It is expected that these languages will be common among different species of automatic computers, and therefore that any automatic computer anywhere will be able to solve the problem if expressed in this language. Business problems are less amenable to this development than mathematical problems, but there are important general automatic programming languages which automatic computers can interpret and use.

Computer manufacturers have encouraged the formation of groups of users of their machines, resulting in an exchange of programs among users. This has been an important factor in the development of automatic programming and a common language for giving programs to computers.

An automatic computer with a library of programs and a general language in which you can instruct the computer to solve a vast variety of problems is rather different from an automatic computer with just the same hardware but with no programs, and all the programming to be done from scratch. It is natural to call the first kind of computer an "educated" computer, and it is easy to see that the "education" of computers will increase with no specified or assignable limits.

Eventually more and more problems of mathematics and business, industry and government, war and peace, society and science, will become programmed for computers. More and more tapes of programs will be available for placing on any computer. The amount of knowledge which a computer will have access to will begin to tower above the amount of knowledge which a human being has access to. If we are willing to use the word "educated," a computer with its storehouse of programs will be more educated than a human being, in a great many different areas.

After all, what is the education of a human being? It means putting into his control the keys to the storehouse of knowledge which the human race has compiled over 5,000 years of recorded history and more thousands of years of unrecorded history. In the training of a human being, to be able to *read* is probably the first and most important ability, for this is the ability which enables the human being to turn the key in the lock to the treasury of recorded knowledge. So also for computers, the capacity to interpret a program, the capacity to take in information, is a key to using a library of programs.

Just as the education of a single human being depends on the information, knowledge, and wisdom collected by great numbers of human beings preceding him, so the education of computers depends on a social enterprise also. Only the processes are different. The computer is fast in learning, the human being slow. The programmed computer remembers exactly everything it is told until its memory is wiped out by a new program; the human being can remember only a part of all that he is told, but that is not voluntarily erasable.

Are there any limitations to the nature of problems that computers, automatic machines for handling information, can handle? Can these machines actually "think"? If not now, will they eventually "think"? Is it correct to call them "giant brains"?

To begin the discussion of this much-argued topic, let us consider first the meaning of the word "think." This word acquired most of its meaning years, in fact centuries, ago. Until 1944, when the first automatic computer first operated, the meaning of the word had not received any shocks from experience with machines.

The applicability of the word to various kinds of situations involving reasoning and judgment was established almost entirely in the years before automatic computing and data-processing machines were invented.

As one result, when the word "thinking" is applied to machines, the connotation of the word "thinking" arouses emotional reactions in people.

As a second result, there is an uncertain and fuzzy area in the meaning of the word "thinking" when it is applied to novel situations. The operation of automatic machines that handle information reasonably and automatically is a novel situation.

Therefore, a good deal of the argument about whether or not a machine can think is fruitless, because it reduces to an empty argument over whether or not some kind of specific activity (for example, adding 2 and 3 and obtaining 5) is or is not to be included under the term "thinking." In the uncertain and fuzzy areas, different people will define "thinking" in different ways.

There is no doubt at all, however, that up until the time when machines began to do reading, writing, arithmetic, reasoning, and looking up data in records, all these activities would have been classified as "thinking." If a dog or chimpanzee or other animal had ever done these things, the animal would have been classified as "thinking."

LENGTH: 1,350 WORDS

VOCABULARY

linguistic pertaining to language
amenable docile, subject to authority, agreeable
connotation emotional meaning, implication

26 · Educating Computers

MAIN SENTENCE Each of these sentences appears in the text. Which one best describes the contents of the passage? _____

1. A *program* for a computer is an exact sequence of instructions that it uses to solve a problem.
2. Computer manufacturers have encouraged the formation of groups of users of their machines, resulting in an exchange of programs among users.
3. Eventually more and more problems of mathematics and business, industry and government, war and peace, society and science, will become programmed for computers.

GENERALITIES Based on the passage, which of the following generalities seem justifiable? _____ and _____

1. No one knew much about thinking before the "giant brains" were built.
2. Automatic computers force us to change our ideas about education and thinking in general.
3. Without a program, a computer cannot become "educated."
4. Computers are machines that open an exciting future for us.

RETENTION Based on the passage, which of the following statements are True (T), False (F), or Not answerable (N)?

1. _____ Essentially a computer performs mathematical calculations.

2. _____ Finding the square root of five is not a mathematical calculation.

3. _____ Most of our knowledge of how men think was gained before computers.

4. _____ A computer is only as "smart" as its program.

5. ____ The man who programs the computer "educates" it.

6. ____ A computer can accept approximately a dozen programs at a time.

7. ____ Computers are "smarter" than people.

8. ____ Computers can be better educated than many people.

9. ____ The author interprets education as learning and storing knowledge.

10. ____ Good programming is based primarily on four principles.

11. ____ Computers have a "language"—that of square roots.

12. ____ Presently, the "language" of different kinds of computers is not standardized.

13. ____ Programs can be preserved on punched paper or on magnetic tape.

14. ____ The computer is slow to learn, but it never forgets.

15. ____ Computers can "forget" all they have been told, but a human being cannot.

16. ____ The first automatic computer was operated in 1944.

17. ____ When applied to machines, the word "thinking" is not well understood.

18. ____ Adding 2 and 3 and getting 5 is a process of thought.

19. ____ If a dog added 2 and 2 to get 4, we would have to say it was thinking.

20. ____ There are sharp limitations to the "thinking" computers can do.

COMPLETION   Choose the best answer for each question.

1. ____ A term not mentioned as a possible substitute for the word "program" is: (a) schedule.   (b) routine.   (c) pattern.   (d) sequence.

2. ____ A good deal of effort among computer manufacturers has gone into: (a) devising a machine language.   (b) university courses.   (c) automatic programming.   (d) making subprograms.

3. ____ The "education" of computers has: (a) only just begun.   (b) no specified limits.   (c) become very important.   (d) taught us how to think.

4. ____ One great advantage of having a standard language for computers is the: (a) possibility of exchanging programs.   (b) ease of educating computers.   (c) help one computer can give another.   (d) economy of manufacture.

5. _____ The most important first step in the educating of a human being is: (a) making him think. (b) showing him certain operations. (c) giving him keys to knowledge. (d) teaching him to read.

6. _____ A computer will be "better educated" than a human when it has: (a) solved harder math problems. (b) taught itself a program. (c) learned more facts. (d) begun to appreciate mathematical functions.

DEFINITIONS In the following passage, each underlined word has a number. In the columns below, match the number of each underlined word with the letter of the word that is closest to it in meaning.

       1   2   3   4

An automatic computer with a library of programs and a general language in

             5   6   7   8

which you can instruct the computer to solve a vast variety of problems is

9   10   11   12   13

rather different from an automatic computer with just the same hardware but

                                   14   15

with no programs, and all the programming to be done from scratch.

Column A	Column B
1. _____	a. great
2. _____	b. quite
	c. education
3. _____	d. collection
4. _____	e. identical
5. _____	f. self-operating
	g. various
6. _____	h. different kinds
7. _____	i. books
8. _____	j. teach
	k. the beginning
9. _____	l. instructions
10. _____	m. dull
11. _____	n. machinery
12. _____	o. unlike
13. _____	p. intelligence
14. _____	q. common
	r. giant brain
15. _____	s. only

27 · Slavery and the Slave Trade

PAUL BOHANNAN

*Slavery and Africa have long been known to one another. How-
ever, the European concept of slavery and the African one are
not the same. Paul Bohannan describes the basic economic and
psychological differences between them.*

The nature of slavery is not always understood by modern Westerners. Both the Europeans and the Africans at the time the trade developed
had a tradition of slavery, but the two traditions were of very different sorts.
African slavery (usually called benign, domestic, or household slavery) was a
domestic institution—there were only a few exceptions on the continent. Domestic slaves are interesting because their economic value was not the most
important thing about them (although they may, like housewives, be of economic value). It was rather their value as political followers and as indicators
of prestige that was dominant.

It is necessary to do *something* with war captives, with criminals, and with
the generally bad lots that are found in small numbers in all societies. The
African answer was to turn them into slaves, which meant giving them a
special (and humble) status in which they—either rejected by or removed from
kinsmen—could be carefully watched at the same time that they were given
security and position. The word "slave" in this sense refers to people who are
attached to domestic groups by non-kinship links of a sort that contain elements of servility. Many slaves could occupy high positions within households
—such was also the case with some slaves in classical societies—and to this
day, an African will take up arms, joining his slave, if the slave is "insulted"
in public by being addressed as such.

SLAVERY AND THE SLAVE TRADE   From *Africa and Africans* by Paul Bohannan, copyright © 1964
by Paul Bohannan. Reprinted by permission of The Natural History Press (Doubleday & Company, Inc.).

A slave was, thus, a kind of kinsman—with different rights from other kinsmen, different positions in the family and household from other kinsmen, but nevertheless a kind of kinsman. Slaves had either to be captured or they had to be acquired from their kinsmen who were "selling them into slavery." This means that, as a form of banishment, some groups took their criminal or generally unsatisfactory kinsmen and performed a ritual which "broke the kinship" and then sold him. The people who bought such men brought them into their own domestic groups and attached them by non-kinship, but kin-like, links to various "huts" within the household. Such slaves did work—often the hardest work—but they married, brought their families into the social group, and formed a thorough-going part of the extended household.

Indigenous African slavery was benign in another sense—there were not very many people involved in it. The wars that Africans fought, until they met Europeans or until the Zulu and Ngoni began their progress through South Africa in the eighteenth century, did not produce very many captives. And very few people are totally unsatisfactory to their kinsmen.

Throughout Africa, slaves were no more than otherwise kinless persons who were attached by non-kinship links into households. The few exceptions are those in which they were attached to kings and courts, and in one or two places such as Dahomey, where there were plantation slaves working for the king (probably a feedback from New World institutions).

One of the most important distinguishing characteristics of the American Negro slaves is that they too were kinless people. We who live in such a loose kinship system as that of middle-class America forget the tremendous importance of kin. But even in works of Harriet Beecher Stowe, one finds the classical distinction between the good master and the bad master: the bad master "broke up families." Every slaveowner in the New World had the right, obviously, to break up families. To this day, in lower-class Negro families, the matricentric family, consisting of a woman and her children with the link to the husband-father weak and ephemeral, is commonly found. When Negroes move into middle- or upper-class culture, this trait disappears. However, in the lower-class culture and through much of the Caribbean area, such is the standard family pattern, left over from the days of slavery. Slaves, even in our own society in the nineteenth century, were kinless people. In the African situation, this is about all that slavery amounted to.

In Europe slavery was a very different institution. It arose on a different basis, had a different history, and led to totally different conditions. European slavery was, from the beginning, primarily economic—perhaps it would be better to say that domestic slavery was the exception, for all that it existed side by side with economic slavery both in the classical world and in the American South. Even in Aristotle's time there were economic slaves being worked to death in salt mines—that expression has been with us for a long time.

Particularly in the medieval world, the form of subservience or servility was scarcely "slavery" in the African sense at all, because it consisted of the institution that European history knows as the "bond servant." Bond service was of an almost purely economic character. For reasons of debt, or some other, it was possible for me to bond myself, or a member of my family, to work until the debt was paid. The whole notion of bond service developed out of a feudal ethic and carried over into the subsequent period.

What happened in the slave trade is that the economically dominated feudal version of servility from the European area met the basically benign, family-dominated slavery from Africa. Like many other aspects of culture, they met first in the market place. Africans saw nothing wrong in selling slaves. Europeans found nothing wrong in buying them—indeed, many of the Negroes in the earliest importations were treated as bond slaves, their bondage limited by contract to a period of years. But the idea that each had about the role of the slave in the world's work was totally different from that of the other. Supply of slaves became expensive, and the "bond" became permanent. From the meeting of the two and the establishment of new nations and new economies, a new institution—New World slavery—emerged.

Given this particular impetus in the form of a labor force, Portugal got a tremendous shot in the arm. Spain was not far behind. And as Portugal went down the coast of Africa, with sea captains under contract to the princes, working on a commission basis, they found themselves by 1460-70 in the Bight of Benin. They built fortresses along the coast at a slightly later date.

The Dutch were not far behind the Portuguese. The Brandenburgers, the Danes, the English by 1540—all got into the trade.

When the Portuguese came down the coast, they found large African kingdoms on the Guinea coast and at the mouth of the Congo. The sources of slaves extend from Cape Verde down the coast deep into Angola. Slaves going into Latin America and Brazil tended, after the first few years, to come from the coast south of the Cameroons; those into the West Indies and North America from the Guinea coast. Portuguese slavers eventually even exported slaves from the east coast, particularly from what is today Mozambique, into Brazil.

The slave trade that the Portuguese found in full tilt along the east coast was of a different sort. It seems to have been somewhat smaller in volume (the records of the west coast trade are good; those on the east coast trade, carried on by Arab dhows, are either poor or unexplored or both), but the whole of eastern Africa was involved in a slave trade, carried out by Swahili contractors for Arab traders who shipped Negroes to Arabia, Persia, and India. The conditions under which they were shipped make the justly infamous middle passage from West Africa to the New World seem benign. The Arabs organized the Swahili traders along the coast. The Swahili organized the immediately inland tribes, who raided farther and farther toward the center of the continent. The captives then had to carry ivory and other goods to the coast; during the trip they were inadequately fed and housed. Livingstone in the nineteenth century made some startling estimates about the vast number of slaves who died on this trip. The slave markets in Dar es Salaam, Zanzibar, and Malindi, and particularly those on Pemba Island, are well described in the eighteenth century and even earlier by Arab travelers. The slaves were packed, like cordwood, into dhows, with sometimes as little as eighteen inches between the decks. Not surprisingly, after the exhausting trip to the coast, many more died at sea.

By the beginning of the nineteenth century, the African continent was more or less in chaos, produced from the slaving operations carried out from both its coasts. The goods that were traded for slaves included large proportions of firearms, and the power structure of African societies underwent vast change. African chiefships and kingships fell to those who controlled the most force, could thereby raid most effectively, and ultimately get the richest. It was with this new power situation, based on the ancient African tradition of kingship, and the wealth produced by the slave trade, that the new empires of the Ashanti, Yoruba, Dahomey, and of the Kongo were enlarged, and on which their new export economy was being erected. The records for Dahomey and Abeokuta and others show that every year the armies of the kings scoured neighboring tribes in slave raids.

Africans did not, of course, take to enslavement kindly. But they did not perish under it as some other peoples have done. They had slavery institutions that they knew; to a degree, they knew how to behave as slaves. Certainly they knew how to survive as slaves. They were neither puzzled nor terrified by the institution itself. The Spanish had done their best to enslave the American Indians of the West Indies; the West Indians had a freedom-or-nothing attitude and seem to have lacked a cultural tradition of slavery. So many of them died that Las Casas (who lived to regret it bitterly) and many other leaders of New Spain sought the royal permission that ultimately led to wholesale importation of African slaves. The African slaves fought it, and many escaped from it into the hills of Surinam (to form the present-day tribes of "Bush Negroes") and into Middle America. But die out they did not.

LENGTH: 1,850 WORDS

VOCABULARY

benign   harmless, mild
servility   slave situation
indigenous   native to the area
Zulu and Ngoni   powerful African tribes
matricentric   headed by the mother—usually said of a family
ephemeral   without substance, lasting a short time
impetus   motivation, urge
infamous   well known for bad reasons

27 · Slavery and the Slave Trade

SCORING: Reading time: _____ Rate from chart: _____ W.P.M.

MAIN SENTENCE	number right _____ × 4 equals _____ points	
GENERALITIES	number right _____ × 4 equals _____ points	
RETENTION	number right _____ × 2 equals _____ points	
COMPLETION	number right _____ × 3 equals _____ points	
DEFINITIONS	number right _____ × 2 equals _____ points	

(Total points: 100)   **total** _____ points

MAIN SENTENCE   Each of these sentences appears in the text. Which one best describes the contents of the passage? _____

1. The nature of slavery is not always understood by modern Westerners.
2. Throughout Africa, slaves were no more than otherwise kinless persons who were attached by non-kinship links into households.
3. The slaves were packed, like cordwood, into dhows, with sometimes as little as eighteen inches between the decks.

GENERALITIES   Based on the passage, which of the following generalities seem justifiable? _____ and _____

1. Many modern Negroes still suffer indirectly from the effects of slavery.
2. The white trader introduced the idea of slavery to Africa.
3. No one, either today or in the past, actually approved of slavery.
4. The African suffered but nevertheless survived in slavery.

RETENTION   Based on the passage, which of the following statements are True (T), False (F), or Not answerable (N)?

1. _____ Slave raids often were carried out by African kings.

2. _____ Slave traders had little or no respect for the humanity of the slave.

3. _____ The Arabs eventually paid dearly for taking part in slavery.

4. _____ Slaves disembarking from Dar es Salaam headed east to Arabia or India.

5. _____ The Portuguese found no civilization in Africa in the fifteenth century.

6. _____ The tradition of kingship is an ancient one in Africa.

7. ____ Slavery helped African kings alter the power structure of societies.

8. ____ In Dahomey, the kings had slave raids on the interior every year.

9. ____ African slavery originally was not economic slavery.

10. ____ The European "bond servant" was quite unlike the African slave.

11. ____ The slaves in Aristotle's time were not economic slaves.

12. ____ In American society, slaves were not kinless people.

13. ____ In Africa, although a slave was not kin, he often had position and security.

14. ____ Historically, indigenous African slavery involved many people.

15. ____ The use of plantation slaves in Dahomey was probably a feedback from the New World.

16. ____ The passage indicates that housewives are a kind of slaves.

17. ____ The Spanish could not enslave the American Indians of the West Indies.

18. ____ The institution of slavery was familiar to Africans in the fifteenth century.

19. ____ Africans saw nothing wrong in selling slaves.

20. ____ A dhow is the name of a trading expedition.

COMPLETION Choose the best answer for each question.

1. ____ In domestic slavery, the slave has no: (a) rights under the law. (b) real economic value. (c) friends. (d) position in the society.

2. ____ Possibly the Africans survived slavery because: (a) the slave traders were kind and helpful. (b) the conditions of slavery were good. (c) society tolerated slavery. (d) they had a tradition of slavery.

3. ____ One of the principal items the African kings got from their slaving operations was: (a) ivory. (b) firearms. (c) ships. (d) art objects.

4. ____ The author is careful to inform us that African slavery: (a) was healthful. (b) was different from that practiced by Europeans. (c) was similar to that practiced by Europeans. (d) resembled the tradition that Las Casas discovered in the West Indies.

5. ____ African slavery originally affected: (a) kings and widows. (b) those who refused to work. (c) cripples and invalids. (d) war captives and criminals.

6. _____ Original African slaves could: (a) marry and raise a family. (b) work in the fields. (c) go home once every year. (d) complain.

DEFINITIONS In the following passage, each underlined word has a number. In the columns below, match the number of each underlined word with the letter of the word that is closest to it in meaning.

                  1   2   3

One of the most important distinguishing characteristics of the American

                         4

Negro slaves is that they too were kinless people. We who live in such a

5   6   7   8   9

loose kinship system as that of middle-class America forget the tremendous

    10   11   12

importance of kin. But even in works of Harriet Beecher Stowe, one finds

      13   14

the classical distinction between the good master and the bad master: the bad

        15

master "broke up families."

Column A	Column B
1. _____	a. enormous
2. _____	b. without family
	c. casual
3. _____	d. writings
4. _____	e. ignore or neglect
	f. traditional
5. _____	g. differentiation
6. _____	h. keeps
7. _____	i. separated
	j. pretend
8. _____	k. discovers
9. _____	l. painfulness
	m. significant
10. _____	n. unimportant
11. _____	o. differentiating
12. _____	p. organization
	q. features
13. _____	r. family
14. _____	s. value
15. _____	

28 · Growth Toward Belonging

HARRY and BONARO OVERSTREET

Alienation is commonly used to describe people who feel apart from their society. Does alienation indicate mental illness? What kind of life can an alienated person hope to live?

The troubled people who come through the doors of the counseling center, mental hospital, and psychiatrist's office are as various as the people on the street outside. Mental and emotional disturbances are no respecter of persons. They take slight account of age, race, education, sex, or prestige. Yet with all their differences, those who thus come seeking help tend to share one problem: they all suffer from some acute disorder of their human relationships. They do not feel close to anyone—themselves or anyone else.

The technical term for their state is *alienation*. It may be so severe a state that the individual is helpless to continue operating in a normal human environment. Or it may be so mild that his associates have not thought of him as a "problem person" except to wonder why he seems anxious all the time or to be caught off guard, now and then, by his moods. However, to some degree, severe or mild, the experience of the *alienated* individual is that of being cut off from his environment. He does not see it as others do; is out of touch with its realities; is unable to make contact; is deeply and fearfully alone. He may indeed talk with other people; and they may reply in the conventional sounds of a common language. Yet his isolation is not broken. The words somehow do not reach across. They do not build bridges of understanding. For he and those to whom he talks are speaking out of different worlds of emotional reference.

The deeply disturbed person, housing a welter of anxieties and inner conflicts, is not only a stranger in a strange land, but a stranger to himself among people who remain intractably strangers to him even if they live in the same house; and he inhabits a land that cannot be other than strange, for he sees it through the lens of his private illusions and fantasies and of his intense preoccupation with his own problems.

The individual patient usually does not suspect the nature of his own difficulty. He only knows what it makes him suffer. Here is a man, for example, who has come desperately seeking help because he cannot concentrate on his job and lives in daily fear of being fired. Moreover, he seems to have lost control of his own moods: he flies off the handle; is constantly at odds with his family; has got shouting mad a couple of times with fellow workers. This man does not tell himself or the therapist that he is suffering from *alienation*. He does not say that the world in which he moves is not that of the people around him: that while he and they are eating at the same table or going up to work in the same elevator, he is alone—always alone—because in his world all events derive their interpretation from his own inner conflicts. What he reports to the therapist is nothing at all like this. More probably he says that he feels so "wrong inside" he must be "going crazy"; that if something isn't done he will "fall apart."

We are talking here, of course, about the extreme case: the case calling for professional help. Such an acutely disturbed individual as this may seem to have little in common with the one whom we think of as just abnormally shy or as a chronic worrier or as given to "off days" when no one can speak to him without being snapped at in return. We all, to be sure, have moods, and abrupt moments of feeling ourselves to be a stranger among strangers. We all have the baffled sense, now and then, that our words do not reach through to the person to whom we are talking. Yet most of us, most of the time, feel that we belong: that a number of people like us; that we are accepted by our friends, family, and working associates. It may not make their blood tingle to see us coming; but neither do they wish, as a rule, that we were going the other way. Just as we earn enough money to get by without ever becoming rich, so most of us earn enough human relationships to get by and to enjoy a certain emotional security.

What, then, can we learn from the disturbed person who suffers an acute and continuous sense of estrangement: who feels no reassuring intimacy with his human fellows; who, in Byron's phrase, stands "among them, but not of them"?

We can learn a good deal from him; for he is not as much a stranger to us as he feels himself to be. Here is a case, indeed, where we can learn from him both *as he is when he comes seeking help*, with his problems untouched as yet by the therapeutic experience, and *as he becomes when he has had a chance to make a dent on those problems.*

We can learn from him *as he is* because the traits that mark his dealings with other people, and that keep him a stranger among them, are only exaggerated versions of the attitudes and behaviors with which the rest of us, all too often, take the fine edge of happiness off our human relationships. Our own mistakes may slip by unnoticed or may seem, each in turn, too small to bother about. The irritations and tensions they breed, and the anxiety and loneliness we suffer in consequence, may be so slight and transient that we dismiss them as "natural" and to be expected. After all, we say, no one and no human relationship is perfect. True as our generalizations on this score may be, it is also true that we derive far less confident happiness from our human associations than we might if we made fewer mistakes that differ *in degree* from those of the deeply disturbed person but resemble them *in kind.*

If a person lives as an emotional stranger in a strange land, with his own inner problems and conflicts dictating what he sees in the world around him, how will he characteristically treat other people?

In the first place, he will be obtuse in his responses to them—as though they had no feelings that needed to be taken into account. The reason, here, is obvious. If a person lives in a world of private reference, with his attention anxiously consumed with his own private problems, he is in effect blind and deaf. He does not see what is to be seen in others nor hear what is to be heard. Thus he has no material out of which to build a sensitive awareness of the people around him. They are there; but the only reality they have is in relation to his own needs and demands. His behavior toward them is, therefore, less a response to what they are or do or feel or need than it is a forcing outward (a projection) of his own inner state. More often than not, it is unfitting and uncalled for. It is obtuse, inept, callous. And it is, we must note, the very type of response that we ourselves are likely to make when we are so preoccupied with our own affairs that the world around us and the people in it seem remote and unreal compared with the inner world of our anxieties and problems.

In the second place, the deeply disturbed person exploits those around him. That is to say, he uses them—or tries to use them—as means to his own emotional ends: to help him feel what he needs to feel. Just as a ruthless employer—the type we think of as exploitative—sees as "good" the employee who works hard and asks little, and as "bad" and a "trouble-maker" the one who speaks up for his rights, so the "problem person" sees the members of his family and his working associates as "good" if they accept the role he assigns them and as "bad" or "selfish" if they do not. If, for example, the emotional economy by which he lives makes him need to lean on others, and be looked after, then they—as he sees the case—should be willing to be leaned on. If he needs to dominate others, then they should submit. Here we have the essence of what Karen Horney has described as the neurotic tendency to turn *need* into *claim*.[1] Here also, we observe, is a tendency often exhibited by people who are far from neurotic in a clinical sense. Many a seemingly normal person does profound harm to his human relationships by never being able to see why his friends and relatives should not do exactly what he wants them to do; or by warming up to people only when they are being useful to him.

Again, the deeply disturbed person is insatiable. Plagued by the conflicts and confusions of his own mind, he is inordinately dependent upon the world around him for substitutes for inner peace and confidence. Since, however, what he thus reaches for is irrelevant to his actual need, no amount of it can be enough. If food is his substitute for love, he becomes the glutton. If power is the prop on which his ego depends, he must exercise it constantly, in excess, and over all comers. If he is proving himself by sexual conquest, no one sexual partner can satisfy him; if by busyness, he must be constantly on the go; if by material possessions, the big car must always lead to the bigger.

Once more, the disturbed individual has an exaggerated sense of being "different." He feels himself to be on the outside of situations where everyone else is on the inside. He cannot believe that other people have feelings like his own or problems to match his. In fact, he cannot afford to believe it; for he needs to see himself as different enough from others that he can cast them in roles unlike his own. If he needs to dominate, he cannot afford to see other people as equal with him in capacity or human rights. If he needs to be dependent, he must believe that other people are different enough from him that they can be expected to look after themselves and him too.

LENGTH: 1,600 WORDS

VOCABULARY

welter commotion
therapeutic medically helpful
obtuse stupid
inept unsuitable, awkward
callous unthoughtful, hardened
insatiable never satisfied
inordinately unusually, excessively

---

[1]Karen Horney, *Neurosis and Human Growth*, Chap. 2. New York: W. W. Norton and Company, 1950.

28 · Growth Toward Belonging

SCORING: Reading time: _____ Rate from chart: _____ W.P.M.

MAIN SENTENCE	number right ____ × 4 equals ____ points	
GENERALITIES	number right ____ × 4 equals ____ points	
RETENTION	number right ____ × 2 equals ____ points	
COMPLETION	number right ____ × 3 equals ____ points	
DEFINITIONS	number right ____ × 2 equals ____ points	
	(Total points: 100) total ____ points	

MAIN SENTENCE   Each of these sentences appears in the text. Which one best describes the contents of the passage? ____

1. The troubled people who come through the doors of the counseling center, mental hospital, and psychiatrist's office are as varied as the people on the street outside.
2. However, to some degree, severe or mild, the experience of the *alienated* individual is that of being cut off from his environment.
3. The patient usually does not suspect the nature of his own difficulty.

GENERALITIES   Based on the passage, which of the following generalities seem justifiable? ____ and ____

1. Basically, all mental illness is the same.
2. Often the mentally ill person seeks a substitute for the love he cannot get from others.
3. People can never tell if someone they know is mentally ill.
4. Severe or mild, *alienation* is a form of mental illness.

RETENTION   Based on the passage, which of the following statements are True (T), False (F), or Not answerable (N)?

1. ____ Mental and emotional disturbances are no respecter of persons.
2. ____ An alienated person usually has remarkable control of his moods.
3. ____ The alienated person breaks his isolation by conversing with friends.
4. ____ The deeply disturbed person sees life through a distortion created by his illusions.
5. ____ Deep *alienation* is often caused by a personality split.

6. ____ The alienated person is not in contact with the world of his friends.

7. ____ Most people live well enough with others and do not feel isolated.

8. ____ To an extent, everyone has the same traits as the alienated man.

9. ____ Most alienated people have no real family to relate to.

10. ____ Often behavior resembles that of the disturbed person in kind, but not in degree.

11. ____ In a way, the alienated person is blind and deaf to the needs and ideas of others.

12. ____ The disturbed person exploits those around him.

13. ____ To a disturbed person, someone who is "bad" is a person who will not do as he wishes.

14. ____ The disturbed person is unusually dependent on the world around him for confidence.

15. ____ Most psychiatrists do not know how to deal with the alienated man.

16. ____ Everyone is alienated to some degree.

17. ____ The disturbed person feels that he is just like everyone else.

18. ____ Whatever the disturbed man substitutes for love actually satisfies him.

19. ____ The alienated man cannot be sensitive to the people around him.

20. ____ Often the alienated man feels as if he is "falling apart."

COMPLETION Choose the best answer for each question.

1. ____ If food is the alienated man's substitute for love, he will become a: (a) cook. (b) gourmet. (c) glutton. (d) consumer.

2. ____ Troubled people are alienated from their relatives and from: (a) their pets. (b) their doctor. (c) themselves. (d) none of these.

3. ____ The normal man and the alienated man have: (a) different emotional references. (b) nearly similar impulses. (c) largely different backgrounds. (d) a sense of genuine conviction.

4. ____ The troubled person only knows: (a) the name of his condition. (b) that his doctor is trying to help him. (c) where he has been. (d) that he is suffering.

5. ____ For a troubled man, talking with other people does not imply: (a) friendship. (b) understanding. (c) convenience. (d) sense.

6. _____ What is learned from studying the disturbed individual is that he: (a) never wants to talk to people. (b) is a lot like everyone else. (c) cannot help himself. (d) wants to use others for his own purposes.

DEFINITIONS   In the following passage, each underlined word has a number. In the columns below, match the number of each underlined word with the letter of the word that is closest to it in meaning.

1   2   3   4

Here also, we observe, is a tendency often exhibited by people who are far

5   6 7   8   9

from neurotic in a clinical sense. Many a seemingly normal person does

10 11   12   13

profound harm to his human relationships by never being able to see why his

friends and relatives should not do exactly what he wants them to do; or by

14   15

warming up to people only when they are being useful to him.

Column A	Column B
1. _____	a. shown
2. _____	b. serious
	c. well-adjusted
3. _____	d. medical
4. _____	e. apparently
	f. to understand
5. _____	g. bring to a boil
6. _____	h. meaning
7. _____	i. disturbed
	j. see
8. _____	k. friendships
9. _____	l. pattern of behavior
10. _____	m. damage
11. _____	n. frequently
12. _____	o. being friendly
13. _____	p. necessary
	q. infrequently
14. _____	r. pretentious
15. _____	s. nice

29 · The Status of Soviet Women

WILLIAM MANDEL

> *In Russia, women have their freedom just as they do in America.
> But Russian society makes far more use of women's talents than
> America does. Women in Russia take up their duties as doctors
> and engineers and professionals at all levels.*

"**D**on't turn to grandma for advice!" warns a headline in a Soviet
magazine for farm women. Her good will is far outweighed by ignorance. She
was probably illiterate until after the Revolution. When grandma was a girl,
many peasant mothers gave birth in the fields. Factory girls often had their
babies alongside the loom in a textile mill or in the mill-yard. Infants died
like flies, and mortality among mothers was shocking. Only one child in twenty
was delivered with qualified assistance. Birth control was unknown; illegal,
unsanitary abortions took a tremendous toll.

Today, prenatal and maternity medical care is universal. The country has
14,000 women's and infants' medical consultation centers which keep expectant
mothers under observation to the time of confinement, teach them proper care
of the child, and treat the sick. These centers supposedly offer birth-control
clinics and instruct in physical and psychological painless childbirth techniques.
As of 1958, half of all Soviet women had in this way been freed of the physical agony of childbearing. The figure today is doubtless higher.

Few contraceptives are produced. Unwanted pregnancies occur. In the
postwar years this led to a rise in illegal abortions. In 1955 the Soviet government gave up trying to fight abortion practices by a combination of education
and aid to mothers married or not, and reinstituted legal, hospital abortion.
It is free when medically justified, and costs $5.50 otherwise. But traditional

concepts of shame remain. *Izvestia* admits that illegal abortions are still common in the case of unmarried girls and even married women who don't want pregnancies to become known.

In publicly owned establishments, all women—industrial workers, office employees, professionals (all professional occupations are salaried positions in the U.S.S.R.), state-farm workers—are allowed eight weeks' prenatal and eight weeks' postnatal leave at full pay. This can be followed immediately by the annual paid vacation if the individual wants it then, and then by three months' unpaid leave if she desires. Only if she remains away from work after this does management have the right to change her job status in any manner. The paid postnatal leave is increased, on doctor's affidavit, in case of a multiple birth or abnormal delivery. Pregnant women and nursing mothers cannot be assigned to night work or overtime. Nor may they be sent on business trips after the fourth month of pregnancy. (Women number 53 percent of all employed college-trained people, including three out of four physicians, two out of three teachers, more than half the economists and statisticians, two out of five agricultural experts and veterinarians, one-third of the lawyers and judges, and three out of ten engineers, so this is a realistic provision.)

Co-operative enterprises meet costs such as maternity leave out of their own funds. Therefore, the law does not set standards for them as high as in publicly owned establishments, for this might be too heavy a burden for weak co-ops.

There is a continuing effort to convince women to have babies, once conceived, as a matter of health. This is aided by such institutions as the round-the-clock nursery, in which mothers can place their infants for the whole week, taking them home only on week-ends and holidays. These are an inestimable boon to unmarried and widowed mothers, and those whose housing conditions are worse than the generally unsatisfactory average. Among women between twenty-five and twenty-nine, the birth rate is four times as high among those having adequate housing as among those who do not live in separate apartments, private homes, or rooms of ample size. The over-all birth rate is among the highest on earth but is dropping steadily. A Soviet study showed that the only possible practical measure to reverse that downward trend would be an even more rapid rise in housing construction than is now the case.

Infant mortality is among the lowest in the world: one in thirty-one, in 1961, and is only one-eighth of what it was in 1913. One reason for this is that the number of doctors in obstetrics and gynecology alone is larger than the entire Russian medical profession before the Revolution.

Each newborn child is registered automatically at the local consultation center, and the first visit by a nurse is the day after the mother has returned from the hospital with her baby. The center follows the child to the age of fourteen. One of its functions is to provide baby formulas and foods, and special diets for older children when needed. These consultation centers all have legal departments that provide free advice (their other services are also free). Thus, the unwed mother, the abandoned wife, the divorced woman whose husband is not paying alimony, can obtain both physical and the legal aid at a single place. In the countryside, the same services are offered at the county health centers. The latest medical advances are available to country people: 60 percent of confinements in the cities are by painless childbirth, and 44 percent in rural areas.

In 1963, year-round day nurseries and kindergartens could accommodate a total of 6.2 million children in the age groups from two months to six years. This represents a doubling of these facilities in five years, and provides by far the highest level of preschool care in the world. Nevertheless, these institutions can care for only one-fifth the number of children in this age group. Therefore the great majority of children continue to be looked after by their own families all day.

Admittance to day nurseries is not controlled by one's income. The fee is only 15 percent of the cost of maintenance, including meals. It is cheaper for a child to be in a nursery than at home. But there are just not nearly enough, although rapid expansion continues. On the other hand, opposition to letting one's child out of the home during these years is still very strong.

The fullest provision of children's facilities is in the summer. Camps, children's health resorts, trail camps, and summer day-camp sites for the permanent kindergartens and nurseries care for seven million children; three million children attend seasonal rural nurseries when the demand for farm labor is at its height. For these children it is, as I have had a chance to see, a lovely life.

Camps and kindergartens—I have observed both—provide love and warmth and successfully teach co-operativeness and respect for what belongs to all, and yet leave room for robust individuality.

I remember the amazement of everyone in my party at the splendid condition of the elaborate dolls in a kindergarten we visited. It was hard to believe that they were in constant use. But there was no doubting the sincerity of the motherly staff. They told us that the children kept them that way just because they were for everyone to use: to spoil your own toy is stupid, but to spoil that which others will use is bad. And what, we asked, when a child does something that is bad—as surely must happen? Of course it happens, they said, but then the earliest opportunity is taken to tell a story or play a game that will illustrate the good way to do the particular thing that had been done wrong. The child is not scolded. Whether the little child ever does it again, or how many times, I do not know.

Officials and educators in the Soviet Union say that expressions of selfishness, superstition, backward traditions in family life, and a lack of interest in or contempt for manual occupations may be traced to the fact that children are still largely raised by doting parents—and particularly grandmothers.

Whether because the war-torn lives of parents and grandparents were so difficult, or for whatever other reason, there is a distinct tendency to coddle children in the family, and to protect them against physical effort. This is something the authorities try to undo in the school system, where a determined effort is made to give a type of training that will break down the widespread feeling that manual labor is beneath the dignity of a person with a high-school education. However, I spent a good deal of time talking to teenagers in Leningrad in 1962, and got no feeling that they looked down upon physical effort or manual labor, although they naturally hoped to go on to work that would use their brains.

Soviet women certainly do not think of themselves solely as mothers. Like American women, they are "joiners," perhaps to an even greater degree. Also like women in other countries, they feel that there is a place for organizations of women alone, although they participate to a high degree in organizations open to both sexes.

As in the United States, women are particularly active in parent associations. But the last several years have seen the emergence of groups called women's councils. They are at present local bodies, although there is some demand for a national organization. These councils may come into being merely to organize a party for children, but in the course of this simple activity someone will bring up the need for a new kindergarten, and the council continues in existence to see this through with the local authorities. Meanwhile the matter of unsatisfactory service in local stores may have come up, and the council will crusade on this, since the stores are all run either by municipal authorities or co-ops. In one Ural Mountain city the size of San Francisco, there are 160 neighborhood women's councils headed by a city-wide representative body. In addition to engaging in the activities mentioned above, they act as public monitors of the health services and of hostels for young working people. They work with the local school system to organize leisure-time activity and recreation for children and adolescents, and press for the introduction of home economics courses. They give much attention to adult education. They are also active in promoting the planting of flowers and greenery throughout the city.

LENGTH: 1,780 WORDS

VOCABULARY

prenatal   before birth
Izvestia   official Russian newspaper
postnatal   after birth
obstetrics   branch of medicine concerned with birth
gynecology   medical science related to women's diseases

29 · The Status of Soviet Women

SCORING: Reading time: _____ Rate from chart: _____ W.P.M.

MAIN SENTENCE	number right ____ × 4 equals ____ points	
GENERALITIES	number right ____ × 4 equals ____ points	
RETENTION	number right ____ × 2 equals ____ points	
COMPLETION	number right ____ × 3 equals ____ points	
DEFINITIONS	number right ____ × 2 equals ____ points	

(Total points: 100)   **total** ____ points

MAIN SENTENCE   Each of these sentences appears in the text. Which one best describes the contents of the passage? ____

1. "Don't turn to grandma for advice!"
2. Soviet women certainly do not think of themselves solely as mothers.
3. As in the United States, women are particularly active in parent associations.

GENERALITIES   Based on the passage, which of the following generalities seem justifiable? ____ and ____

1. If women are to become professional people, centers must be established for the care of children.
2. Soviet women probably dislike having to become doctors and engineers.
3. There are many Soviet professional women because there are few men.
4. Childbirth and birth control are probably more serious national problems in Russia than in the United States.

RETENTION   Based on the passage, which of the following statements are True (T), False (F), or Not answerable (N)?

1. ____ Older Russian women are likely to have been engineers like their granddaughters.

2. ____ Soviet women's councils are much like American parent associations.

3. ____ Unlike American women, Soviet women are not "joiners."

4. ____ The Soviet government seems to think children are spoiled by grandmothers.

5. ____ The normal Russian family does not have a tendency to coddle its children.

6. _____ The author believes that the teenagers he spoke with do not look down on manual labor.

7. _____ The Soviet government takes no official recognition of unwed mothers.

8. _____ The introduction of painless childbirth was significant in modern Russia.

9. _____ Soviet women prefer normal childbirth to the painless method.

10. _____ Soviet nurseries are cold and inhuman in their treatment of children.

11. _____ Children in the nurseries are not permitted to touch elaborate dolls.

12. _____ Admittance to the day nurseries is controlled by one's income.

13. _____ The nurseries could accommodate only 20 percent of the children of nursery age.

14. _____ The nurseries take care of children from two months to six years of age.

15. _____ The Soviet birth rate is related to adequate housing facilities.

16. _____ After their fourth month of pregnancy, Soviet women cannot be sent on business trips.

17. _____ In 1955, the Russian government legalized all abortions.

18. _____ The infant mortality rate in Russia is among the lowest in the world.

19. _____ Less than half the total college-trained work force in Russia is women.

20. _____ In Russia, prenatal and maternity care are universal.

COMPLETION   Choose the best answer for each question.

1. _____ The Soviet government advises modern women not to turn to grandma for advice because: (a) grandma probably is uneducated. (b) grandmas coddle the children. (c) grandma is so old she is undependable. (d) old people have no place in Russian society.

2. _____ The maternity-leave provision in public-owned businesses is: (a) realistic. (b) idealistic. (c) unnecessary. (d) quite wasteful.

3. _____ The over-all birth rate in Russia is one of the highest on earth, but: (a) not much higher than ours. (b) much lower than Japan's. (c) is still rising every year. (d) is declining steadily.

4. _____ The time of the year when facilities for children are most active is in: (a) the fall. (b) the summer. (c) the weeks right after birth. (d) business hours.

5. ___ When the child is mischievous in the nursery he is: (a) sent home. (b) carefully spanked. (c) not scolded. (d) given to his grandmother.

6. ___ In pre-Revolution Russia, the total number of doctors was less than the present number of: (a) engineers. (b) obstetricians and gynecologists. (c) citizens in San Francisco. (d) new-born children.

DEFINITIONS In the following passage, each underlined word has a number. In the columns below, match the number of each underlined word with the letter of the word that is closest to it in meaning.

     1   2   3   4   5   6

Admittance to day nurseries is not controlled by one's income. The fee is only

               7   8   9

15 percent of the cost of maintenance, including meals. It is cheaper for a

                                       10   11

child to be in a nursery than at home. But there are just not nearly enough,

    12   13   14   15

although rapid expansion continues.

Column A

1. ___
2. ___
3. ___
4. ___
5. ___
6. ___
7. ___
8. ___
9. ___
10. ___
11. ___
12. ___
13. ___
14. ___
15. ___

Column B

a. less expensive
b. acceptance
c. growth
d. with
e. goes on uninterrupted
f. merely
g. sufficient
h. even though
i. earnings
j. cost
k. child care centers
l. certain
m. very fast
n. exciting
o. unimportant
p. unlikely
q. regulated
r. upkeep
s. approximately

30 · Man's Genetic Future

CURT STERN

> *The "best" biological specimens should mate with each other,
> but they usually do not. Will this random mating cause the race
> of man to deteriorate? Curt Stern reassures us that the world's
> gene population is healthy.*

Assuming the human species is here to stay, what is likely to happen to us genetically? Will the stock improve, deteriorate or remain the same? Is the future predestined, or can we direct it?

To answer such questions we must consider mankind's hereditary endowment as a whole and the distribution of this endowment among individuals. Let us assume, as we may for the purpose of this discussion, that the human germ cell has exactly 20,000 genes. That means that every one of the more than two billion people on earth today has acquired a set of 20,000 genes from the father and a similar set from the mother. These are shuffled like two decks of cards to produce new sets of 20,000 genes in the individual's own germ cells. Everyone has the same 20,000 kinds of genes but some genes appear in more than one form. Many probably occur in only one variety and are the same for everyone; others may show two, three, four and up to 100 varieties. In any case, the total pool of genes in the earth's population at present is some 80 trillion (two billion people times 20,000 pairs of genes each). This is the storehouse from which the genetic future of man will be furnished.

The number of different possible combinations of the varieties of genes is huge, so huge indeed that of the hundreds of billions of sperms one man produces during his lifetime, no two are likely to be identical in the combination

MAN'S GENETIC FUTURE From *Scientific American*, February 1952. Reprinted by permission of *Scientific American*.

of genic varieties. The shuffling of the genic cards makes it unlikely that any person on earth (with the exception of identical twins) has ever exactly duplicated any other person in genic make-up, or will in the future.

This does not mean, however, that our inheritance is an entirely random affair. If men and women were completely promiscuous in mating—socially, racially and geographically—then one genic combination would be as likely as any other, and people might vary individually much more than they actually do. There are times and places where man does approach such random mating, for example, during great migrations and large military occupations, when one group may sow its genic varieties among those of another group. As a rule, however, a potential child within a given group does not draw on the whole storehouse of mankind's genes. Usually his genes will come from a socially, nationally and racially segregated part of the store.

Yet for thousands of years the barriers separating the store of human genes into compartments have been progressively lowered, and with the increase of human mobility in our era of world-wide transportation many barriers will undoubtedly disappear. Tribes, minor races and other subgroups will vanish. A diffusion of genes from one group to another is bound to occur, however slowly and gradually, and in time it will tend to eliminate all partitions in our storehouse.

Will this be good, bad or immaterial for mankind? We cannot answer this question without evaluating the racial differences of the present. Have the present combinations of genic varieties originated in a haphazard way or are they the result of selective forces in the earliest prehistory of mankind which adapted the different races to specific environments? It is probable that both chance and design have played a role. Thus the racial differences in blood types (Rh and so on) seem to be just accidental and of no adaptive significance. On the other hand, it is likely that the differences in pigmentation and breadth of nose between the Africans and the Caucasians were evolved to fit the differing climates in which these peoples lived. Does this mean that the leveling of the genic partitions will make the world's peoples less fit to cope with their respective environments? Such a conclusion might be justified if we could assume that the originally adaptive traits have the same significance today as they had 100,000 years ago. But has not man created new influences which effectively alter his environment in such a fashion that the external physical factors continuously decline in importance? Housing and clothing, food and medicine, occupation and training have changed radically, and it may well be that these new factors have superseded the old ones.

What of mental differences among races? Whether or not such differences exist has not been established; exact knowledge of the genic distinctions between groups is most lacking where it most matters. This is not only because psychologists have found it difficult to invent standard tests to measure the inborn capacities of different races but also because there is great variability in mental traits within any one group.

The 20,000 pairs of genes in the fertilized egg control a multitude of interactions whose full complexity far transcends our understanding. In every trait of the individual numerous genically induced reactions are involved. There is no absolute, one-to-one relation between a specific gene and a specific trait; it is necessary for the process that results in the specific trait, but it does not invariably produce the trait in question. A gene for clubfoot, for instance, makes for an inclination, a potentiality, toward the appearance of clubfoot, but whether this potentiality will become reality depends on the interplay of life processes. A slight variation in timing or in the environment may decide one way or the other. The clubfoot defect may appear in one foot, in both feet or in neither.

The amount of variation in some life processes is small, in others large. A man's blood type, for example, remains the same throughout his life, but the color of his hair changes. Are the traits that distinguish different races variable in expression or invariable products of their genic endowments? It seems as a first approximation that genes for physical traits are more rigid in expression than those for mental traits. The Caucasian's hair remains straight or wavy and the Negro's kinky, regardless of any change in environment or training. It is otherwise with mental traits. A normal man's genetic endowment provides him with a wide potential for mental performance, from very low to very high. As with a rubber balloon, the state of expansion of his mind at any given time is hardly a measure of its expansibility. In human evolution those genes that allow the greatest mental adaptability, that possess the greatest plasticity of expression, seem to have undergone preferential selection in all races. If this is actually so, then the different genic varieties for mental traits may be comparably evenly distributed among all human groups, and the disappearance of the present barriers subdividing man's genic storehouse would not greatly affect mankind's mental potentialities.

What role will differences in reproduction play among the various socioeconomic groups within populations? It is well known that the lower socioeconomic layers of Western societies have higher birth rates than the upper ones. Do these layers differ in their stocks of genes? We cannot say with any certainty. The difficulties of research in this important field are great. We do not know, for instance, to what extent intelligence scores reflect true genetic factors in addition to education and environment, which they certainly reflect to a large degree. Nevertheless, the evidence strongly suggests that hereditary mental differences between socio-economic groups do exist. The mean intelligence scores of children at the higher socio-economic levels are consistently higher than those of lower groups, whether the tests are made in the U.S., in the U.S.S.R. or in any other country. That environment is not the sole reason for such differences is indicated by comparative studies on comparable groups of children, particularly twins reared together and separately. It is hard to avoid the conclusion that there are mean differences in the genetic endowment of different socio-economic groups, although the individual endowments within each group cover the whole range from very low to very high. Since the groups that seem less well endowed intellectually produce the most children, a deterioration of the genetic endowment of the population should result.

This large-scale difference in reproduction rates is a rather recent phenomenon. It is primarily the result of birth control, which did not become an important social practice until the second half of the 19th century. So far the upper and middle groups of Western countries have adopted birth control much more widely than the lower ones. But there is reason to believe that the use of contraceptive measures will spread through the whole population, and that the group differentials in fertility will be diminished, although perhaps not obliterated.

Before we become too alarmed over the possibility that the genetic stocks of Western peoples may deteriorate, it would be well to obtain an estimate of the rate of this suspected deterioration. Such analyses as have been made suggest that the decrease of valuable genic varieties is probably much smaller than a naive consideration would suggest. High intelligence undoubtedly is based not on single varieties of genes but on the cooperation of many genes. The valuable varieties must be present, singly or in partial combinations, even in the great mass of individuals who score low in intelligence. From there they can, in the course of a single generation, reconstitute an appreciable number of the "best" combinations. In other words, the population at large constitutes a great reservoir, and the possible loss of valuable genic varieties possessed by the small upper layers of the population tells only a part of the story.

LENGTH: 1,660 WORDS

VOCABULARY

gene the unit of matter that carries hereditary characteristics from parents
  to offspring
genetic referring to genes
promiscuous random, haphazard
supersede to replace, take the place of
transcend to go beyond
induced caused
endowments talents, gifts
obliterated destroyed
naive innocent, uneducated

30 · Man's Genetic Future

SCORING: Reading time: _____ Rate from chart: _____ W.P.M.

MAIN SENTENCE	number right ____ × 4 equals ____ points	
GENERALITIES	number right ____ × 4 equals ____ points	
RETENTION	number right ____ × 2 equals ____ points	
COMPLETION	number right ____ × 3 equals ____ points	
DEFINITIONS	number right ____ × 2 equals ____ points	

(Total points: 100)   **total** ____ points

MAIN SENTENCE   Each of these sentences appears in the text. Which one best describes the contents of the passage? ____

1. Everyone has the same 20,000 kinds of genes but some genes appear in more than one form.
2. A diffusion of genes from one group to another is bound to occur, however slowly and gradually, and in time it will tend to eliminate all partitions in our storehouse.
3. Tribes, minor races and other subgroups will vanish.

GENERALITIES   Based on the passage, which of the following generalities seem justifiable? ____ and ____

1. The possibilities for human variety are quite limited.
2. Eventually birth control will affect our gene pool.
3. Racial and tribal mixing is likely to have little or no effect on the mental ability of offspring.
4. Inheritance is almost entirely a random affair.

RETENTION   Based on the passage, which of the following statements are True (T), False (F), or Not answerable (N)?

1. ____ No two sperms a man produces are likely to be identical.

2. ____ The present pool of human genes is about two billion.

3. ____ There is a gene that determines the size of a person's ear.

4. ____ An individual's genic make-up must be duplicated elsewhere on earth.

5. ____ A man gets 20,000 genes from his mother and 20,000 from his father.

6. ____ Random mating among humans is rather common.

7. ____ Man's genes are segregated by geography, race, nation, and language.

8. _____ Social class is unimportant in segregating gene stores.

9. _____ Increased mobility will affect radically the segregated gene stores.

10. _____ Some differences between races seem to be unrelated to environment.

11. _____ A new child draws on the genic storehouse of all mankind.

12. _____ Other factors, in addition to environment, have affected man's evolution.

13. _____ Some differences exist among the mental traits of various races.

14. _____ There is often a one-to-one relation between a specific gene and a specific trait.

15. _____ Genes for physical traits are more decisive than those for mental traits.

16. _____ The genes of a normal man permit him a wide potential for mental performance.

17. _____ There is no evidence to suggest a genic difference between socio-economic groups.

18. _____ High intelligence is based on a single set of genes.

19. _____ Contraceptive measures may become almost universal.

20. _____ Royalty has the "best" gene patterns known in Western culture.

COMPLETION   Choose the best answer for each question.

1. _____ The author compares the mixing of genes received from father and mother to: (a) mixing soup. (b) stirring a pool. (c) cleaning a deck. (d) shuffling cards.

2. _____ Lower socio-economic groups in both the U.S. and the U.S.S.R. have consistently lower: (a) birth rates. (b) mean intelligence scores. (c) eyebrows. (d) measures of expansibility.

3. _____ In human evolution, those genes that allow man the greatest mental adaptability have: (a) undergone preferential selection. (b) tended to disappear. (c) been affected by genic segregation. (d) remain unchanged.

4. _____ If one genic combination was as likely as another, people probably would: (a) die at birth. (b) have a great degree of mobility. (c) vary individually more than they do. (d) stay the same.

5. _____ Much knowledge of genes is not yet available because scientists have yet to invent a test to show: (a) genic patterns. (b) inborn mental capacity. (c) genic inheritance. (d) proper socio-economic grouping.

6. _____ One physical trait that has little or no relationship to environment is: (a) hair color. (b) clubfoot. (c) eye color. (d) blood type.

DEFINITION   In the following passage, each underlined word has a number. In the columns below, match the number of each underlined word with the letter of the word that is closest to it in meaning.

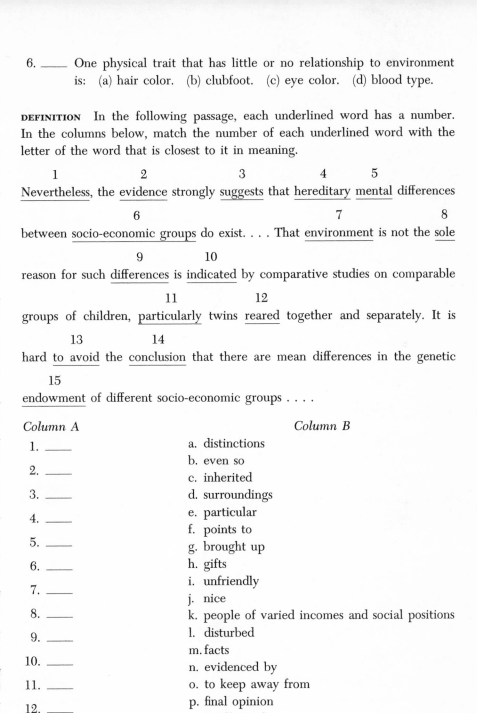

Nevertheless, the evidence strongly suggests that hereditary mental differences

between socio-economic groups do exist. . . . That environment is not the sole

reason for such differences is indicated by comparative studies on comparable

groups of children, particularly twins reared together and separately. It is

hard to avoid the conclusion that there are mean differences in the genetic

endowment of different socio-economic groups . . . .

Column A

1. _____
2. _____
3. _____
4. _____
5. _____
6. _____
7. _____
8. _____
9. _____
10. _____
11. _____
12. _____
13. _____
14. _____
15. _____

Column B

a. distinctions
b. even so
c. inherited
d. surroundings
e. particular
f. points to
g. brought up
h. gifts
i. unfriendly
j. nice
k. people of varied incomes and social positions
l. disturbed
m. facts
n. evidenced by
o. to keep away from
p. final opinion
q. intellectual
r. with emphasis on
s. only

31 · Growing Old in the U.S.A.

GIBSON WINTER

> *Most young people cannot imagine themselves growing old, and the older citizen often has trouble understanding the young. A selection from the book* Love and Conflict *discusses such differences in attitude and their possible influence in preventing the old from living useful, happy lives.*

Our emphasis on productive work makes old age seem like the end of life. People have always been forced to withdraw from productive work in later years, but now they withdraw into a vacuum. In most societies, retirement from work meant entrance into the honored position of elder. One could give time to counseling the young, passing on the traditions, and sitting in the seats of the venerated. Life did not end with retirement. New life and new responsibilities followed withdrawal from hunting, fishing, war parties, or bearing children. There is no such honored position for the elder in our way of life. We honor the new, the youthful, the more efficient. Methods are changing year by year and only the most youthful can keep up with the new. Older people do get somewhat more set in their ways. This is the conserving strength of the elder in a society. He represents the wisdom of the old ways. We, on the other hand, have no place for the old ways. Even as children, we use the word old-fashioned as a term of disdain. Old age comes to mean "useless" in a society that worships the latest method and the newest invention.

We also deprive old age of its meaning by our confidence in man's control of circumstances. Despite the threat of hydrogen bombs, modern man has unlimited confidence in his ability to control his destiny. We have conquered some diseases. Give us a little more time, and we shall conquer all diseases. If oil runs short, we shall resort to atomic power. If there is strife in a factory, we can bring in the experts on human relations who will adjust all the tensions. In fact, we have to emphasize our control of the uncertainties of life in order to stimulate our pursuit of new knowledge and techniques. If this confidence flags, our efforts may diminish and the security which we seek may be jeopardized.

Older people discover that these youthful dreams are not the whole truth. Some things can be controlled, but sooner or later death approaches. Old friends are dying one at a time. George had a heart attack last year. Eleanor is ailing. The precariousness of life hits us as we grow older. Family, friends, loyalty, and religious faith take on new importance in later years. Some would cynically call this tendency of older people an attempt to find substitutes for their youthful vigor. Others would say that one can only achieve a real sense of values in our society after he has passed through the American dream of success to the realities of life. Whatever our interpretation, Americans despise the values which older people must discover if their lives are to have meaning. We are so confident of our control over life that we make older people seem senile in their sensitivity to human weaknesses.

Older people have to face some of the shabbiness of the American dream if they are to come to the faith that makes sense out of life. They have to look upon their successes and achievements in a broader perspective. Success, after all, is but one of many values in life. Older people remember the relationships which were broken by harshness. They see the importance of God's forgiveness. They live long enough to see some of the results of their good and bad deeds. Needless to say, their words about faith seem foreign to the young. This is just another sign that dad is getting old. He doesn't understand any more. He is losing touch, but it's nice that dad has found religion.

These are a few of the ways in which our way of life isolates older people. Our provisions for the aged also reflect this separation. Our medical knowledge has brought miraculous skill in perpetuating life. Men and women are kept alive in hospitals during months of ravaging disease. Drugs help, but soon they lose their effectiveness. These illnesses are costly. Many older couples spend their life's savings on these so-called "terminal" illnesses. Consequently homes for the aged are reluctant to accept older people who are not in good health. Despite these precautions, most homes for the aged are burdened with the care of bedridden patients. Many older people must be placed in nursing homes. Many others are sent to state mental hospitals which have whole sections maintained for older people. Some of these older people linger for years without a visitor or friend. They lie helplessly in bed, while overworked attendants make a vain effort to keep them clean and provide some attention.

Old-age pensions and social security have undoubtedly improved the lot of older people. Until pensions for older people can provide independence with a decent standard of living, however, we cannot deny that our provision for the aged reflects our view that they are no longer of value.

We find it difficult to face the real needs of older people because we ourselves are afraid of all that old age means. We realize that old age contradicts the values which we now cherish—youth, vigor, success, the new and the more efficient. It is difficult to see the realities of old age unless we can face the uncertainty of human life. We confess that we cannot face these facts about life by the way that we overlook the hardships of aging in our time. We know these hardships. We see them all about us. Nevertheless, we cannot really see them, because it is too disturbing to face their implications.

Even when older people can receive good accommodations and a decent standard of living, they still suffer from personal isolation. Old peoples' homes have been a boon to many, but they do not overcome the estrangement from children, younger people, and family life. The course of human life is lived in neighborhoods and homes. Daily life involves laundry, cooking, going to work, having arguments, and a hundred routine things. Older people are removed from this stream of life when they enter a home for the aged. Some of them like the quiet of such a setting and the fellowship with others of their age. Many, however, age more rapidly, become bedridden, and deteriorate under such conditions. Welfare agencies have been attempting to place older people in private homes to overcome this deterioration. Isolation from the stream of life intensifies the process of aging. One cannot escape the feeling that he is rejected by the community. Premature illness and the need for bed care become substitute ways of gaining attention. Old age becomes living death rather than a new stage of life.

New developments in our society may transform some of these conditions for older people. There is strong pressure to continue to improve pension and social security provisions. If this trend is strengthened, older people may gain a degree of independence which will place their destiny more in their own hands. We treasure our freedom to decide the circumstances of our lives, but thus far we have withheld this privilege from many older people. It remains to be seen whether we are willing to extend this privilege to them.

The shorter working week may also contribute to the freedom of older people by allowing time for outside interests during the productive years. More men and women are using their leisure time to develop avocations. Many of them, to be sure, are using leisure time to supplement their incomes with additional work, but the four-day week will undoubtedly create a serious question about the use of leisure time. Unless young adults develop creative interests, they will find TV and recreational pursuits dull and uninteresting. Leisure time is very unevenly distributed in our society, since managerial and professional people often work seven days a week, while production workers find time to carry two jobs in order to increase their incomes. Nevertheless, professional and managerial personnel usually have too many outside interests, whereas production workers have had too little energy to develop other interests. If production workers gain more leisure time and use it to develop avocations, they may well look forward to retirement from industry. In fact, the shoe may be on the other foot. Industry may be inducing workers to continue after retirement age, thus utilizing their technical skill for the problems of production. Workers, on the other hand, will have the choice of continuing in productive work or pursuing their avocations. Such a development is still in the field of working time, but it may enhance the freedom of choice for older people.

Automation is another industrial development which may benefit the older worker. Opinions differ on this subject, since the implications of automation for industrial life are still uncertain. A good case can be made, however, for the fact that automation will put a premium on technical competence and minimize youthful vigor. Most workers are quite naturally concerned over the degree of unemployment which will be created by automation. Nevertheless, automation may increase the need for technical training and thus lengthen the training period for workers. A labor scarcity is a real possibility if educational and training requirements are considerably increased. Such a development would more than offset the reduction in number of workers. This, at least, is a reasonable possibility which Peter Drucker has suggested. If this happens, the pressure to make the retirement age more flexible will be increased. Older skilled workers may be in great demand. Knowledge of complex processes is not easily gained and requires a minimum of physical strength. Older workers may have considerably more choice about their retirement in the not too distant future.

These rather optimistic considerations about old age should be countered with two rather obvious considerations. We Americans tend to live up to the limits of our income. We get a raise and think that now we shall have plenty to spare. In a few months that raise has been absorbed in a slightly higher standard of living for the family. It is hard to say just where the money went, but we have used it on a multitude of little things. There is no reason to expect that pension provisions will ever match this higher standard of living which has been achieved in the productive years. Older people have fewer expenses, since they are no longer supporting children. Nevertheless, their standard of living is bound to drop with retirement. Furthermore, American standards of thrift have changed radically since World War II. Credit buying has become standard practice. Most couples today are carrying rather heavy debts. Cars are purchased on credit. Mortgages are not new on the American scene, but many more couples are buying homes and paying on long-term mortgages. Many older people in our day have had some savings for their later years. The present generation, however, may have some equity in a house but they will have no other savings. Both of these facts, the drop in the standard of living and the lack of savings, will undoubtedly handicap our own generation as they approach retirement. These conditions may induce them to put off retirement in order to maintain their incomes. If they have greater freedom to retire or pursue avocations because of automation, they may be more inclined to continue working because of financial pressure. In any case, the financial prospects for older people look somewhat better in the years to come.

LENGTH: 2,050 WORDS

VOCABULARY

vacuum   emptiness
venerated   respected
disdain   scorn, disapproval
jeopardized   threatened
estrangement   alienation, separation
avocation   hobby

31 · Growing Old in the U.S.A.

+---+

SCORING: Reading time: _____ Rate from chart: _____ W.P.M.

MAIN SENTENCE	number right _____ × 4 equals _____ points
GENERALITIES	number right _____ × 4 equals _____ points
RETENTION	number right _____ × 2 equals _____ points
COMPLETION	number right _____ × 3 equals _____ points
DEFINITIONS	number right _____ × 2 equals _____ points

(Total points: 100)   **total** _____ points

+---+

MAIN SENTENCE   Each of these sentences appears in the text. Which one best describes the contents of the passage? _____

1. Older people do get somewhat more set in their ways.
2. Old age comes to mean "useless" in a society that worships the latest method and the newest invention.
3. We find it difficult to face the real needs of older people because we ourselves are afraid of all that old age means.

GENERALITIES   Based on the passage, which of the following generalities seem justifiable? _____ and _____

1. Societies other than ours have found ways of making the old useful.
2. America is the country in which problems of the aged are most serious.
3. Efficient control of our environment is partly responsible for our feeling that old age is a useless period of life.
4. People who are old also have the tendency to worship youth.

RETENTION   Based on the passage, which of the following statements are True (T), False (F), or Not answerable (N)?

1. _____ The qualities we cherish are youth, vigor, success, and efficiency.

2. _____ We have not faced the facts of aging in our time.

3. _____ Most young people harbor an unexpressed sympathy for the elderly.

4. _____ In homes for the aged, the elderly often suddenly become spry and more lively.

5. _____ Isolation from the stream of life intensifies the process of aging.

6. _____ Developing a creative hobby in youth helps people in old age.

7. ____ The leisure time of people in labor and management is often taken up with work.

8. ____ Automation will hurt rather than benefit the older worker.

9. ____ Longer training periods for workers will be one result of automation.

10. ____ In the future, older workers may have more choice about retirement.

11. ____ The financial prospects for older people look bad.

12. ____ American standards of thrift have not changed since World War II.

13. ____ Old people's homes have been a booming business since 1945.

14. ____ No old people want to spend their lives in a home for the aged.

15. ____ Social security and pension plans make life easier for older people.

16. ____ Homes for the aged are reluctant to take unwell people.

17. ____ Homes for the aged are drab and dull.

18. ____ Our society has great confidence in its ability to solve problems.

19. ____ Old age makes us more sensitive to family, friends, religion, and death.

20. ____ Emphasizing productive work makes old age seem the end of life.

COMPLETION Choose the best answer for each question.

1. ____ Our society has no use for: (a) elderly people. (b) early retirement plans. (c) pension plans. (d) old ways.

2. ____ Americans despise the values older people must discover: (a) later in life. (b) if their lives are to have meaning. (c) in spite of the efforts of youth. (d) even if they do not want to.

3. ____ Our way of life tends to: (a) isolate older people. (b) soften older people. (c) coddle older people. (d) patronize older people.

4. ____ We see the hardships of old age, but we do not respond to them because: (a) they are not important enough. (b) old people will not let us. (c) we cannot face the meaning of those hardships. (d) our life is too fast.

5. ____ Old people's homes do not overcome the estrangement from: (a) work. (b) routine. (c) friends. (d) family.

6. ____ When one is consigned to a home for the aged, he cannot overcome the feeling that: (a) the home is not a good place to be. (b) he has been rejected by the community. (c) no one will know how to care for him. (d) old age is here at last.

DEFINITIONS   In the following passage, each underlined word has a number. In the columns below, match the number of each underlined word with the letter of the word that is closest to it in meaning.

          1   2   3   4
New developments in our society may transform some of these conditions for

                      5   6   7   8
older people. There is strong pressure to continue to improve pension and

                  9   10
social security provisions. If this trend is strengthened, older people may gain

      11   12
a degree of independence which will place their destiny more in their own

                13   14
hands. We treasure our freedom to decide the circumstances of our lives, but

                    15
thus far we have withheld this privilege from many older people.

Column A	Column B
1. ____	a. pattern
2. ____	b. certain amount
	c. changing conditions
3. ____	d. keep on
4. ____	e. value
5. ____	f. distribute
	g. specific features, characteristics
6. ____	h. culture, way of life
7. ____	i. change
	j. make better
8. ____	k. kinds
9. ____	l. influence, force
10. ____	m. fate, future
11. ____	n. kept back
12. ____	o. benefits
13. ____	p. situations
	q. limitations
14. ____	r. intense
15. ____	s. diploma

32 · Memories of a Mississippi Childhood

ELEANOR BLUM

Eleanor Blum tells how, as a young girl in a small Mississippi town, she became aware of the existence of prejudice only when a new neighbor questioned things the long-time residents took for granted.

I grew up in the 1920's and early 1930's in a tree-shaded little Mississippi town of 35,000 nestling at the tail-end of the Appalachians in a countryside of sandy soil, short-staple cotton, lean hogs, and skinny chickens. We were only a few miles from the village of Philadelphia which splashed into headlines last summer, although at that time it was scarcely more than a number of stills and an Indian reservation. Poor folks country, some called our part of the state, to distinguish it from the flat, black-soiled delta to the west where cotton staples grew long, and where the plantations had been and where the slaves had been. Few of us in our part of the state had ever owned a slave; the soil was not fertile enough to have supported the institution. Placed in a literary context we were Lillian Hellman's *Little Foxes;* we were Faulkner's Snopeses without his Sartorises.

A Johnny-come-lately among Mississippi towns, we got our start in the 1880's by accepting the railroad when older communities rejected it as an intrusion of privacy and dirty to boot. With the coming of the railroad, subsistence farmers moved into town to work in the yards or to start businesses, followed by Jewish peddlers. Those who were good businessmen prospered, and they and their children helped shape the town. Jew or Gentile, it made no difference. If you made money you were respected regardless of creed.

MEMORIES OF A MISSISSIPPI CHILDHOOD   From *The Antioch Review*, Volume XXV, Number 2. Reprinted by permission of The Antioch Press, copyright holder and first publisher.

My own family was Jewish, although not descended from this group, and from first-hand experience I can say that I never knew prejudice. If I wanted to be snide I might say that the town was kind to its Jews, or that, prejudice being somewhat of a burden to maintain, there is room for only one under-privileged minority in a community. Rather, however, I think money and class are strong ties. Even more important, the Southern culture is all-pervasive, leaving little room for another. Within a generation our Jews had lost their orthodox ways. Chopped chicken livers made way for country ham; bagles and lox, for hot biscuits and chicken fried in lard. Our colored cooks could not cope with the intricacies of kosher rites. The few orthodox families who arrived later were somehow of a lower caste, running delicatessens and stores catering mostly to Negroes. They were accepted neither by Gentiles nor fellow Jews. But given time they would make the grade if they made the money.

It was a comfortable and pretty town. The rolling terrain, the prevalence of trees and flowers softened and flattered the mishmash of architecture ranging in middle-class neighborhoods from late Victorian and imitation colonial to 1910 bungalows and pseudo-Spanish stucco, which was the latest word in the 1920's. Water oaks arched over the principal avenues and giant magnolias shaded the front yards. Honeysuckle and columbine twined around fences, attracting hummingbirds. Crepe myrtle trees were everywhere, their branches all summer and well into autumn heavy with grape-like clusters fashioned in-tricately from shocking-pink blossoms. Chinaberry and fig trees grew in back-yards of middle-class homes and front yards of Negro quarters, for even our plant life had a segregation system. What with this abundance of flowers and also of fruits and vegetables, the summers as I grew older began to seem end-less and so excessively beautiful that I welcomed the bleak and restful monot-onies of winter. Home from college on weekends, I would drive alone through remote countryside after the first frost, finding a stark beauty in the fields of withered corn and cotton stalks and in the long stretches of brown sedgegrass.

However, if you belonged to a middle-class white family your only cause for worry about overabundance was aesthetic. Certainly, it never made for extra work—the tending, the picking and the preserving—which we would have had to perform ourselves in other parts of the country. For a pittance, we hired Negroes to tend our gardens, our homes, and us.

I believe that the proportion of colored to white was half-and-half, but facts like this were too much taken-for-granted to be discussed as long as the supply of servants exceeded the demand, as it always did. Domestic service was the largest single source of income to most Negro families. Although some of the men performed semi-skilled labor like construction work, or truck driving, or loading or unloading cotton, an equal number were houseboys, delivery boys, janitors, and chauffeurs. Because pay was meager, men seldom made enough to support their families, so that women, too, hired out as cooks, nurses, and housemaids, or took in washing. And even this would not have brought in sufficient income except for that wonderful institution, the basket.

Middle-class white families ate bountifully of hot food freshly prepared three times a day and served at the dining-room table, set with white cloth and silencer. Only poor whites ate in the kitchen, which, for us, was the cook's domain. We served far more than we could eat, but nobody who was anybody lived skimpily. An abundant table was the mark of gentility.

It was also a mark of gentility for the lady of the house to look the other way while the servants took home the leftovers in a large basket. However, a steady diet of scraps made slim pickings, and once again the mistress turned her head while the servants supplemented with flour, lard, butter, cornmeal, coffee. "They eat you out of house and home" was the phrase most often used to describe this practice, but the words were uttered fondly, as one might speak of a child's failings.

The commonsense solution, higher wages, never crossed anyone's mind, and if it had I am sure it would have been rejected on the grounds that "they" were natural-born thieves and would have helped themselves anyway. We did not, of course, really believe this. If we had we would not have permitted them to care for our homes and children. Too, we knew full well that valuable articles like clothing, silver, and jewelry did not disappear. But we preferred largesse to logic.

I became aware of this lack of logic at age ten. A family named Morgan, transferred from Indiana by Sears Roebuck, had rented the bungalow next door. People from so far away were a novelty, and although the neighbors on the whole liked the Morgans, we thought them strange. For example, why did Mrs. Morgan prefer to do her own work rather than to hire a servant and spend her time like the rest of the ladies at bridge, gossip, movies, driving, and shopping?

One summer afternoon while she was visiting us, Mother broached this question. Kate, the maid, had just appeared with napkined tray holding tumblers of Coca-Cola brimful of ice crushed by hand and decorated with wedges of lemon.

"My, Kate, how pretty!" Mrs. Morgan exclaimed. Kate, beaming gratitude, bowed out.

"You know, Mrs. Morgan," Mother said (women of that more formal generation never got on first-name terms), "I could get you one just like her. They're not expensive."

"It's not that," Mrs. Morgan admitted reluctantly. "I just don't want one."

"But why don't you want one?" Mother persisted.

"Well, it's just that I don't feel comfortable around them," Mrs. Morgan confessed. "How do I know they're clean?"

"Mrs. Morgan!" Mother exclaimed, as horrified as if she herself had been accused of being dirty, which in a way she had. "If they weren't clean, do you think we'd let them cook for us? Do you think we'd let them nurse our children?"

"But if they are clean," Mrs. Morgan reasoned, treading delicate ground carefully and apologetically, "then why do you mind their sitting by you at restaurants and movies? Why can't the children all go to school together? Not all white people are so clean, either," she digressed, naming a few examples from the fourth grade which Mildred and I had attended the previous winter. "Why do you let them cook for you but not sit down at the table with you?" She was not being sarcastic. There had been no Negroes in her Indiana community and she was genuinely bewildered by the inconsistencies.

"But you don't understand," Mother replied huffily. "It's just that they're different from us. We love them and take care of them and we just couldn't get along without them." She recounted numerous examples of the care we took of them, the castoffs we bestowed, the times we went to bat at the police station. "You just don't understand," she concluded sadly.

And I am sure Mrs. Morgan did not, nor did my Mother, nor did I. Our relationship with our Negroes did not function on the level of understanding. It functioned on the level of pure, unsullied emotion.

The Negroes did not seem to mind. Such resentment as may have existed lay so far below the surface that it was unapparent to the whites they served. If they harbored bitterness, they hid it well. But I doubt that they did—not at that time. I think that they accepted their poverty, their servitude, their shanties on stilts as part of God's law, like seasons and birth and death. And so did we.

LENGTH: 1,800 WORDS

VOCABULARY

subsistence farmers   those who live on what they grow
snide   unkind, nasty
orthodox   strict, formal
pseudo-Spanish   not genuine Spanish
aesthetic   pertaining to the beauty in art
largesse   a gift generously given
digressed   wandered from the subject
unsullied   pure, without taint

32 · Memories of a Mississippi Childhood

SCORING: Reading time: _____ Rate from chart: _____ W.P.M.

MAIN SENTENCE	number right _____ × 4 equals _____ points
GENERALITIES	number right _____ × 4 equals _____ points
RETENTION	number right _____ × 2 equals _____ points
COMPLETION	number right _____ × 3 equals _____ points
DEFINITIONS	number right _____ × 2 equals _____ points

(Total points: 100)   **total** _____ points

MAIN SENTENCE   Each of these sentences appears in the text. Which one best describes the contents of the passage? _____

1. For a pittance, we hired Negroes to tend our gardens, our homes, and us.
2. Our relationship with our Negroes did not function on the level of understanding.
3. Even more important, the Southern culture is all-pervasive, leaving little room for another.

GENERALITIES   Based on the passage, which of the following generalities seem justifiable? _____ and _____

1. Southerners in Miss Blum's childhood thought carefully about the relationships established between Negroes and whites.
2. There was nothing sinister about the white attitude toward Negroes.
3. No one, Negroes least of all, would have wanted the situation changed.
4. Everyone seemed to accept unquestioningly things as they were.

RETENTION   Based on the passage, which of the following statements are True (T), False (F), or Not answerable (N)?

1. _____ Most orthodox Jews in the community lost their orthodox ways.

2. _____ Money had little to do with a person's acceptance in this town.

3. _____ Miss Blum's town was comfortable and pretty.

4. _____ The black delta country was elsewhere in the state.

5. _____ Community leaders tried not to be prejudiced.

6. _____ Jews were outcasts in much the same way Negroes were.

7. _____ Miss Blum's part of the state was called Poor Folks Country.

8. _____ Most of the people in her part of Mississippi had owned slaves.

9. _____ Most Negro men worked at semi-skilled jobs.

10. _____ Only poor whites ate their meals in the kitchen.

11. _____ A mark of gentility was to permit servants to take food scraps home.

12. _____ Mrs. Morgan honestly failed to understand the standard Southern attitude.

13. _____ Miss Blum's town frequently attracted guests from out of state.

14. _____ Most of the ladies spent their time playing bridge, gossiping, and shopping.

15. _____ Mrs. Morgan actually wanted a Negro servant.

16. _____ At the time Miss Blum describes, she was a fifth grader.

17. _____ The company Mr. Morgan worked for refused to hire Negroes.

18. _____ The relations of the town with Negroes functioned on the level of emotion.

19. _____ Miss Blum feels the Negro resented the treatment he received.

20. _____ Even plant life seemed to have a segregation system.

COMPLETION   Choose the best answer for each question.

1. _____ Miss Blum says that at home she welcomed the restful monotonies of: (a) spring.   (b) summer.   (c) winter.   (d) fall.

2. _____ In Miss Blum's town, the proportion of Negro to white was: (a) 2 to 1.   (b) 1 to 2.   (c) 3 to 1.   (d) 1 to 1.

3. _____ Servants took food home to their families probably because: (a) they were born thieves.   (b) their white employers were so generous. (c) they could sell it elsewhere.   (d) they were paid so little.

4. _____ One of the marks of gentility in this small town was: (a) an abundant table.   (b) refusing to talk to strangers.   (c) having no kitchen. (d) hiring Negro servants.

5. _____ From the town's treatment of Negroes, Mrs. Morgan thought Negroes must have been: (a) angels.   (b) dirty.   (c) well loved.   (d) necessary.

6. _____ The largest single source of income for Negro families was: (a) work in the cotton fields.   (b) truck driving.   (c) nursing.   (d) domestic service.

In the following passage, each underlined word has a number. In the columns below, match the number of each underlined word with the letter of the word that is closest to it in meaning.

              1   2

If I wanted to be <u>snide</u> I might say that the town was <u>kind</u> to its Jews, or

     3   4   5   6

that, <u>prejudice</u> being somewhat of a <u>burden</u> to <u>maintain</u>, there is <u>room</u> for

              7   8   9   10

only one <u>underprivileged</u> <u>minority</u> in a <u>community</u>. Rather, however, I think

  11   12   13   14

<u>money</u> and <u>class</u> are strong <u>ties</u>. Even more important, the Southern <u>culture</u> is

     15

<u>all-pervasive</u>, leaving little room for another.

Column A	Column B
1. ____	a. instead
2. ____	b. schoolroom
	c. Negroes
3. ____	d. complimentary
4. ____	e. heavy load
	f. keep up, carry on
5. ____	g. less numerous class
6. ____	h. nasty
7. ____	i. way of life
	j. a place
8. ____	k. intolerance
9. ____	l. social position
10. ____	m. stealthy
11. ____	n. poor, deprived
12. ____	o. spread everywhere
	p. bonds
13. ____	q. wealth
14. ____	r. nice
15. ____	s. town

33 · Do Schools Teach Art and Music All Wrong?

ANONYMOUS

Are art and music teachers producing technicians rather than people who understand and respond to music and art? In the struggle to produce scientists and mathematicians, America may have forgotten how to develop the artistic abilities of her young.

Watch a class of bright junior high school students expertly manipulate the far-out concepts of "modern math." Follow them into a class of art or music and you may very likely see the same quick minds being fed a diet of trivia hardly worth their attention.

The contrast points up a problem that troubles not only professional educators but a growing number of leaders in other fields. What kind of citizen are we educating? Will he be highly sophisticated in the sciences but limited in the humanities and next to illiterate in the arts? And if his schooling is out of balance, isn't there danger that the society he creates will be out of balance, too?

Sometimes they put it this way: Perhaps in our anxiety to outdo the Russians in space we have forgotten that one of the essential differences between their system and ours is in the attitude toward the humanities and, particularly, the arts. Aren't we weakening ourselves at the very point where a free society enjoys its greatest strength and advantage?

Maybe, comes the answer, but those fears surely are exaggerated. Considering the harsh facts of the world we live in, youngsters are probably getting all the music and art they need and have time for. If there is an extra period

DO SCHOOLS TEACH ART AND MUSIC ALL WRONG? Reprinted by permission from *Changing Times*, The Kiplinger Magazine (June, 1965 issue). Copyright © 1965 by The Kiplinger Washington Editors, Inc., 1729 H Street, N.W., Washington, D.C. 20006.

or two, perhaps they ought to be given some economics or more English grammar or a vocational subject, something that will be of practical use in daily life. Certainly creative activities aren't being neglected—just look at those corridors lined with pictures and listen to those bands and orchestras!

The schools are teaching more young people than ever to blow clarinets, tootle on tubas, paste up collages and construct mobiles. Yet, to a large extent, this feverish "creative" activity is misleading. For one thing, only a minority of students, especially in junior and senior high schools, are involved. Few secondary schools require any music or art. Nearly half don't even offer art as an elective. Elementary schools generally devote a substantial amount of time to some kind of music, but they give hardly more than an hour a week to art, and most teachers who give the instruction have had little training.

But even at schools with lots of activity, there's plenty of reason to doubt the value of what does go on. There's so much emphasis on the production of art and the playing of instruments that hardly any time goes into the development of understanding and appreciation. Learning to play the clarinet in the school band may improve a student's dexterity and ability to read certain types of music, but it does not seem to turn him into a more perceptive listener. Nor does the creation of backdrops for a school play or posters for a school anti-smoking campaign give him a basis for understanding and appreciating good art.

Not only do the schools overemphasize performance, according to a recent Rockefeller report, *The Performing Arts,* but what is just as bad, they devote too much time and effort to inconsequential material. "The objective often seems to be solely to entertain rather than to educate."

In general, music and art courses are so imbalanced and ineffective that they give the average student nothing on which to build his tastes. "All of us who are professionals in music or art education," writes Illinois Professor Bennett Reimer in the *Music Educators Journal,* "know that great numbers of youngsters terminate all contacts with the arts after they leave high school, and that precious little has been left with them in the way of artistic standards, appreciation for art, and desire to continue to develop their aesthetic sensitivity."

Probably the most penetrating—and constructive—criticism of the schools comes from some three dozen topflight musicians, scholars and teachers who met recently. Their report makes these strong points.

►Most of the music offered in the schools is "appalling." Too much of it is tasteless and corrupted by fake arrangements, reflecting the mind-drugging stuff we all get constantly at restaurants, in the movies or with TV cowboy shows.

►Authentic music, such as the great classics, is rare in the schools. Even jazz, "a precious national heritage," isn't presented honestly. Instead, the schools cater to fads—show music, rock and roll, hybrid dance tunes, sentimental ballads and citified country music.

►The potential of children is constantly underestimated. They are given weak "educational" recordings and songbook arrangements that are nothing but "pseudomusic" and dull. "The repertory of vocal music is chosen for its appeal to the lowest common denominator and for its capacity to offend the smallest possible number."

►The audiovisual aids used in music courses are pretty poor; in fact, they're "antimusical." Many films shown in elementary schools, for example, give the kids dialog, pictures and animations but hardly anything that has to do with music itself.

►Although there's been a modern revolution in music as deep as the revolution in science, you'd never know it from visiting the schools. Even less attention is paid to the great music of our times than is paid to the giants of the past. The only difference between a school music book of today and one of 30 years ago is the multicolor art work.

►The massive growth in performing activity has not been matched by growth of artistic maturity, says the report. The repertory is narrow and counterfeit. The majority of teachers are "trapped by the pressures of public performance and of community and student tastes into a deplorable routine that produces superficial results." Even gifted youngsters get very little benefit out of school performances. "A society that prizes creativity, originality and individualism seems to have known best how to produce the musical technician, follower and teammate."

►A major reason for all this is the poor training of teachers. Even those who specialize in music get heavy doses of vocal and instrumental training but very little background in the history or analysis of great works of music.

No such intensive report is available on art in the schools. But the situation is not much different. Few elementary schoolteachers have any background in the subject. And secondary teachers of art usually have a vocational-technical training rather than a grounding in the history and appreciation of art. As a result, not many high schools even attempt to offer those aspects of the subject.

The belief is growing among educators, and many others, that the only way to deal with the present art and music curriculum is to revise it drastically. This doesn't mean the end of painting and performing or other participation by youngsters. But it does mean higher standards for what they participate in, less exclusive attention to performance and greater effort to breed musical and artistic taste in all students. Instead of being used as "learning tools" or as therapeutic activities to help children "meet their needs," these courses would be taught as basic subject matter highly worthwhile in its own right.

In music, children would continue to dance, sing, learn how to play instruments. But they'd also learn how to compose, how to understand musical ideas and how to listen actively to the very best in old and modern music. High school students would be urged to take a music elective, possibly more than one course. And they would get, not a skimpy survey of history, but challenging material such as the works of Bach, Mozart, Beethoven, Brahms and Stravinsky, to engage their emotions and minds.

In art, the child would continue to paint and draw freely "to express himself." But he would also receive aid in improving his techniques. As he moves up through the intermediate grades, he would be taught basic aesthetic principles and be introduced to art history and such masters as Michelangelo, Rembrandt, Turner, Delacroix, Matisse, Picasso, Klee, Chagall. Secondary schools, says Professor Howard Conant of New York University in his book *Art Education,* would stop emphasizing mask-making and copper enameling and the like. All students would be required to take an art course of some kind and would learn to analyze and appreciate the very finest historic and modern examples of painting, sculpture, architecture and design.

Topflight artists and musicians would be brought into the schools as consultants and to work with classes on a resident basis. Community resources —museums, orchestras, radio and TV stations—would be fully used. And, of course, the education of art and music teachers would have to be revamped to reflect the new approach.

Most important, standards would not be compromised. Students at all age levels would get the real thing, not "kiddy adaptations." "It is a universal law in art," writes Professor of Music G. Wallace Woodworth of Harvard, "that the good will drive out the bad. . . . Receptiveness to beauty is one of the earliest characteristics of children, and unless it is snuffed out by exterior circumstances, it still lives in young people of high school and college age."

Is it really important to put all this emphasis on art and music courses? Those who say yes have several strong reasons:

►Art and music have always been recognized as among the highest and most enduring attainments of man. We remember civilizations for their creative output: ancient Greece, Renaissance Italy, the Ming Dynasty. Education should help preserve this heritage by teaching young people to understand and value the finest achievements of men so that their own standards and goals will be high.

►Creativity, originality, independence, nonconformity—these are traits we seek to develop in bright young people to make them more useful to society in all fields. These characteristics are nourished by enjoyment of the arts. The research scientist who loves music, for example, has become a stereotype.

►Never have good music and art been so widely available. Never have so many people been interested. As we move into the age of automation, longer life and increased leisure, more and more people will have an opportunity to turn to the arts for some of their most satisfying pleasures. The time to begin preparing them is now.

►Finally, art and music should be taught more seriously for purely educational reasons. They are rigorous intellectual and emotional disciplines. They sharpen the senses, awaken the imagination, shape the personality. Every youngster, whatever his capacities, can benefit from them.

"It is the paradox of art," says Professor Woodworth, "that enjoyment and discipline go hand in hand. The young boy and girl need desperately to experience beauty and to express emotion through a discipline."

LENGTH: 2,180 WORDS

VOCABULARY

sophisticated   well educated, knowledgeable
collages   artistic works consisting of pieces of newspaper, cloth, flat objects pasted on a surface and often connected with lines and color
mobile   form of sculpture having movable parts suspended from wires and capable of being set in motion by slight currents of air
dexterity   skill and ease in using one's hands
inconsequential   unimportant
aesthetic   pertaining to the beauty in art
hybrid   combination of different or incongruous things
pseudomusic   not genuine music
repertory   collection
therapeutic   corrective, helpful
revamped   changed, reworked
paradox   apparent contradiction

33 · Do Schools Teach Art and Music All Wrong?

SCORING: Reading time: _____ Rate from chart: _____ W.P.M.

MAIN SENTENCE	number right _____ × 4 equals _____ points	
GENERALITIES	number right _____ × 4 equals _____ points	
RETENTION	number right _____ × 2 equals _____ points	
COMPLETION	number right _____ × 3 equals _____ points	
DEFINITIONS	number right _____ × 2 equals _____ points	

(Total points: 100) **total** _____ points

MAIN SENTENCE   Each of these sentences appears in the text. Which one best describes the contents of the passage? _____

1. Considering the harsh facts of the world we live in, youngsters are probably getting all the music and art they need and have time for.
2. But even at schools with lots of activity, there's plenty of reason to doubt the value of what does go on.
3. In general, music and art courses are so imbalanced and ineffective that they give the average student nothing on which to build his tastes.

GENERALITIES   Based on the passage, which of the following generalities seem justifiable? _____ and _____

1. The Russians are overtaking us in the area of art and music.
2. Oddly enough there is some concern among Americans about programs in music and art.
3. Much of the music offered in the schools is the same as that heard on TV and in jukeboxes.
4. One of the best ways of changing the downward trend is to give students more substantial musical and artistic experiences.

RETENTION   Based on the passage, which of the following statements are True (T), False (F), or Not answerable (N)?

1. _____ No teachers are aware of the seriousness of the situation.

2. _____ The author of this article is a teacher.

3. _____ "Educational" approaches are often thin, weak, and second-rate.

4. _____ Most music students presently learn a great deal about Bach.

5. _____ Too many schools emphasize mask-making at the expense of understanding art.

6. ____ Students need special adaptations of great music for listening.

7. ____ Receptiveness to beauty is an early characteristic of children.

8. ____ Art and music have not had great cultural importance in the past.

9. ____ Individual creativity is linked to independence and originality.

10. ____ The research scientist who loves music is a stereotype.

11. ____ Appreciation of art and music is unimportant in America today.

12. ____ One recommendation is that art and music be taught as disciplines.

13. ____ Enjoyment and discipline are said to be closely related in art.

14. ____ The schools try to teach difficult art and music to the students.

15. ____ "Kiddy adaptations" do not develop understanding of art and music.

16. ____ Often youngsters are subjected to trivia instead of serious music.

17. ____ Schools apparently use Bach, Brahms, and Mozart in music courses.

18. ____ The emphasis in many schools is on production of art rather than on understanding it.

19. ____ The average school student has nothing on which to build his tastes.

20. ____ Music and art are not important enough to be taught in the schools.

COMPLETION   Choose the best answer for each question.

1. ____ Probably the most constructive criticism of schools comes from: (a) the perceptive student. (b) teachers themselves. (c) educated parents. (d) knowledgeable journalists.

2. ____ A good way to gain an understanding of art is through: (a) making posters for an anti-smoking campaign. (b) developing more artistic techniques. (c) the aid of a teacher. (d) analysis of works of art.

3. ____ A major reason for such poor instruction in the schools is the: (a) poor preparation of teachers. (b) indifference of parents. (c) lack of instructional aids. (d) quality of the students.

4. ____ The only difference between a school music book of today and that of 30 years ago is the: (a) concern for concert music. (b) multicolor art work. (c) complexity of arrangements. (d) exclusion of religious songs.

5. ____ Rather than a grounding in the history and appreciation of art, teachers often have: (a) no training at all. (b) a real distaste for art. (c) no interest in teaching art. (d) vocational or technical training.

234   ANONYMOUS

6. _____ G. Wallace Woodworth of Harvard says that the good art and music will: (a) go unliked in the schools. (b) drive out the bad. (c) continue to be produced. (d) never be meaningful in high school.

DEFINITIONS In the following passage, each underlined word has a number. In the columns below, match the number of each underlined word with the letter of the word that is closest to it in meaning.

1   2   3   4

All students would be required to take an art course of some kind and would

5   6   7 8   9   10

learn to analyze and appreciate the very finest historic and modern examples

11   12

of painting, sculpture, architecture and design. Topflight artists and musicians

13

would be brought into the schools as consultants and to work with classes on a

14   15

resident basis.

Column A	Column B
1. _____	a. compelled
	b. attend and complete
2. _____	c. contemporary
3. _____	d. three-dimensional art
4. _____	e. race track
	f. independent
5. _____	g. value, enjoy
6. _____	h. antiquated
	i. sort
7. _____	j. older
8. _____	k. first-class
9. _____	l. examine closely
	m. arrangement
10. _____	n. destroy
11. _____	o. living-in
12. _____	p. illustrations
	q. advisors
13. _____	r. program
14. _____	s. best
15. _____	

34 · How Good Are American Cars?

JOHN R. BOND

The editor of Road and Track *presents convincing reasons for the superiority of American cars. He explains why American cars are so highly valued in other countries and why they are so good.*

American cars are highly prized, greatly respected throughout Europe, where competition is extremely keen. Our cars cost anywhere from 50 to 150 percent more there than at home because of duties and discriminatory levies, yet 144,510 American passenger cars were exported in 1963.

Why are our cars so popular overseas? Because they run and run and run. Our engines use little oil and ordinarily need no major repairs for at least 50,000 miles, usually much more. The chassis components stand up better than overseas products on bad roads. The bodies do not rattle or corrode. A well-used American car with 100,000 miles on the odometer will still bring a fantastic price—in other lands.

Durability and reliability are taken for granted by the American consumer. This circumstance explains why, with the single exception of the Volkswagen, the American public has become so disenchanted with the small imported car. Many of the latter proved to be economical on fuel, but not so economical when repair charges and depreciation were added up at the end of two or three years.

Today every American car manufacturer has a large engineering department and extensive acreage devoted to proving grounds. The auto companies have found, sometimes through sad experience, that it is cheaper to test a new design exhaustively than to produce a relatively untried model and face expensive service problems or corrections in the field.

A combined total of a million miles or more of testing is virtually standard procedure before any new model is introduced. A typical example is Rambler's all-new six-cylinder engine, announced in mid-1964. One test car with the new engine racked up 107,000 miles with no major attention except routine maintenance. At that mileage the oil consumption was still less than one quart per thousand miles.

An interesting sidelight of this particular Rambler test was that the company used off-duty Chicago policemen for drivers. American Motors' engineers stated that their regular test drivers notice incipient malfunctions and report them for correction. Policemen drive like most ordinary people and keep going till the car quits. In all, AMC built ten experimental test engines (very expensive) and logged 2 million miles on these and pilot production-line samples.

Tests were run also at such diverse places as Phoenix, Arizona, and Bemidji, Minnesota. More than 15,000 hours were logged on dynamometer testing in Kenosha and Detroit.

Such thorough procedures as those described for AMC's Rambler "232" engine are not at all unusual; they are typical throughout the American automotive industry. Equally important, such testing is not confined to the power plant.

The seats in a five-year-old car, for example, do not fall to pieces as they did before the war. Why not? Every major auto manufacturer in the United States has an extensive testing laboratory, filled with strange and weird-looking machines. Seats are tested by a machine which forces a wooden model of a derriere into the cushion a given distance, then releases it. The process is repeated every three seconds and continues for a million cycles (if nothing fails). Spring sag, spring breakage, and upholstery durability are evaluated accurately.

These laboratories perform several functions. Their first and most obvious duty is to test newly designed components for function and durability before production commences. A second duty is to test items submitted by outside suppliers. A simple stoplight switch is a good example. Samples submitted for approval must pass a test of one million cycles without failure. Once a supplier is selected he must expect further checks on the quality of his product; such tests as are required are a continuous process on a spot-check basis. It is not unusual for an entire shipment from a supplier to be turned down because half of a batch of twenty samples failed prematurely.

Laboratory tests are of course an important adjunct to the normal road-test program. A shock absorber that will stand up for 500,000 cycles within a week in the laboratory will probably outlast the car in normal use. Engineers call this accelerated testing, and talk of correlation between lab and road tests. Testing procedures are developed so that a week in the laboratory is equivalent to five years or more on the road. This saves time and money—especially important in an industry which has new models almost every year.

No part of the car is too small or too insignificant to escape the laboratory. The outside rearview mirror is a good case in point, and here is a brief outline of the procedure used by the Ford Motor Company.

Sample mirrors are given a ninety-six-hour salt-spray bath to test for plating quality. Other samples get a sixteen-hour corrosion-abrasive test, considered even more severe than the salt bath. Qualification details are spelled out in specification sheets, even to the amount of porosity permitted in the die-cast mounting and the quality of the mirror glass. ("First surface" type of glass is specified, the best on the market, in order to avoid a double image.) Sample mirrors are also installed on test cars which run on a very rough proving grounds circuit for 40,000 miles, deemed equivalent to 100,000 miles on ordinary roads.

Other sample mirrors get an interesting lab test of the ball joint used for the adjustment feature. This joint must not stick or freeze, yet it must also retain its ability to stay put if the car owner wants to make an adjustment. Mirrors are cycled in the lab by a series of special machines which oscillate the mirror back and forth and in two different directions. At intervals during the cycling the temperature is lowered to minus 20 degrees Fahrenheit, raised to 120 degrees Fahrenheit. After 3,500 gyrations the ball joint must still have 70 percent of its original frictional characteristics to pass. As a result of these tests over the years, Ford specifies a special lubricant for the ball joint, which eliminates sticking yet inhibits wear during the cycling test. The testers have also found that stainless steel (rustproof) mounting screws are essential. After preproduction mirrors are approved, samples from every batch supplied by the vendor are checked on a regular schedule to ensure maintenance of quality control.

The Delco "Delcotron" alternator adopted by GM cars in 1964 is an excellent example of thorough testing. Delco, as a large supplier for GM, has its own test laboratory. Before this new alternator was ever placed in production, Delco engineers tested various samples and designs for the equivalent of 70 million miles. Other tests included 2.2 million miles on the dynamometer and 25 million actual miles on the road—all this from a supplier. The auto manufacturer has his own additional qualification tests before acceptance.

Some tests are more dramatic than others. At Chrysler the writer watched brake hoses on test. These are the vital connecting links between the hollow steel brake lines and the bouncing wheels of your car; failure of only one of the four flexible lines would mean that you had no brakes. A battery of machines actually whips them to tatters, and this test runs twenty-four hours a day.

A few years ago Pontiac introduced a car with a curved or bent drive shaft connecting the engine and the rear wheels. One of the tests involved a laboratory duplicate of the backbone-like chassis: engine in front, the drive shaft inside its backbone-like tunnel cover and the complete rear axle assembly. A dynamometer replaced each rear wheel. Automatic controls actuated the engine's throttle, and once every thirty seconds the "car" started up from a standstill, raced up to 80 mph at full throttle, then came to a full stop. The curved drive shaft had to take this enormous strain without failure for 100,000 miles. Before the design and material specifications were finally settled, nearly 100 different shafts were tested. Needless to say, Pontiac Tempest's unique curved drive shaft gave absolutely no trouble in service.

In 1938 Chevrolet had 13,000 square feet devoted to lab tests; today it has over 100,000 square feet for this purpose, located at the GM Tech Center just outside Detroit.

Chevrolet has a test fixture for the front suspension which strokes the two wheels to duplicate driving over railroad ties for a distance of 1,000 miles. This severe test is computed on the basis of 250,000 cycles of the machine. Another test machine at Chevrolet simulates a loading equivalent to a front-wheel side skid. The suspension must not fail in 500,000 cycles.

Rear suspension systems get similar abuse. When Chevrolet first introduced its coil-spring system, it took a test car down to the racetrack at Darlington, South Carolina. The car was elaborately instrumented, and the driver made several laps at over 120 mph. Then the engineers took the recorded data back to the laboratory and built a special test machine to simulate the stresses and strains imposed on the rear end at the track. Cornering loads equivalent to 625,000 racing miles were duplicated before the rear suspension was approved for production.

Accessories, optional at extra cost, are very popular with car buyers, especially since these accessories are thoroughly engineered by the car manufacturer and built to give long life without the need for attention or repairs.

Automatic transmissions are the most popular extra-cost item: 77.6 percent of all cars produced in the United States last year were so equipped. As with engines, these complex assemblies are not redesigned every year. Chevrolet's Powerglide, for example, has been refined in detail, but it has been fundamentally unchanged since it was first introduced in 1949. But as with engines, a new or revised automatic transmission is thoroughly tested for millions of miles before production commences. The value of this policy was amply demonstrated by the Lincoln division of Ford two years ago. At a new-model preview, Ford let members of the press drive one of the new Lincolns, then immediately drive a year-old model with over 100,000 test miles on the odometer. There were some differences, but the average driver would not be able to notice them.

Chrysler's durability test procedure for its optional four-speed manual transmission is interesting, and the company says that it is somewhat more grueling than the requirements of competitors. Chrysler specifies a life test of twenty hours in first gear, twenty-eight hours in second gear, and thirty-five hours in third, under load. The load is varied for each gear and is equivalent to the strain of running continuously on a hill steep enough to force the engine to operate at wide-open throttle. Years of experience with this accelerated laboratory technique have shown it to be equivalent to over 100,000 miles of driving by the average owner.

Air conditioning is an optional accessory becoming more popular each year. In 1964 some 1.4 million cars left the factory equipped with air conditioning. The industry expects that the demand will rise rapidly; 76 percent of the three luxury cars produced in 1964 had air conditioning, as compared with only 17.89 percent of all cars produced.

The air-conditioning systems are not redesigned every year. The design of component parts is, however, under a continuous process of development, both to improve cooling performance and to reduce costs. A standard performance test is to put a black car out to bake in the sun, windows closed. A test driver then steps in, fires up the engine, turns on the air conditioning, and clocks the time required for the interior to come down to 70 degrees Fahrenheit. One and a half minutes for a drop from 120 degrees to 70 degrees is not unusual.

Another critical test for an air-conditioned car is the performance of its engine-cooling system. The A/C system imposes extra loads on the engine and requires a larger heavy-duty radiator. Also, an engine at idle tends to boil because there is no forward movement of the vehicle to provide a blast of air for engine cooling. For this test most manufacturers specify that on a day when the temperature is 110 degrees, the engine must not boil when idling for at least thirty minutes. For durability of the A/C components, they require 40,000 miles over the rough-road route, equivalent to 100,000 miles of ordinary driving.

Testing includes many other accessories. For instance, jacks are tested, and trailer hitches also get careful consideration. In fact, nearly all cars are available today with special options designed and tested solely for the benefit of those motorists who pull trailers. The companies even test roof racks, which surprisingly enough have in the past given a lot of trouble. The test load for a large roof rack is usually 250 pounds. Among other things, they test with a loose load at 90 mph, then put on the brakes for a crash stop.

Now let us consider some of the criticisms of our cars. It is true that our most popular, so-called standard, cars have grown larger and heavier since the war. This is a simple result of the great American desire to "get ahead." The mass market for post-war cars has proved to be for something bigger and better than just transportation. And there is nothing wrong with this attitude; if the bulk of sales are in what used to be the Buick-Chrysler category, why blame Chevrolet, Ford, Plymouth, and Dodge for supplying products to meet the demand? These four cars, with weights approaching two tons (unloaded), account for more than half of all sales. All four are big cars in the truest sense of the term, and though gasoline consumption is not nearly so economical as the pre-war standard of twenty miles per gallon, the fact remains that the consumer is willing to pay for more luxury, more performance.

As for the compacts, the figures show conclusively that only one out of five buyers is interested in economy. All these cars weigh under 3,000 pounds, and weight is the all-important factor when it comes to economy, whether we are talking about fuel, oil, tires, or even first cost. American compacts are far superior to comparable imports, primarily because they are designed, tested, and built to give genuinely economical transportation. They may not give thirty miles per gallon, but cost-conscious buyers know that the annual fuel bill is not a significant factor in computing the cost of owning an automobile.

Forced obsolescence has been much maligned. When production quantities exceed 350,000 units per year, the tooling is worn out anyway. Hence, the technical innovations evolved each year by engineers can just as well be incorporated when tools, dies, and machines are replaced. While Henry Ford may have saved a dollar or two per Model T (by making no important design changes), he spent over 100 million dollars in 1927 to make the change to the Model A. Yet only 4.5 million Model A's were produced before complete re-tooling was required for the 1932 V-8. From that time on, Ford retooled every year for a new and improved model. Even Ford capitulated to the inexorable march of technological advances.

The detractors of the American car like to point out that most major technical innovations come from Europe. This may well be true if one talks of who was first. But it remained for Detroit to produce the soft-riding independent front suspension at a reasonable cost in 1934. It was Reo in Lansing which first offered an automatic transmission in 1933. Duesenberg in Indianapolis pioneered four-wheel hydraulic brakes in 1921. American tire engineers developed the balloon tire in 1924, the extra-low-pressure tire in 1949, the low profile in 1964. Goodyear pioneered the caliper-disk brake on the Crosley in 1949. The super-charger, first used on the Chadwick car in 1908 and later adapted to high altitude flying by GE, helped us to win World War II.

Current European cars often abound in technical or novelty features, but it takes American engineering, design, testing, and manufacturing to make these features practical and available to great numbers of people at a cost they can afford.

An oft-quoted example of European "leadership" is the widespread use of independent rear suspension. In the United States, we have only the Corvette and Corvair with this system of rear-springing.

I have talked with dozens of engineers in and around Detroit on this subject. They all agree that independent rear suspension has some advantages, but they also agree that the ride is not noticeably improved, that erratic handling is difficult to overcome, and that the high manufacturing cost is not justified by the results. The Corvair would not be possible without independent rear suspension because of its rear-mounted engine. The Corvette needs a similar type of suspension in order to get adequate traction with its tremendous power-to-weight ratio (up to 425 horsepower, weight only 3,200 pounds).

Independent suspension gives a much improved ride on small, light cars, but on 4,000-pound American cars the ratio of sprung to unsprung weight, even with solid one-piece rear axle assemblies, is not critical. The latest American development—positioning the rear axle more positively and accurately by means of three or four rubber-cushioned links—gives excellent results at low cost. The links are arranged to negate acceleration squat and brake lift; they give good cornering control and freedom from transmission of axle-gear noise.

The typical American car is astutely designed to supply a simple need: comfortable, reliable transportation at a reasonable cost. I regard the modern American car, at well under $1.00 per pound, as one of the best buys in the world today.

LENGTH: 2,400 WORDS

VOCABULARY

discriminatory levies   unfair taxes
chassis   the body of a car
incipient   early, beginning
dynamometer   a device to measure force or power
adjunct   companion, auxiliary
deemed   judged, thought
oscillate   to swing back and forth, vibrate
simulate   imitate
obsolescence   the condition of being out of style or out-moded
inexorable   inevitable, unyielding
astutely   shrewdly, intelligently

34 · How Good Are American Cars?

SCORING: Reading time: _____ Rate from chart: _____ W.P.M.

PURPOSE	number right ____ × 4 equals ____ points
GENERALITIES	number right ____ × 4 equals ____ points
RETENTION	number right ____ × 2 equals ____ points
COMPLETION	number right ____ × 3 equals ____ points
DEFINITIONS	number right ____ × 2 equals ____ points

(Total points: 100)   **total** ____ points

PURPOSE   Which of the following phrases best expresses the purpose of the passage? ____

1. to show that even things like rearview mirrors can be important to automobile manufacturers
2. to demonstrate that European cars are not so good as American cars
3. to show that exhaustive testing makes American cars better and safer

GENERALITIES   Based on the passage, which of the following generalities seem justifiable? ____ and ____

1. European car buyers prefer American cars to their own products.
2. Car manufacturers, whether they redesigned or not, probably would have to retool every year.
3. Testing is important, but it does not reduce the cost of most automobiles.
4. Americans first made most of the important automotive innovations.

RETENTION   Based on the passage, which of the following statements are True (T), False (F), or Not answerable (N)?

1. ____ The American car costs somewhere near $1.00 per pound.

2. ____ Americans bought small foreign cars as an economy measure.

3. ____ European engineering makes novelty features available to a mass-market of car buyers.

4. ____ Independent rear suspension is not necessarily an "advanced" technique.

5. ____ The author does not discuss any criticisms of American cars.

6. ____ A critical test for an air-conditioned car is the performance of its engine cooling system.

7. ____ In 1964, Detroit produced 7.6 million cars.

8. ____ Like engines, automatic transmissions are redesigned every two years.

9. ____ Accessories at optional cost are very popular among car buyers.

10. ____ The Delco alternator is an excellent example of thorough testing.

11. ____ Brake hoses were tested by having them whipped to tatters.

12. ____ Before the war, the seats in a five-year-old car might have fallen to pieces.

13. ____ A shock absorber that will stand up for 50,000 cycles of testing will probably outlast the car.

14. ____ Few parts of the car are tested in the laboratory.

15. ____ One of the most interesting tests is the one made on hub caps.

16. ____ Pontiac recently introduced a well-tested, curved drive shaft.

17. ____ The Rambler "232" engine has eight cylinders.

18. ____ American cars are popular overseas because they run for a long time.

19. ____ Foreign cars use less gas but need repairing more frequently than American cars.

20. ____ Many durability tests simulate 100,000 miles of actual wear.

COMPLETION   Choose the best answer for each question.

1. ____ One function of the laboratory is to test new components and designs, but another function is to test: (a) drivers' reflexes. (b) European products. (c) items from outside suppliers. (d) old components and designs.

2. ____ Once a supplier is selected, he must: (a) file a record of sales each month. (b) answer to the general public. (c) continue to have his product tested. (d) not raise his price or his costs.

3. ____ One other testing area, besides the laboratory, which is mentioned is: (a) the home. (b) the racetrack. (c) the police station. (d) the showroom.

4. ____ Last year 77.6 percent of all cars produced in the U.S. were equipped with optional: (a) air conditioning. (b) tachometers. (c) rearview mirrors. (d) automatic transmission.

5. ____ The author suggests that the bulk of car sales is in what used to be the: (a) Buick-Chrysler category. (b) Reo-Oldsmobile category. (c) Ford-Plymouth category. (d) Crosley-Goodyear category.

6. ____ A make of automobile not mentioned in the article is the: (a) Dusenberg. (b) Chadwick. (c) Corvette. (d) Cadillac.

DEFINITIONS In the following passage, each underlined word has a number. In the columns below, match the number of each underlined word with the letter of the word that is closest to it in meaning.

1   2   3   4

As for the <u>compacts</u>, the <u>figures</u> show <u>conclusively</u> that only <u>one out of five</u>

5   6

buyers is <u>interested</u> in <u>economy</u>. All these cars weigh under 3,000 pounds, and

7   8

weight is the <u>all-important</u> <u>factor</u> when it comes to economy, whether we

9   10

are <u>talking about</u> fuel, oil, tires, or even <u>first cost</u>. American compacts are

11   12   13   14

<u>far superior</u> to <u>comparable</u> <u>imports</u>, primarily because they are <u>designed,</u>

15

tested, and built to give <u>genuinely</u> economical transportation.

Column A	Column B
1. ____	a. purchase price
2. ____	b. smaller cars
3. ____	c. discussing
	d. similar
4. ____	e. low cost, thrift
5. ____	f. shapes
	g. much better
6. ____	h. really
7. ____	i. twenty percent
8. ____	j. without doubt
	k. element
9. ____	l. desired
10. ____	m. statistics
11. ____	n. concerned about
	o. foreign cars
12. ____	p. most significant
13. ____	q. transactions
	r. planned
14. ____	s. unlikely
15. ____	

35 · The Mystery of Thirst

LORUS and MARGERY MILNE

> *Thirst is something we take for granted, but which for all our knowledge of science, we know relatively little about. The Milnes discuss the nature of human thirst, what causes it, and how the human body reacts to it.*

Somehow it seems fitting for one of the earliest mentions of thirst to come from the deserts of Egypt. About forty centuries ago, the henchman Sinuhe, who served as administrator under King Amenemhet I, was felled by thirst as he crossed the Isthmus of Suez. In one of the treasured records of ancient Egypt is the story of his despair, with his tongue stuck to the roof of his mouth, his throat burning, his whole body demanding something to drink. "This," he told himself, "is the taste of death."

Today, these sensations are still a real hazard. No man can survive for three weeks if his water supply is cut off completely. With water he might last a month without food. Yet we appear to have a plentiful supply of water in our bodies: between 50 and 60 per cent of our adult weight. Our leeway is roughly a fifth of this amount. If we lose more, we die. If we lose less, we survive and can replenish our inner store. It makes no difference whether the loss is so sudden that it occurs in a single day, as sometimes happens to people lost in hot deserts, or comes over a period of weeks. In 1821 a prominent Frenchman committed suicide by persistently refusing to drink anything; he held out for seventeen days. On the fifteenth day, he might have saved himself. Castaways who have been fifteen days without water have survived the ordeal.

Most of us never come anywhere near such extremes of thirst. Yet all of us experience this sensation. Amazingly, we respond to its gentle urgings in the most casual ways and still manage to maintain our inner diffuse reserves of water with outstanding accuracy. From our hidden "water pool" we lose daily about two-thirds of a quart by perspiration and as moisture in the air we exhale. On a normal balanced diet, we discharge about a quart of water merely to flush out the waste products of each day's metabolism. At the same time, we gain about a third of a quart as "metabolic water" synthesized daily through the digestion of even dry foods. But without wet foods and liquids in our diet, we would quickly incur a serious deficit. Under the faint prodding of thirst, we make good the deficit almost automatically. Automatically, too, we compensate for extra losses or extra gains. How do we know when we've had enough? The sense of thirst is so vague that we are hard put to say just where we feel it.

Children soon learn that their fathers and mothers are reluctant to ignore a request for water. How many parents today do as ours did: order us to hold a little water in the mouth for a few minutes, to "let it quench our thirst" and incidentally keep us quiet? The notion that dryness of the mouth causes thirst goes back a long way, and was made respectable a few decades ago by the great endocrinologist Walter B. Cannon. Unfortunately, it is not an adequate explanation. Dryness which comes from nervousness, long-winded public speaking or breathing through the mouth during vigorous exercises, as well as from a reduced flow of saliva, can be relieved with a little lemon juice or a sour pickle that will stimulate the salivary reflex. These palliatives will not conceal true thirst for more than a few minutes.

We feel thirst so often when we are dehydrated, when our dehydration is leading to a reduction in the flow of saliva and a dryness of the mouth, that we condition ourselves into believing dryness and thirst to be synonymous. Actually, we can become desperately thirsty while our salivary glands, stomach, blood stream and bladder are all loaded with water. Deliberately or unconsciously, bartenders make use of this in selling their wares. They encourage thirst by putting out free dishes of salty, mouth-watering tidbits: pretzels, potato chips, popcorn, peanuts. Saliva flows freely. Yet the back of the throat reports that it is parched. How about another drink? The parching is internal, caused by a fractional increase in the salt content of the blood, upsetting the normal ratio of water and salt. A meal of salty ham or fish similarly can drive a person almost wild with thirst until the kidneys discharge the salt and get the blood ratio back into its proper range. These urges vanish, however, if the back of the throat is painted with an anesthetic solution.

Recent exploration of the brain with electrical probes has shown that the true site of the thirst sensation is a small region, the hypothalamus, close to the pituitary gland. Here we have strange little sense organs that monitor the water-to-salt ratio in the blood coursing through capillary beds of the carotid artery. A decrease in this proportion measuring no more than one to two percent below normal apparently starts messages along an indirect route. From the hypothalamus the response may be an unidentified hormone to which the lining cells in the back of the throat are sensitive. Once stimulated by it, however, the throat cells relay nerve messages to the cerebral cortex and induce the conscious senses of thirst. No wonder we are vague about this "feeling." In reaching a better understanding of it, the scientists have also been able to contradict the old adage about leading a horse to water. Now they *can* make it drink, by sending electrical stimuli along fine wires to its hypothalamus. The animal will become so thirsty, in fact, as to return compulsively to the watering trough even right after it has drunk its unstimulated fill!

Satisfying thirst is a matter of getting the water-to-salt ratio in the blood back into the proper range. This can be accomplished by eating juicy fruits just as successfully as by drinking water or other liquids. In tropical countries where the water supplies are often contaminated, our own preference is to rely upon oranges and other fruits we can peel rather than boil water from public supplies for twenty minutes or treat it with chemicals. This method can prevent the development of thirst even where the air is so dry that seven to nine quarts of water are lost into it daily by evaporation from skin and lungs.

All of us are limited in the number of ways we can maintain the water-to-salt ratio in the blood by the comparative inefficiency of human kidneys and by our lack of special salt-secreting glands. We cannot manage as a seal does on a diet of raw fishes, chiefly because our kidneys require in flushing out products of protein digestion more water than can be gained from the fish flesh. A seal, by contrast, is efficient in excreting nitrogenous wastes, and the animal conserves water by losing none in the form of sweat. Nor can we drink sea water, as albatrosses and many bony fishes do, because we would have to excrete more water than we take in merely to get rid of the added salt. Each quart of sea water contains about thirty-five grams of salt; to get rid of it we would have to discharge nearly two quarts of liquid. The albatross and other tube-nosed birds drink sea water with impunity because their nostrils contain special glands which extract from the blood all superfluous salts and let them drip away in mucus to the outside world. Bony fishes in the sea achieve the same end with salt-secreting cells in the surface of the gills.

No mammals are known to make a habit of drinking sea water as a source of moisture. Yet the desert-dwelling kangaroo rats can be trained to do so. They are adapted in many peculiar ways to living where free water of any kind is rarely encountered. Kangaroo rats avoid the dry air of day, and even keep themselves from losing water by carrying any air-dried seeds to their burrows in fur-lined cheek pouches. In the burrow the trophies absorb water vapor from the soil, and the kangaroo rat then eats them. It is efficient in conserving water by re-absorbing the precious material in its kidneys until its liquid waste is more than twice as salty as sea water. Metabolic water can then suffice, letting the animal live its whole life without a drink. To a kangaroo rat, a sip of sea water represents surplus water, whereas to us it is merely extra salt.

Probably the camel could manage on sea water almost as well as the kangaroo rat. A camel's adaptations are many, and make us wonder why man's body could not be fitted similarly to conserving precious water. Yet most of its specializations are beyond human reach. We cannot let our bodies chill down to 95 degrees Fahrenheit in the cool desert night, to warm up slowly in the morning sun and reach a temperature of 105 degrees before we begin to sweat. We cannot route from the liver to the stomach (rather than the kidneys) a large part of our nitrogenous wastes, and reuse the material in synthesis of proteins —as the camel seems to do. If we could, it would save us from throwing away valuable water, and at the same time reduce the incidence of protein deficiency (kwashiorkor)—one of the world's most widespread diseases today. We cannot even conserve the water in our blood stream while losing it from the rest of the body's reserve, as a camel does. After seventeen days without water, a camel is very much alive, although it may have lost a tenth of its plasma water and a third of its other body water; it can recoup its losses in ten minutes if given access to a drinking trough.

Almost the only way in which we can imitate the camel is by wearing layer after layer of loose wool garments in the desert sun as the Arabs do, shielding the skin from the heat and reducing the need for water loss by perspiration to cool the skin. The camel's thick hair, sticking out several inches over surfaces exposed to the sun, is only part of this adaptation, however. The remainder lies in the camel's distribution of fat, which is largely restricted to the hump on its back rather than spread uniformly below the skin where we store so much. By the time a camel's body temperature has risen to 105 degrees, its skin surface is at about 103 and the outward flow of heat is relatively unimpeded. We can achieve equal dissipation of heat only by cooling the body surface five degrees or more through the evaporation of sweat, costing us water we may have difficulty replacing. Yet without this cooling, the fatty insulation below the skin's surface so limits heat flow that our body temperature would rise to dangerous levels.

Seemingly the camel's adaptations include also a superior ability to identify acceptable water. It will readily take bitter solutions we would refuse except as a last resort. In deciding whether water is fit to drink, we rely heavily upon odor and taste, particularly upon the receptors affected by salt. Yet these too can fool us. Curiously, we show a preference for solutions containing traces of salt. Pure water, which we describe as tasteless and odorless, we may even shun as "flat" and "uninteresting" in flavor.

At the Veterinary College in Stockholm, Dr. Yngve Zotterman and his colleagues have discovered that the frog's tongue possesses special taste endings that respond specifically to water and to highly dilute solutions of sodium chloride. Does this mean that the frog detects water as a distinct taste? The Swedish scientists suggest that the frog has this ability and uses it in detecting any leakage of fresh water into the mouth when immersed. Since frogs do hide themselves in the muddy bottoms of ponds during the winter months, the idea seems reasonable. But does man detect a specific taste in water, other than through identification of salt, sweet, sour, bitter, or odorous materials dissolved in it?

No one seems to know what gave a tin dipperful of farm spring water its delicious taste. It wasn't the dipper alone, for the same utensil used to raise a sample of distilled water to the lips fails to conceal the striking difference. Most people who perform this test are ready to agree that really pure water is fine for automobile batteries, but scarcely fit to drink. Rain water, which is sun-distilled, shows the same lack of character. Even spring water that has stood for weeks in a closed glass container has a "livelier" flavor.

It is strange that we should react in this way for, more than anything else, fresh water supplies determine where man can live. We recognize today not only personal thirst, but also civic thirst and industrial thirst. The growth of a city is determined by the extent to which its water supply can be augmented. The success of many industries, from steel-making to farming, depends upon the availability of vast amounts of water.

In the United States today, each man, woman and child shares in a demand averaging 200 gallons of fresh water per person per year for drinking, 15,000 gallons per person per year for washing, cooking and operating our living quarters, plus 160,000 gallons per person per year for industrial purposes, and 230,000 gallons per person per year for irrigation. For 180 million people, this amounts to about a seventh of all the water that runs down our streams and rivers into the ocean. With a predicted population of 360 million in the year 2000, a comparable thirst at private, civic and industrial levels will total a third of the fresh waters available.

Before too many years pass, man must either devise salt-extracting machines to let him produce fresh water from sea water, or find human populations along our coasts curbed by chronic thirst. Even then, the transport of large amounts of desalted sea water to the dry interiors of great continents is unlikely to be worth while economically—not on the scale required by agriculture, industry and large cities. Inland communities seemingly must depend indefinitely upon satisfying thirst from natural rainfall. In the future they may become fresh-water oases, with man hurrying from one to the next—perhaps wishing he were as well equipped to do so as a camel.

LENGTH: 2,650 WORDS

VOCABULARY

synthesized put together, made up, compounded

endocrinologist specialist in glandular defects

palliative something that lessens the effects or symptoms of a condition without curing it

dehydrated dried up

hypothalamus region of the brain that regulates body temperature and many metabolic processes

pituitary gland gland at the base of the brain, which regulates many of the body's functions

capillary thin blood vessel, tiny tube

carotid artery major artery in the neck

nitrogenous filled with nitrogen

reuse to use again

35 · The Mystery of Thirst

PURPOSE Which of the following phrases best expresses the purpose of the passage? _____

1. to reveal that the sense of thirst is so vague we cannot identify it
2. to clarify the relationship between dryness and thirst
3. to show that we recognize not only a personal thirst, but a civic thirst

GENERALITIES Based on the passage, which of the following generalities seem justifiable? _____ and _____

1. In the future, citizens will have more respect for water than we do.
2. Camels and kangaroo rats are more highly specialized than man.
3. Water is tasteless and odorless except to frogs.
4. The study of thirst is complicated by the different kinds of thirst man feels.

RETENTION Based on the passage, which of the following statements are True (T), False (F), or Not answerable (N)?

1. _____ The seal does not perspire.

2. _____ Man can live without water for fifteen days.

3. _____ Man can live with water but without food for three months.

4. _____ Juicy fruits can sustain man in even the hottest of climates.

5. _____ The salivary glands function when stimulated by salt.

6. _____ Metabolic water is water that is found normally in our food.

7. _____ Fresh water supplies have little effect on where man chooses to live.

8. _____ The albatross depends wholly on fresh water supplies.

9. _____ The gull is a tube-nosed bird.

10. _____ Not one mammal is known to drink sea water as a source of moisture.

11. _____ Dry air has a high proportion of salt.

12. _____ Dryness of the mouth is not an indicator of true thirst.

13. _____ The hypothalamus can go without water for more than a week.

14. _____ There is no artificial way to stimulate thirst.

15. _____ True thirst cannot be satisfied with lemon juice.

16. _____ It is possible to commit suicide by refusing to drink water.

17. _____ Our body is 85 percent water.

18. _____ The camel might be able to thrive on sea water like the kangaroo rat.

19. _____ The Arab wraps himself in layers of wool to keep the sun from his skin.

20. _____ The success of many industries depends on availability of vast amounts of water.

COMPLETION   Choose the best answer for each question.

1. _____ The man who said, "This is the taste of death," was an: (a) old time seal hunter.   (b) eminent Frenchman.   (c) Arab merchant.   (d) Egyptian.

2. _____ Our body weight is close to 60 percent water; our leeway before death occurs is roughly one: (a) third of this amount.   (b) quarter of this amount.   (c) fifth of this amount.   (d) half of this amount.

3. _____ The true site of the thirst sensation is: (a) the back of the neck.   (b) near the pituitary gland.   (c) on the edge of the tongue.   (d) behind the salivary glands.

4. _____ Our feeling of being upset by excess salt in our system is caused by inefficient: (a) arteries.   (b) liver secretions.   (c) kidneys.   (d) glands.

5. _____ One of the world's most widespread diseases is: (a) nitrogenous wastes.   (b) protein deficiency.   (c) thirst.   (d) croup.

6. _____ Inland communities seem to depend completely upon: (a) water from the sea.   (b) still rivers.   (c) natural rainfall.   (d) fresh-water oases.

In the following passage, each underlined word has a number. In the columns below, match the number of each underlined word with the letter of the word that is closest to it in meaning.

1   2   3   4   5   6

Seemingly the camel's adaptations include also a superior ability to identify

7   8   9   10

acceptable water. It will readily take bitter solutions we would refuse except

11   12   13

as a last resort. In deciding whether water is fit to drink, we rely heavily upon

14   15

odor and taste, particularly upon the receptors affected by salt.

Column A	Column B
1. ____	a. willingly
2. ____	b. depend
	c. contend
3. ____	d. recognize
4. ____	e. have, contain
5. ____	f. apparently
	g. skill
6. ____	h. ready, proper
7. ____	i. acrid liquids
	j. taste buds
8. ____	k. specialized characteristics
9. ____	l. preposterous
	m. more effective
10. ____	n. final opportunity
11. ____	o. higher
	p. sensitive to
12. ____	q. oasis
13. ____	r. not accept
14. ____	s. drinkable
15. ____	

36 · The World's Greatest Automobile Collection

KEN PURDY

> *William Harrah, owner of the Harrah's Club gambling casinos in Las Vegas and Tahoe, has the world's greatest collection of classic cars. Ken Purdy, the famous car buff, tells about the problems of restoration Harrah faces.*

Since the end of World War II there has been a remarkable resurgence of interest in the automobile, not only as a means of transportation but as an instrument of sport and as an artifact. Museums dedicated to the preservation of the motorcar have sprung up all over the Western world. Some of them are impressive. Probably as many as 250,000 people a year visit the Montagu Motor Museum at Beaulieu in England. The Daimler-Benz Museum in Stuttgart-Untertürkheim concentrates on the products of the oldest motorcar manufactory in the world, founded by the two men most frequently cited as the actual inventors of the automobile: Gottlieb Daimler and Karl Benz, who never met. The Museo dell'Automobile Carlo Biscaretti di Ruffia in Turin has an extraordinarily varied collection; Fritz Schlumpf of France owns some 130 specimens of a single make, the legendary Bugatti.

More collections existed in America during the 1940s and 1950s than there are now: the collections of James Melton and Cameron Peck have been broken up; the Pollard collection of Detroit is unrestored and unshown; in California Briggs Cunningham's sizable collection is private. Brooks Stevens has a fine inventory of about 150 motorcars in Milwaukee, and the Ford Museum in Dearborn has a notable collection. The elegant collection of Henry Austin Clark, Jr., at Southampton, Long Island, continues to be on view from June 1 to October. But the biggest collection, and the finest, is in Reno, Nevada.

William Harrah of Reno is the world's premier collector of automobiles. He has 990, give or take a few. (His master records may lag forty-eight hours or so behind the reports of his buying staff, so that he does not always know the exact census.) Harrah's purpose in amassing this astonishing number of motorcars is not mere acquisition. His is not the string-saver's compulsion, and except for two makes, Ford and Packard, he is not personally motivated. For many years Harrah owned Fords and Packards in preference to other makes, and he thinks them both important in the history of the motorcar. As this was written, he had acquired ninety-seven Fords and forty-six Packards. Partly because of this kind of duplication, the Harrah collection favors U.S. over European cars by about twelve to one.

Harrah wants to accumulate that number of automobiles that will, assembled under one roof, demonstrate the history of the vehicle. Harrah still has about 200 cars on his wanted list. His buyers are busily searching them out, while the rest of his staff—painters, upholsterers, mechanics, wheelwrights—look after those already on hand. The Harrah collection occupies the full-time attention of 102 men and women.

Many cars come into the collection's receiving department as "basket cases," rusted, dented, broken, after perhaps three decades under the leaky roof of a farm shed. Occasionally, one may arrive under its own power. They may come, four at a time, in the huge Peterbilt tractor-trailer pickup rig, its sleeper cab fitted with the three bits of equipment that distinguish all Harrah regular-use cars: air conditioning, fire extinguisher, seat belts. However a car looks on arrival—and some look very good indeed—it is not good enough to go on the floor of the Number 1 exhibition building in the complex that houses the collection in Sparks, Nevada, just outside Reno. First it will be checked against factory specifications. The automotive library, housed in the main exhibition building, is the largest in private ownership. The staff can reproduce detailed specification sheets, blueprints, catalogues, magazine estimates, and road tests on many thousands of automobiles.

Every new acquisition is checked. Perhaps an original Rochester carburetor has been changed for a Stromberg; or the wheels are wearing the wrong size of tire; or three body stripes are too close by a millimeter. Researchers who are knowledgeable and intent will fill out a report, and the car will go to the shops. If it is a modern motorcar and has been well cared for, it may be ready in a couple of weeks. If it is an antique, with wood framework rotted out, bodywork missing, its engine a lump of rust, it may be worked on for months.

Among old-car buffs, restoration is a term loosely used. It may mean merely washing and polishing the car, daubing paint over any obvious rust spots, and making the engine run somehow. In Great Britain, cars wearing the original paint and upholstery are esteemed, and American methods are held to be vulgar, except by those collectors, such as C.W.P. Hampton of Sussex, who can afford them. To Harrah's technicians, a restored automobile is one that has been restored to the condition in which it left the factory. Underrestoration is thought unprofessional and slack; overrestoration is heinous. For example, steering-wheel spokes that were originally plated in nickel must not be done in chromium. The fact that chromium is better looking and easier to maintain is neither here nor there; nor does it matter that few visitors will be able to tell the difference.

What matters is the original specification. Harrah thinks no effort or expenditure excessive if it is necessary to establish an original specification. For example, he has paid $165 to make a set of 1928 Pierce-Arrow pedal pads, although a mint set of 1929's was available, indistinguishable from the 1928's except by advanced experts. Harrah will never order a part made unless it appears impossible to find an original, but he has on occasion cast whole engine blocks, and a few months ago his head metalworker was building a 1910 Pope-Hartford crossflow radiator, welding up a complex of some seventy-five flat oblong water tubes one eighth of an inch high. Harrah does not think it unreasonable to spend weeks determining the exact construction methods and materials used for the interior of a door, and then seal the work off forever with upholstery.

Harrah is obsessed with perfection, and so a screwhead is as important as a steering wheel. He sees no difference. Philip Frohman, architect of the National Cathedral in Washington, insisted that a molding 250 feet from the ground be moved by a fraction of an inch. From the floor, an expert with a binocular couldn't tell the difference, but Frohman couldn't understand why his action should be thought remarkable: the molding was in the wrong place, and he knew it. Therefore it was imperative to move it.

When a car has been restored, it is tested on the road by Lee Jellison, a master mechanic who functions as automotive operations manager, and by the general manager of the collection, Ralph Dunwoodie. If these two pass it, Harrah takes it on the road. He rejects approximately 40 percent of the cars as unsatisfactory and sends them back for more work. If there is something amiss, he will almost certainly find it.

He has watched the car in restoration, and he knows every corner of it. "He sees, and holds in his hand," one of the mechanics told me, "every part that comes in here. Everything is spread out on a bench for him, with a ticket showing where it came from and what it cost."

A "part" can be a set of rear springs for a 1912 Garford or a head-lamp lens for a 1934 Cadillac. It can be anything from a bulb horn to a custom-built touring body. Harrah's chief buyer, Edward Cattlett, is a shrewd and indefatigable man. One room in one of the parts warehouses is solid with brass horns, headlights, sidelights, taillights. If a body-shop man needs a component part, he can take it out of inventory, have it bought, or have it made; and whether it's a mudguard brace or a "King of the Belgians" touring-car body complete doesn't really matter. When I was last in Reno, a replica pre-World War I Rolls-Royce body was being built. Finished, it will be indistinguishable from the original in every particular except one: Harrah's upholsterers can and do duplicate old diamond pleating or any other kind of leatherwork; his wheelwrights can make a wooden wheel for a 1910 Palmer-Singer; and his painters could do 1910 coach-painting too, but they do not. The coach-painting technique was to lay down ground coats of color and cover them with many layers of clear varnish. The job took thirty days, and the finish lasted a year. Everyone uses modern paints today. Most collectors couldn't afford the old technique. Those who, like Harrah, can afford it in money cannot afford it in time.

The income that enables William Harrah to consider reasonable an attempt to demonstrate the history of the automobile through 1,000 perfectly conditioned, beautifully housed and lighted specimens comes from the largest gaming establishment in the world, the fabulous complex of Harrah's Clubs in Reno and in Lake Tahoe on the California frontier. Like all Nevada gaming houses, they run twenty-four hours a day. Unlike many of the others, they run to near-capacity most of the time. Harrah runs the same games, at the same house percentages, that other places run, but there is a startling difference in air, in tone. The root of the matter is shiny cleanliness and good taste. A marquee sign detailing the show-business acts with which all the big Nevada houses divert the client is lighted and moving, but only just: it's no jungle of neon or flashing bulbs; it's a big rectangle of pearlescent white squares, moving slightly from side to side, and so, flickering in the backlight. It's better looking by far than any other such come-on in town, and it probably pulls more business.

One enters Harrah's through a $40,000 air door—it keeps out flies, warm air, all but determined dogs, and relieves the client of the necessity of so much as turning a knob. Within, the place shines. It is startlingly clean. The slot machines glitter. (Incidentally, it is the vogue now to play two at one time.) The felt surfaces of the crap tables obviously were vacuumed not long since. There are ashtrays everywhere—one in each slot machine, for example—and they are all empty, or they hold at most one cigarette butt. In the case of a major catastrophe—a dropped drink, for instance—a cleanup man will be on the scene within a minute, and probably sooner. There are square yards of mirror on the walls and ceiling, and it all glistens like new ice. And it is all Argus glass, one-way mirror. Behind it are galleries from which every foot of floor in the club can be observed, and in these galleries men sit at small tables with field glasses in their hands. They're looking for cheaters, for known criminals, for employees who do not smile and say thank you to the customers, and for overflowing ashtrays as well.

When Harrah came into Reno after the war, an unknown in the gaming world, he had three basic ideas: that a really successful gambling house would employ pleasant people who would run strictly honest games in a surgically clean atmosphere. On this system he has prospered, to state the matter mildly. Since Harrah's is privately held, public disclosure of profit and loss is not required, and since gambling is entirely a cash business, even the Internal Revenue people can only estimate, on the basis of spot checks. He has between 2,500 and 3,000 people on his payroll according to season; his expenses run to around $114,000 a day. The closest anyone who knows will come to disclosing Harrah's income is the term the Rolls-Royce people use when asked the horsepower of their cars: "It is adequate." Harrah's income is adequate for his purposes, even if those purposes include the maintenance of 1,000 motorcars. The collection may in time contribute substantially to its own support: admission is one dollar, refundable at Harrah's Club in Reno if it is presented within twenty-four hours.

The just-washed, shiny-bright tone that marks the gaming rooms obtains everywhere over the five acres that house the Harrah collection. There are separate shops for sandblasting, for steam cleaning and washing, for bodywork, for upholstering, and they are all as nearly spotless as possible. The main restoration shop, housed in the same building with the executive offices, the library, and the best of the cars, looks like a small demonstration factory: machine shop, massive overhead electric hoists, soft fluorescent lighting. A dozen projects are simultaneously in hand. Three mechanics are rebuilding a Stutz Bearcat, one of the earlier, bucket-seat models, a bright buttercup yellow. Every part they are working with has been painted or polished; there is nothing in sight that would stain a white glove. Next to them a young man wearing a cinnamon-brown pointed beard is striping a 1913 popcorn wagon. He does striping only, and he will work on the wagon from ten in the morning until five the next morning. There is a big rush on it, as there is on the Stutz: both must be ready for a major meeting of the Nevada Horseless Carriage Club in a few days.

LENGTH: 2,155 WORDS

VOCABULARY

resurgence   reappearance, rising again
artifact   any object made by human work, a work of art
Museo dell'Automobile Carlo Biscaretti di Ruffia   the Carlo Biscaretti di Ruffia Museum of the Automobile
premier   the first
acquisition   the act of obtaining, a thing that is acquired or obtained
wheelwright   one who makes or fixes wheels
heinous   terrible, awful
mint   brand new, perfect
indistinguishable   impossible to be told apart
obsessed   dominated or excessively troubled by, preoccupied with
imperative   of first importance
amiss   wrong
indefatigable   tireless
replica   reproduction, imitation
specimens   examples
pearlescent   shiny, like pearl
the vogue   the style
Argus glass   a mirror that can be seen through from one side

36 · The World's Greatest Automobile Collection

PURPOSE Which of the following phrases best expresses the purpose of the passage? _____

1. to show that English fortunes cannot compete with American fortunes in the field of automobile restoration
2. to help us understand why a man like Harrah would spend all his time and money keeping together a fleet of old cars
3. to give an idea of the immense effort and attention needed to amass a truly first-class collection like Harrah's

GENERALITIES Based on the passage, which of the following generalities seem justifiable? _____ and _____

1. Harrah does not like the idea of people coming to look at his collection.
2. The original specifications of each car act as a kind of standard of achievement for Harrah.
3. Harrah is interested in every detail of restoration undertaken by his staff.
4. One monument Harrah has always looked up to is the National Cathedral in Washington, D.C.

RETENTION Based on the passage, which of the following statements are True (T), False (F), or Not answerable (N)?

1. _____ Harrah's regular use cars all have air conditioning.

2. _____ Harrah has preferred Fords and Packards to other makes of cars.

3. _____ Daimler and Benz became friends in Germany.

4. _____ Perfection is important to Harrah.

5. _____ Harrah now has 10 cars on his wanted list.

6. _____ A restored car must be exactly as it was when it was first bought.

7. _____ Some restorations take only a few weeks.

8. _____ Harrah has two Packards for every Ford he owns.

9. _____ One man in Europe has 990 Bugatti automobiles.

10. _____ Briggs Cunningham's collection has 500 cars in it.

11. _____ Harrah's collection is housed in Sparks, Nevada.

12. _____ English antique car owners prefer cars with the original paint on them.

13. _____ The cars Harrah has restored do not have to be driven.

14. _____ Harrah collects some trucks as well as passenger cars.

15. _____ Harrah leaves all the work of restoration to his staff

16. _____ Harrah was a good friend of Philip Frohman, the architect.

17. _____ To restore a car, many parts have to be built.

18. _____ Harrah's Clubs earn a little more than 114 million dollars a year.

19. _____ The Rolls-Royce people are interested in Harrah's collection.

20. _____ Harrah sends 60 percent of his restored cars back for more work.

COMPLETION   Choose the best answer for each question.

1. _____ An automobile not mentioned in the text is: (a) Ford.   (b) Garford. (c) Cadillac.   (d) Plymouth.

2. _____ Harrah does not use the old technique of painting cars with varnish because: (a) it is too costly.   (b) he prefers modern finishes.   (c) no one can paint in the old style.   (d) he cannot afford the time.

3. _____ The author uses the example of Frohman's insisting that a molding be moved a fraction of an inch where no one could see it to show that both Frohman and Harrah are: (a) going too far.   (b) not sure what they want.   (c) perfectionists.   (d) tremendously observant.

4. _____ Harrah paid $165 for a set of 1928 Pierce-Arrow pedal covers even though: (a) he did not have a 1928 Pierce-Arrow.   (b) no one could see them once they were in place.   (c) he had a slightly used set on hand.   (d) he had a mint set of 1929 covers.

5. _____ The Harrah collection employs the full-time attention of: (a) 102 men and women.   (b) 24 men and women.   (c) 6 men and women. (d) 62 men and women.

6. ____ Harrah's ultimate goal is to have enough cars to: (a) illustrate the history of the automobile. (b) show up C.W.P. Hampton of Sussex, England. (c) be the "King of the Belgians" among collectors. (d) realize a childhood dream.

DEFINITIONS In the following passage, each underlined word has a number. In the columns below, match the number of each underlined word with the letter of the word that is closest to it in meaning.

      1   2   3   4   5

The income that enables William Harrah to consider reasonable an attempt to

    6   7   8

demonstrate the history of the automobile through 1,000 perfectly conditioned,

            9   10   11

beautifully housed and lighted specimens comes from the largest gaming

  12   13   14

establishment in the world, the fabulous complex of Harrah's Clubs in Reno

                  15

and in Lake Tahoe on the California frontier.

Column A	*Column B*
1. ____	a. intentional
2. ____	b. business firm
	c. development
3. ____	d. permits
4. ____	e. effort
5. ____	f. examples
	g. wonderful
6. ____	h. earnings
7. ____	i. border
	j. restored
8. ____	k. to think, to regard
9. ____	l. within reason
10. ____	m. gambling
11. ____	n. show, act out
12. ____	o. collection or group
	p. displayed
13. ____	q. perform
14. ____	r. inculcate, cultivate
	s. antiquity
15. ____	

37 · Life!

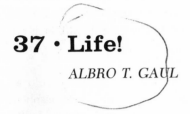

ALBRO T. GAUL

*For centuries the world has considered the possibility of life on
other planets. This article considers what such life might be like.*

There has been much speculation about life on the moon and the
planets. At first, thinking people believed that these other worlds were really
images of the earth, in a sense, and that things were pretty much the same
there as here. Today we know that this is not the case at all, and we should
be very surprised if we found there anything much resembling earth. Modern
astrophysics has made some statements that would discourage us from expecting
much life anywhere. On the other hand, the chemist, the biochemist, and the
biologist have learned a great deal about life, and so with all this information
put together, we can determine whether or not life could exist on other worlds.

The biologist defines life by its several characteristics. Life reproduces itself.
Living things grow by producing new cells, each a living unit. Living things
take in food. Living things cast out wastes. Living things use respiratory gases.
Living things have metabolism (they burn their food for energy) hence they
are chemical organisms.

With our definition of life, we are now prepared to tackle the possible kinds
of life.

Here on earth, living things use the oxygen in the atmosphere. They com-
bine this oxygen with their foods. The foods are largely carbohydrates made
of carbon, hydrogen, and oxygen, or they are fats (with a higher percentage of
carbon and hydrogen), or they are proteins (made of carbon, hydrogen, and
oxygen, with nitrogen in the form of amino groups, plus assorted atoms of

LIFE!   From *The Complete Book of Space* by Albro T. Gaul. Copyright © 1956 by Albro T. Gaul.
Published by arrangement with The World Publishing Company, Cleveland and New York.

sulphur, phosphorus, and other elements). These, when combined with oxygen, form water and carbon dioxide, while the nitrogen-sharing amino group becomes plain ammonia, which is converted to urea or uric acid in some animals.

Suppose, therefore, we had a planet which had a chlorine atmosphere. Chlorine is also an oxidizing agent, and it would, therefore, burn the same foods to hydrochloric acid (instead of water), carbon tetrachloride (instead of carbon dioxide), and carbon dichlorodiamine (instead of urea). Although we shudder at the thought of breathing chlorine, which is highly poisonous to us, it is chemically possible that living things could use it.

Suppose we encountered a large hot world. It is large enough to hold an atmosphere, and hot enough to vaporize sulphur. It will have an atmosphere of sulphur, and any oxygen that it might have had would have combined with metals quickly because of the heat. Our "life" on this planet could oxidize its foods with sulphur, which behaves in a chemical sense much like oxygen.

But this hot world holds another problem. Our life is based on the use of carbon compounds. Our food is largely carbon compounds, even our vitamins are made of carbon compounds. On this hot world, the carbon compounds may be too active for living things to use. They may have adapted themselves to the use of carbon's chemical relative, silicon. Although we usually think of silicon as a component of sand and window glass, it behaves very much like carbon. During the Second World War, silicon was substituted for carbon in the manufacture of synthetic motor oils. These oils would not break down in high temperature engines, while carbon oils were constantly being burned. So our sulphur world may use silicon as a base substance. Such a world would be cold when the temperature dropped to 800 degrees Fahrenheit, but this is only slightly above the temperature of the hot side of the planet Mercury.

There are, of course, limits to the temperature ranges in which we would expect to find life. These ranges are limited by the freezing and boiling points of the solvents. Our common biological solvent is water. Salts, acids, alkalis, sugars, etc. all dissolve in water and are used by living things largely in the dissolved condition. It is impossible for us to imagine a world of life with any solvent except water. Therefore, we cannot think of life as existing much below 32 degrees Fahrenheit nor much above 212 degrees Fahrenheit. Depending on atmospheric pressures, other solvents would tend to boil away at temperatures much above the boiling point of water. Moreover, many of our minerals would become liquid in our silicon-sulphur world. Tin, lead, magnesium, bismuth, zinc, and selenium would all be liquids, while earth's gaseous elements would swell by the addition to the "air" of bromine, iodine, mercury vapor, phosphorus, and sulphur. In such a world we cannot say that "life," by definition, is impossible, but we certainly have no notion what it would be like. All water would be scalding steam, and whatever solvent this life could use, we have no way of knowing.

Another side of this story is told by the spectroscopes. Our findings about the distribution of the chemical elements in our universe bear out the fact that every star and every galaxy seems to be composed of the same elements. We cannot imagine a star system in which oxygen is lacking, nor can we find stars without hydrogen. We do not know how many stars have planets, but among those which do, some must have temperature ranges between the freezing and boiling points of water. These planets probably have life.

In other words, we can set up in our minds all sorts of conditions and we can make up plans for living things, but, when it comes right down to it, we cannot get away from liquid water as the chief supporter of life. The special properties of water, its solvent powers, its surface tension, its ionization, its specific gravity, its high specific heat (calorie requirements for temperature change), all lead us to believe that life without water is impossible. No other chemical has these properties, and life seems to depend on just these properties. No other compound is as abundant as water. Here on earth, the antarctic has living rotifers which live despite the freezing weather. The hot springs of Yellowstone have fishes which live near the boiling point of water. We can find life along the whole temperature range of liquid water. And so it may be on other planets.

I am afraid that we are stuck with our concept of life in a carbon-oxygen world with a water requirement. Perhaps future expeditions may turn up some entirely new life forms on waterless or oxygen deficient worlds, but, until they do, we cannot guess at their life chemistry.

The simplest living things are single celled animals and plants, the protozoa and the bacteria. Our life forms are based on this unit cell structure. The cell membrane separates the living creature from the mineral world without. We can, however, imagine a simple living thing without a definite cell structure. The virus particle almost fits such a description, since it is simple and has no cell structure, but the hitch with the virus particle is the word "living." A virus alone has no metabolism, is unable to reproduce, and does none of the things by which we define life.

We should expect, then, to find our extraterrestrial life patterned somewhat after our familiar cell structure. An advanced plant or animal must have some organization to hold its shape and make its parts function, and such a creature must have cells.

The larger the beast, the more complicated it must be. It must develop an internal transportation system—call them xylem sap tubes, or arteries and veins if you want. As it increases in size, its surface area does not keep pace with its weight, as will be proved by a simple problem in solid geometry. Therefore, since respiratory gases must be absorbed, and since large bodies need more of these gases, some sort of gill or lung system must develop to fulfill the greater requirements.

We cannot imagine a large animal without the basic systems—nervous, circulatory, respiratory, digestive, and reproductive. We can imagine a circulatory system without an oxygen carrier, because our insects' blood is that way. But the insect has a tubular respiratory system which carries air directly to all parts of the body. Even so, this limits the size of insects to no more than a one-inch diameter. Proportionately larger animals could use the same system if the oxygen content of their planet's atmosphere were greater. All in all, life, to be life at all, must be pretty much as we know it. True, the systems of the animals can be completely different. They might sit on their food and digest it through their skin (somewhat like the inside-out stomach of the starfish), and they might do everything in a wholly strange fashion, but they would be doing the same things that we do.

According to modern biology, animals probably appeared on the earth before plants. Therefore we would expect the same natural laws to make conditions favorable for animal life on other planets before the development of plants. We believe that plants exist on Mars. If our theory is correct, then Mars must have animal life, too.

Our concept of the start of life begins with the cooling earth. Waters condensed and rained, and formed oceans. The atmosphere, largely adsorbed in the rocks, was still very thin. Ultraviolet rays, in a strength unknown to us on today's air-blanketed earth, beat down upon the waters. Slowly carbon dioxide seeped into the water from the rocks and from the thin air. The carbon dioxide plus the water, plus strong ultraviolet rays, automatically formed many complex organic chemicals. This process went on for thousands of years, until the sea was a vast organic soup. Finally, the correct combination of organic chemicals was formed, and a simple, primitive, amoebalike creature resulted. Life had started.

We think that this creature was amoebalike instead of plantlike because plants all manufacture food through the presence of the green pigment, chlorophyll. Chlorophyll is a very complex chemical and would be much harder to manufacture than the relatively simple chemicals that go into the make-up of a simple animal. All animals eat plants, either directly or indirectly, while the plants make sugars and starches from carbon dioxide and water. What then did these simple animals eat? The organic soup of the seas, of course!

It will be interesting to find out if life on other planets bears out this theory, particularly since we assume a more or less similar origin and ancient history for all the planets in our system.

Another aspect of biology insists that there must be a balance of life. Plants remove carbon dioxide from the air and liberate oxygen. Animals take oxygen from the air and liberate carbon dioxide. Animals eat plants and give off wastes which the plants use as organic fertilizer. Thus plants and animals are together in a closed cycle. Again, we cannot imagine Mars with a seasonal plant crop, but without animals to eat the plants or restore carbon dioxide for the use of plants.

Higher animals, those of larger size and consequently more efficient organization, all have certain basic requirements. They must have balanced systems. This implies a form of body symmetry, and indeed we find only two kinds of symmetry among most of our animals. The simpler animals are round. Small protozoans are nearly spherical, and have radial symmetry. The larger animals, the shrimps, the insects, dogs, horses, and elephants have a different symmetry. In these animals one side closely balances the other: this is bilateral symmetry. Even man has his right side nearly identical to his left side, and he is, therefore, bilaterally symmetrical. Wherever we go we should expect the larger creatures of a planet to be bilaterally symmetrical.

Therefore, as we head out into space, the biologist in our crew will expect to find new kinds of life. But he will be greatly surprised if the basic chemistry of the living thing is much different from ours. If he finds plants he will expect to find animals. If he finds large animals they will have well-developed systems of organs, and will be symmetrical. This will hold as true on the planets of some yet undiscovered star as it is on earth.

This completes the fundamental principles of space flight from the point of view of the scientific and ground personnel. The candidates for membership in the crew will add to this theoretical training with mock training flights and emergency activities of all kinds. They will also be briefed on the modern understanding of the conditions which exist on the various worlds to which they are destined. Let us examine the facts which the astronomers can supply about our universe, in terms of what equipment we shall need and how we can survive on each body. After all, we must be prepared for different emergencies on Mercury than the ones we should meet on Pluto.

LENGTH: 2,110 WORDS

VOCABULARY

astrophysics the science of the physical properties of stars and planets
spectroscope device for examining elemental structure through color analysis
rotifers wheel-shaped microscopic life usually found in stagnant fresh water
extraterrestrial beyond the earth
adsorbed condensed and held in

37 · Life!

SCORING: Reading time: _____ Rate from chart: _____ W.P.M.

PURPOSE	number right _____ × 4 equals _____ points
GENERALITIES	number right _____ × 4 equals _____ points
RETENTION	number right _____ × 2 equals _____ points
COMPLETION	number right _____ × 3 equals _____ points
DEFINITIONS	number right _____ × 2 equals _____ points

(Total points: 100)   **total** _____ points

PURPOSE   Which of the following phrases best expresses the purpose of the passage? ____

1. to prove there is life on other planets
2. to suggest that we cannot imagine life that is not in a carbon-oxygen world
3. to show that plants appear on a planet before animals

GENERALITIES   Based on the passage, which of the following generalities seem justifiable? ____ and ____

1. Life in its earliest stages depended on the presence of a "soup" of organic chemicals.
2. Astrophysicists have the most important, recent information about the nature and quality of life and the possibility of life elsewhere.
3. The processes of life are essentially chemical in nature.
4. The presence of mild ultraviolet rays is essential for life.

RETENTION   Based on the passage, which of the following statements are True (T), False (F), or Not answerable (N)?

1. ____ Plants use animal wastes to support their own life.

2. ____ The first forms of life on this planet were chlorine forms.

3. ____ All life is bilaterally symmetrical.

4. ____ Mars has a seasonal plant crop.

5. ____ Life on earth has a variety of basic chemistries.

6. ____ If we find plants on a planet, we should expect to find animals.

7. ____ Life, wherever we find it in space, must be much as we know it.

8. _____ A circulatory system without an oxygen carrier is imaginable.

9. _____ The starfish has its stomach outside its body.

10. _____ Life as we conceive it began with the cooling earth.

11. _____ A virus alone has no metabolism, is unable to reproduce, and does none of the things by which we define life.

12. _____ Life on earth covers the whole temperature range of liquid water.

13. _____ No other chemical has the special properties of chlorine.

14. _____ There are no stars without hydrogen.

15. _____ Silicon is closely related chemically to carbon.

16. _____ During World War II, silicon was used in place of mercury.

17. _____ A cell is a unit of life.

18. _____ Chlorine is an oxidizing agent much like oxygen.

19. _____ There is evidence to discourage us from expecting extraterrestrial life anywhere.

20. _____ Our common biological solvent is hydrochloric acid.

COMPLETION   Choose the best answer for each question.

1. _____ The spectroscope demonstrates that every star and every galaxy seem to be composed of: (a) hot gases.   (b) the same elements.   (c) different chemistries.   (d) gases, liquids, and solids.

2. _____ It is impossible to imagine life without: (a) animals and plants.   (b) a cell structure.   (c) respiratory gases.   (d) a biological solvent.

3. _____ Creatures metabolize their food when they: (a) plant it.   (b) see it.   (c) eat it.   (d) excrete it.

4. _____ The larger the animal the more: (a) destructive it becomes.   (b) complicated it becomes.   (c) symmetrical it becomes.   (d) organic it becomes.

5. _____ If the theory of the passage is correct and if Mars has plant life on it, then it also must have: (a) animal life.   (b) water.   (c) air.   (d) oxygen.

6. _____ The theory for the beginning of life on earth suggests that the simplest forms of life first resulted from the interaction of air, water, carbon dioxide, and: (a) chlorine.   (b) ultraviolet rays.   (c) chlorophyll.   (d) organisms.

DEFINITIONS   In the following passage, each underlined word has a number. In the columns below, match the number of each underlined word with the letter of the word that is closest to it in meaning.

    1   2   3   4

Suppose we encountered a large hot world. It is large enough to hold an

     5   6

atmosphere, and hot enough to vaporize sulphur. It will have an atmosphere

                    7   8

of sulphur, and any oxygen that it might have had would have combined with

  9   10   11   12

metals quickly because of the heat. Our "life" on this planet could oxidize its

 13   14   15

foods with sulphur, which behaves in a chemical sense much like oxygen.

Column A	Column B
1. _____	a. turn to gas
2. _____	b. met or found
	c. high temperature
3. _____	d. determined
4. _____	e. way
	f. imagine
5. _____	g. whatever
6. _____	h. spheroid
7. _____	i. sufficient
	j. joined
8. _____	k. earth
9. _____	l. moon
10. _____	m. contain, retain
	n. gases surrounding planets and stars
11. _____	o. heavy elements
12. _____	p. nourishment
	q. counted on
13. _____	r. burn up
14. _____	s. acts
15. _____	

38 · The Restless Decade

BRUCE CATTON

The nineteen twenties are thought to be the most exciting, wild,
free, and exuberant ten years of our century, a time of wealth,
booze, and Flappers. A famous historian takes a hard look at this
decade to see just how wild it was.

The decade of the nineteen twenties was at one and the same
time the gaudiest, the saddest, and the most misinterpreted era in modern
American history.

It was gaudy because it was full of restless vitality burgeoning in a field
where all of the old rules seemed to be gone, and it was sad because it was
an empty place between two eras, with old familiar certainties and hopes
drifting off like mist and new ones not yet formulated. It was misunderstood
because so many of its popular interpreters became so fascinated by the things
that floated about on the froth that they could not see anything else.

Most of the tag lines that have been attached to it are wrong. It was, we
are assured, the period when *everybody* did fantastic things. Everybody detested
Prohibition, patronized bootleggers, made atrocious gin in the bathtub and
worse beer in the basement, and, inspired by the products of these activities,
danced the Charleston. Everybody bought stocks on margin or Florida lots on
binder clauses and confidently expected to become rich before old age set in.
Everybody put his moral standards away in moth balls, so that neither the
scandalous doings in Washington nor the murderous forays of the Chicago
gangsters seemed very disturbing. Everybody, in short, was off on a prolonged
spree, and the characteristic figure of the era was the Flapper, the girl who

THE RESTLESS DECADE   From the August 1965 issue of *American Heritage*. Reprinted by permission of *American Heritage* and Bruce Catton.

bobbed her hair and wore short skirts with nothing in particular beneath them and put in her time piling in and out of open cars populated by collegians in coonskin coats.

It makes an entertaining picture—it made one at the time, in a way, for the people who were in it—but it is at best only a partial picture.

The first thing to remember is that the word "everybody" is much too inclusive. There were a great many people in the United States in the nineteen twenties, and most of them were serious, hard-working people who did their best to earn a living, bring up their children, live decently by the best light they had, and lay away a few dollars for their old age. Most of them never saw the inside of a speakeasy, most never really tried to make gin or beer at home, and anyone over the age of twenty-six who danced the Charleston regretted it immediately—it was an exercise in all-out acrobatics rather than a dance, and only the young could manage it. Acceptance of the Prohibition law was so widespread that repeal of the Eighteenth Amendment was not voted, or ever seriously considered, until after the decade had ended. Certainly the vast majority bought neither stocks, bonds, nor Florida real estate and never had the faintest notion that with a little luck they could soon stroll down Easy Street. They were just as deeply disturbed by Teapot Dome and Al Capone as anyone would be today, and if these and other phenomena helped to destroy confidence in public leadership, it ought to be added that the kind of leadership that was given to the American people in those years was pretty poor.

Nevertheless, the decade did have its own peculiar character—because it was a time of unending change.

It was a hollow time between wars. The 1914–18 war, which had been ever so much more cataclysmic than anybody had imagined any war could be, was over, but it had left smouldering wreckage all over the landscape; and if the next war was not yet visible, there was ominous heat lightning all along the horizon to warn that there had been no real break in the weather. The certainties the adult American was used to, in 1920—the basic assumptions about world society which he had always taken for granted—were obviously either gone forever or rapidly going. Europe, which had always seemed to be the very center of stability, had collapsed. Of the great empires which had maintained order and set standards, some had vanished without trace and the survivors were mortally injured; Europe was a center of disorder, with monstrous doctrines either being followed or vigorously preached; and the one certainty was that things would get worse before they ever got better.

There was an immense, all-pervading disillusionment. The nation's highest ideals had been appealed to during the war, so that to win the war seemed the holiest of causes; the war had been won, but it was hard to see that anything worth winning had been gained; the idealism had been used up, and people had an uneasy feeling that they had been had. The Prohibition act contributed to the letdown. Here was a social experiment which, as President Herbert Hoover correctly said, had been adopted with the noblest of motives, but nothing was working out as had been anticipated, and the problems the law was supposed to solve seemed to have been made worse; the majority was not yet ready to discard the law, but it was beginning to see that something somewhere was awfully wrong with it.

So lots of people became materialists. The light of faith was flickering low; the average citizen had his own, private faith in the relationship between himself and his Maker, but his faith in the world itself and in the values on which it operated was not robust. It was easier, indeed it was almost necessary, to center one's attention on the material things that were going on in this country.

A great deal was going on, and it was immensely stimulating. The world was in the act of shifting gears—not without grating—starting to move with bewildering speed, and if the destination was wholly unclear, the speed itself was exhilarating.

The age of the automobile was arriving. In 1920 the average American did not own an automobile and did not suppose that he ever would; by 1930 the automobile was a necessity of daily life, and the incalculable change it was going to inflict on America—change for city, town, and countryside, for ways of living and habits of thought—was already visible. At the same time the era of mass production was coming into full effect, and mankind (most especially in America) was beginning to lay its hands on the fabulous capacity to solve any problem on earth so long as the problem was purely material. This of course was most unsettling, because it brought with it the uneasy awareness that the real problem was going to be man himself and not his ability to reshape his environment, and no one was ready to tell people what they ought to do about themselves. But it was a miraculous age. The instruments, skills, and techniques—airplanes, electronics, automation—that would change the world forever were appearing. Albert Einstein, who was known to the few Americans who had ever heard of him as an oddball professor type who thought that space was curved, had already published the formula that was to lead to the atomic age.

It was an exciting decade; in many ways a good time to be alive. If the spirit of the nineteen twenties took on a materialistic cast, nobody can be blamed. It was good simply to look at the surface and enjoy it.

The surface contained elements of sheer fantasy. Along with everything else, the age of mass communications was here, in exuberant, uninhibited blossoming, and the public ear could be reached as never before. In some ways those were the years of the sportswriter, the press agent, and the newspaper columnist—not the purveyor of gossip, but the man who found amusement and a large audience by discussing the items that floated about on the froth. It was the time of the big headline and the loud-speaker, which were reserved for the purely spectacular.

So the most famous people in America were a strange assortment—movie stars, gangsters, Channel swimmers, professional athletes, imaginative amateur murderers, and eccentrics of high and low degree. Before 1920, moving-picture actors and actresses were outsiders; now they were at the top of the ladder, living in the limelight as no one ever did before or since. Before 1920, prize fighting had been disreputable, outlawed in most states, tolerated in a few; now the heavyweight champion was a hero, an ideal for American youth, a man whose performances could command a box-office sale of a million dollars or more. Once in the mid-Twenties the author of a quiz program played a sly trick: by posing two innocent questions he showed that although every adult American could name and identify the star halfback at the University of Illinois, no one outside of the academic profession knew the name of that university's president.

As Westbrook Pegler said, this was the Era of Wonderful Nonsense. Publicity was the thing, and it had no standards of value except pure sensation. An American girl swam the English Channel, nonstop; the mayor of Chicago ran for re-election with the promise that he would hit the King of England on the nose if chance allowed; the President of the United States, asked how such nations as England and France could ever repay their enormous war debts without coming to utter ruin, replied drily: "They hired the money, didn't they?" A countrywoman who tended pigs was carried into court on a stretcher to testify in an earth-shaking murder trial, and for a few days everybody in the country (well, a lot of people, if not quite everybody) was talking about the Pig Woman . . . and all of these things were of equal weight, they made the headlines for a few days, and then life went on as before.

Stock prices went up and up, Florida real-estate prices did likewise; supposedly realistic analysts said that this was only natural because "everybody" was in the market, and the happy theory that everybody in the United States had plenty of money overlooked the fact that farmers and wage earners were being caught in a terrible squeeze in which their bitterest protests went unheeded. A conservative senator announced that congressmen who protested about this situation were simply "sons of the wild jackass" whose cries need not be noticed, and one of the country's best-known economists said that inflated stock prices need worry no one because the nation had reached a new, permanently high plateau in which all of the old standards could be ignored.

If all of this was exciting it was not really satisfying, and people knew it. They were hungry for something they were not getting—an appeal to idealism, to the belief that the greatest values cannot be expressed in cash or set forth in headlines. The amazing response to Charles A. Lindbergh's flight proves the point.

Lindbergh flew from New York to Paris in 1927. The Atlantic had been flown before, it was obviously going to be flown again—two or three highly publicized expeditions were poised at New York, getting ready, while the nation waited—but what he did seemed like nothing anyone had ever imagined before. He was young, boyish, unspoiled, the kind of youth people had stopped believing in, a young man nobody had heard of before, and he came to New York, waited for a good weather report, and then took off, unaided by any of the elaborate devices that would make such a flight routine nowadays. When he landed in Paris it seemed as if mankind had somehow triumphed over something that greatly needed to be beaten. After he had vanished into the over-ocean midnight, and before any word of him had come back, people waited in an agony of suspense, and when it was announced that he had indeed landed in Paris, unharmed and on schedule, there was literally rejoicing in the streets.

It was odd, and revealing. After years in which it seemed as if everybody who got any kind of fame was on the make, here was a young man who apparently had done something great for nothing. Lindbergh became the hero of the decade. We have not felt quite that way about anybody since; he lifted up the heart, and all of a sudden it was possible to believe in something once more. The response to what he did was a perfect symbol of what everybody had been lacking.

It seemed like a miracle . . . but at last the glitter faded, and like everything else, this bright deed was buried under a spate of words. There were too many words in those years. Everybody listened, and nobody got much out of it. Much of the talk came from men who were not qualified to address a large audience. At the beginning of the decade, radio had been nothing much more than a useful device by which a sinking ship could call for help; in a very few years it was central to the mass-communications business, and the man who spoke into the microphone was suddenly a power in the land. E. B. White summed it up by remarking that man's "words leap across rivers and mountains, but his thoughts are still only six inches long."

It was a time for long thoughts, but long thoughts were not often being thought, and when they were it was hard to find an audience for them. The world was passing across one of the significant watersheds in human history and the crest of the pass seemed to be situated right in the United States, but it was hard to think about anything except that, for the moment, the path led upward. The people of the nineteen twenties really behaved about the way the people of all other decades have behaved. They did a great deal of hard work, doing some of it extraordinarily well, when you stop to think about it;

they carried their own individual loads of worry and aspiration and frustration along with them; and if they did some foolish things, they precisely resembled, in the doing of them, both their ancestors and their descendants.

Yet the essential point about the Twenties, the thing that makes us think of the decade as a separate era, was its curious transitional character, which was not like anything ever seen before—or since. The Twenties were years that no one who lived through them can ever forget, and they were also a time nobody in his senses would care to repeat, but you do have to say one thing for them: when the great catastrophe came, one decade after the Twenties had ended, the generation the Twenties had raised proved to be strong enough to stand the shock.

LENGTH: 2,710 WORDS

VOCABULARY

gaudy   bright, showy
burgeoning   blooming, growing
formulated   planned, organized
atrocious   terrible, awful
Teapot Dome   a political scandal in the Twenties
Al Capone   notorious gangster of the Twenties
cataclysmic   overwhelming, suggesting the end of the world
robust   vigorous, filled with life
exhilarating   exciting, energizing
incalculable   unknown, that which cannot be figured out

38 · The Restless Decade

> **SCORING:**   Reading time: _____ Rate from chart: _____ W.P.M.
>
> | | |
> |---|---|
> | **PURPOSE** | number right ____ × 4 equals ____ points |
> | **GENERALITIES** | number right ____ × 4 equals ____ points |
> | **RETENTION** | number right ____ × 2 equals ____ points |
> | **COMPLETION** | number right ____ × 3 equals ____ points |
> | **DEFINITIONS** | number right ____ × 2 equals ____ points |
>
> (Total points: 100)   **total** ____ points

PURPOSE   Which of the following phrases best expresses the purpose of the passage? ____

1. to explain the reasons for the repeal of Prohibition
2. to put the Twenties in a clear perspective
3. to replace some of the fantasies about the Twenties with facts

GENERALITIES   Based on the passage, which of the following generalities seem justifiable? ____ and ____

1. No one lived the way people were said to in the Twenties.
2. Materialism caused the collapse of the economy of the Twenties.
3. The Twenties grew into a period of idealism in spite of itself.
4. In the Twenties, people lived in much the same way they do now.

RETENTION   Based on the passage, which of the statements are True (T), False (F), or Not answerable (N)?

1. ____ There are few exaggerations about life in the nineteen twenties.

2. ____ Catton suggests that the Twenties was a period of transition.

3. ____ Probably few would care to live through the Twenties again.

4. ____ Lindbergh flew from Paris to New York in 1927.

5. ____ No one had ever flown the Atlantic before Lindbergh.

6. ____ Lindbergh's plane was a type never flown before.

7. ____ Catton says Lindbergh's feat got more attention than it deserved.

8. ____ The article implies that most people lived in the Twenties in nearly the same way that people of other decades have lived.

9. ____ Farmers and wage earners enjoyed prosperity with everyone else.

10. ____ Florida real estate was a depressingly bad investment for most people.

11. ____ The implication is that the President of the United States expected the war debts of England and France to be paid back promptly, even if it meant ruin for those nations.

12. ____ Westbrook Pegler called the Twenties the Era of Wonderful Nonsense.

13. ____ Publicity had highly idealistic moral values.

14. ____ Before the Twenties, movie stars were not considered cultural heroes.

15. ____ Einstein had written his famous formula during the Twenties.

16. ____ World War I had been won, and all were content.

17. ____ In America, the aims of World War I had assumed a "holy" character.

18. ____ America was disillusioned because little had been gained by World War I.

19. ____ Low motives prompted politicians to enact Prohibition.

20. ____ Life in the Twenties is commonly considered highly artificial.

COMPLETION   Choose the best answer for each question.

1. ____ The names of movie stars and gangsters were well known because: (a) the public had become dishonest. (b) no one else did anything exciting. (c) publicists focused on the materialistic surface of life. (d) most other people were unromantic and dull.

2. ____ One quiz program master showed the thinness of public knowledge and interest by asking a contestant to identify the: (a) formula that Albert Einstein had devised. (b) star halfback and president of the same university. (c) most important makes of automobiles. (d) plane that Lindbergh flew.

3. ____ Two great forces, on the scene in the Twenties, which were to change American life were: (a) Prohibition and gangsterism. (b) movies and radio. (c) the automobile and mass production. (d) war and peace.

4. ____ What made the nineteen twenties such an unsettling period was the disappearance of: (a) the old certainties, faith in God and man. (b) a genuinely stable Europe. (c) political honesty and good faith. (d) the traditional American way.

5. ____ Catton admits that the kind of leadership given to the American people in this period was: (a) quite remarkable. (b) with one or two exceptions better than in the previous era. (c) characterized by serious indecisiveness. (d) poor.

6. _____ Catton calls the Twenties America's gaudiest, saddest, and most: (a) disturbing era. (b) dull era. (c) misinterpreted era. (d) exciting era.

DEFINITIONS In the following passage, each underlined word has a number. In the columns below, match the number of each underlined word with the letter of the word that is closest to it in meaning.

1   2   3   4

The first thing to remember is that the word "everybody" is much too inclusive.

5

There were a great many people in the United States in the nineteen twenties,

6   7   8   9

and most of them were serious, hard-working people who did their best to earn

10   11   12

a living, bring up their children, live decently by the best light they had, and

13   14   15

lay away a few dollars for their old age.

Column A	Column B
1. _____	a. overly
2. _____	b. save
	c. keep in mind
3. _____	d. retirement
4. _____	e. clear
	f. numerous
5. _____	g. raise, train
6. _____	h. sober
7. _____	i. modesty
	j. hide
8. _____	k. knowledge
9. _____	l. a small amount
10. _____	m. respectably
	n. comprehensive
11. _____	o. gain by work
12. _____	p. energetic, industrious
	q. initial
13. _____	r. beam
14. _____	s. tried sincerely
15. _____	

39 · The Reasons for Religious Faith

MILTON STEINBERG

Are there any reasons for believing in God? Milton Steinberg thinks that logic and close examination are as useful in religious areas of thought as in scientific areas. His views of God are somewhat unorthodox.

Religion's world outlook centers about God.

Before attempting to indicate what we mean by that word, let us first make clear what we do not mean.

"God" does not denote an old man on a throne somewhere up in the sky. That notion is in part a survival of the infancy of the human race, in part a hangover from our personal childhood, from those days when, having first heard about God and possessing only limited intellectual resources, we pictorialized Him according to our naïveté. However the conception is come by, it is far less innocent than is generally supposed. It impels many a person to regard himself as an atheist, simply because he does not believe that there really is an old man in the heavens. On the other hand, it condemns individuals capable of ripe spirituality to the stuntedness, perhaps lifelong, of puerile, unsatisfying, and undignified convictions.

To believe in God, maturely, intelligently, is to believe that reality did not just "happen," that it is no accident, no pointless interplay of matter and energy. It is to insist rather that things, including man's life, make sense, that they add up to something. It is to hold that the universe, physical and moral, is a cosmos, not an anarchy—made a cosmos instead of an anarchy, meaningful rather than mad, because it is the manifestation of a creating, sustaining, animating, design-lending Spirit, a Mind-will, or to use the oldest, most familiar and best word, a God.

Here at last we come to the crux of our investigation. Are there any reasons for maintaining that the world is of this character rather than that, that Deity rather than Nullity moves behind and through it?

There are such reasons, not one but a number, all good, indeed compelling.

1

God is the only tenable explanation for the universe.

Here we are, creatures of a day, in the midst of a vast, awesome world. Sometimes it strikes us as a big, blooming tumult. But through the seeming confusion some traits persist, constant and all-pervading.

Thus, the universe is *one*, an organic unity, subject everywhere to the same law, knitted together with interdependence.

Again, it is *dynamic*, pulsating with energy, movement, life.

It is *creative*, forever calling new things into being, from stars and solar systems to new breeds of animals, new ideas in the minds of men, new pictures on the artist's canvas.

It is *rational* in the sense that everything in it behaves according to law! Electrons and protons according to the rules of their being, plants in harmony with their nature, animals after the patterns of their respective kinds, and man in consonance with the mandates not only of chemistry, physics, and biology but of psychology and the moral order as well. Everywhere: form, design, predictable recurrence, law.

The universe, furthermore, is *purposive;* at least it is in some of its phases. An insect laying its eggs in a place where the larvae yet to be born will be assured of food as they will require it; a spider weaving its web, a bird building a nest, an engineer designing a bridge, a young man charting his career, a government drawing up a policy, a prophet blueprinting a perfected mankind—all these are instances, rudimentary or advanced, conscious or instinctual, of planning ahead. Purposiveness is indisputably an aspect of reality, and no theory can be said to explain the latter if it does not account for the former as well.

The universe further contains *consciousness*. It has produced man. At least in him it discloses intelligence, a thirst for truth, sensitivity to beauty, a desire for goodness. And man is a component of reality. Whence it follows that no explanation of the entirety can be acceptable if it does not illumine the existence and nature of this most complex, challenging and mysterious of its components.

This then is the world in which we live: one, dynamic, creative, rational, and inclusive of elements of purpose, consciousness, and goodness. For such a universe the religious theory is by far the best "fit." Only *it* accounts at all adequately for the striking features just enumerated. That is why men of all eras, cultures, and capacities, including most of the world's great philosophers, have tended so generally to arrive, no matter what their point of departure, at some kind of God-faith. For, once one begins to reflect on the nature of things, this is the only plausible explanation for them.

But what about the evil of the world? Can the God-idea account for *that?* Not entirely, and not to anyone's complete satisfaction. This fact unquestionably counts against faith. On the other hand, there are many interpretations of evil from the religious viewpoint whereby its existence can be reconciled, partially if not thoroughly, with the existence of God.

But even if evil were a total mystery on which theology could not make so much as a dent, the God-faith would still be indicated. For, at the worst, it leaves less unexplained than does its alternative. If the believer has his troubles with evil, the atheist has more and graver difficulties to contend with. Reality stumps him altogether, leaving him baffled not by one consideration but by many, from the existence of natural law through the instinctual cunning of the insect to the brain of the genius and heart of the prophet.

This then is the intellectual reason for believing in God: that, though this belief is not free from difficulties, it stands out, head and shoulders, as the best answer to the riddle of the universe.

2

The second reason for belief in God is that man cannot live joyously, hopefully, healthily, perhaps not at all, without it.

Consider what the universe and man look like under the assumption of atheism.

Reality appears totally devoid of point or purpose. Like everything else, man is seen as a by-product of a blind machine, his history a goalless eddy in an equally directionless whirlpool, his ideals random sparks thrown off by physiochemical reaction in the colloidal solution, compounded by chance, which is his brain. Everything adds up in the end to exactly nothing.

What is the consequence of such a view for man and society? Can it be other than discouragement, demoralization, despair? What else shall one say of it except that "that way madness lies."

Now consider what face the universe takes on once God is assumed.

Because there is Intelligence behind it, its countenance is now intelligible, not vacant. The things that exist both within and without ourselves cease to be capricious, irrational, and isolated episodes. To the contrary, they are bound together into unity, reasonableness, and pattern by the Mind and Being before which, by virtue of which, they exist.

The spectacle unfolding before our eyes, this awesome pageant which has for its actors stars and atoms, plants, animals, and men, our private worlds of thought and feeling—this is a pageant after all, executing a design, spelling out a message.

What is more, it is a friendly visage which, given God, the universe turns upon us. The suns flaming in space are not altogether alien to us; trees, blades of grass, and beasts are all our kin, near or remote; and we humans, for all our differences and contentions, are brothers one to another by virtue of the Father we share.

As the God-faith transforms the cosmic countenance, so it illumines the darkness within ourselves. It dispels the misgiving lest our strivings serve no purpose, lest our ideals be mere idiosyncrasies, without validity beyond our-selves and hence doomed to extinction with us. Instead, our aspirations come to be seen as refractions of God's purpose, our struggles as elements in the working out of the divine scheme. Before us opens an exit from our human impasse. Frail and short-lived though we be, we can still transcend our limita-tions by serving God's will, advancing His design and so partaking, by identi-fication, of His infinity and eternity. Finally, the God-faith sends us into the battle for the good in ourselves and society with heightened morale. We know, as we join issue with the forces of evil, that we do not fight alone. In the face of seemingly insuperable odds we can reassure ourselves with the words of the prophet: "Fear not; for they that are with us are more than they that are with them" (II Kings 6:16).

Such are the emotional states distilled respectively by denial of God and by the affirmation of Him. Between them, who can hesitate?

3

Man's moral life requires belief in God.

Under atheism, as we have just seen, all ideals depreciate in value. Regarded as the creations of cosmic chance, if not indeed as the expression of mere human preference, they lose in validity and authority, until, in the end, the reasonableness of their continued observance comes under question. Men begin to ask themselves what logic there may be to devotion and self-sacrifice on behalf of ethical principles and human welfare, if these principles are as root-less and man's career as pointless as the atheist position implies.

That this is the upshot can be seen from Bertrand Russell's *The Free Man's Worship*, one of the noblest and most thoughtful statements of irreligion ever penned. Mr. Russell is a rare atheist; he is a thorough enough logician to follow his premise to its consequences, and is too earnest to prettify them once he has discovered their true character. He grants point blank that from his point of view there is neither basis nor sanction for moral ideals.

These, he concedes, are altogether alien and inappropriate in a blind world machine. Nevertheless, Mr. Russell concludes, he will cling to them. Not that he has any foundation or logic to justify them. He accepts them, as he is frank to admit, arbitrarily, capriciously, in part because, thanks to indoctrination and habit, he has come to love them; in part, *zu l'hachis*, as it were, to defy and spite an uncomprehending and soulless universe. All of which is noble, if a bit theatrical, of Mr. Russell. But it is far from constituting an adequate basis for ethics. And it leaves unanswered the question of what Mr. Russell would have to say to persons who insist on logic to their morality and who wait for arguments more convincing than a dramatic gesture before they will be persuaded to dedicate their lives to the classic ethical code.

The very origin of our higher moral aspirations supports the thesis immediately before us, that a close connection exists between them and religion. Ethical conceptions such as the worth of the individual, human brotherhood, the future regeneration of mankind are not self-evident. None of the great, ancient civilizations, not even the Greek or Roman, attained to them. Even in our time acceptance of them is far from universal.

LENGTH: 2,190 WORDS

VOCABULARY

denote   specify, mean
naïveté   innocence, lack of experience
puerile   childish
cosmos   an orderly and highly organized system, the universe
anarchy   the absence of government, lawless confusion
animating   moving, driving
nullity   nothingness
tenable   capable of being held or maintained
tumult   excitement, agitation
consonance   accord, agreement
mandates   orders, commands
purposive   having a design or purpose
discloses   tells, reveals
enumerated   singled out, explained
devoid   empty
eddy   a drift, backwash
physiochemical   pertaining to the physical and chemical properties of matter
colloidal   pertaining to a mixture of one substance in another
countenance   face, expression
capricious   whimsical
visage   face
idiosyncracies   personal quirks
refractions   reflections

impasse barrier, a situation in which no further progress is possible
transcend go beyond, overcome
zu l'hachis irrationally, without reason
aspirations hopes, dreams

39 · The Reasons for Religious Faith

```
SCORING:    Reading time: _____ Rate from chart: _____ W.P.M.

    PURPOSE          number right _____ × 4 equals _____ points

    GENERALITIES     number right _____ × 4 equals _____ points

    RETENTION        number right _____ × 2 equals _____ points

    COMPLETION       number right _____ × 3 equals _____ points

    DEFINITIONS      number right _____ × 2 equals _____ points

                        (Total points: 100)  total _____ points
```

PURPOSE Which of the following phrases best expresses the purpose of the passage? _____

1. to refute the arguments of the logical atheists like Russell
2. to show that the world outlook of religion centers about God
3. to give reasons for believing in God as creator of the universe

GENERALITIES Based on the passage, which of the following generalities seem justifiable? _____ and _____

1. The writer's appeal is reasonable and not emotional.
2. No one wants to be forced into atheism because he is unable to believe in God.
3. Bertrand Russell's logic may be reduced to emotionalism.
4. The traditional conception of God is unsatisfactory for the writer, Milton Steinberg.

RETENTION Based on the passage, which of the following statements are True (T), False (F), or Not answerable (N)?

1. _____ Many people think of God as an ancient king sitting on a throne.

2. _____ The author refuses to think of God as having a human shape.

3. _____ Bertrand Russell has chosen nullity rather than deity.

4. _____ The passage suggests that people who have a traditional belief in God will have a stunted religious experience.

5. _____ The universe is a vast tumult lacking constancy and consistence.

6. _____ Natural laws of physics support the author's argument.

7. _____ The author admits there is little or no purpose in the world.

8. _____ Most of the world's philosophers have tended not to believe in God.

9. _____ Evil in the world cannot be fully explained by the author's argument.

10. _____ A reason for belief in God is that man cannot live joyously without it.

11. _____ The author believes his argument is free from difficulties.

12. _____ Under atheistic assumptions, in the end everything adds up to nothing, according to the author.

13. _____ The author suggests that an atheistic view implies madness.

14. _____ With the assumption of God, all takes on meaning and intelligibility, according to the author.

15. _____ Under atheism the value of all human ideals depreciates.

16. _____ Self-sacrifice, the author contends, is meaningless if one is an atheist.

17. _____ Bertrand Russell is an atheist.

18. _____ The author's idea is that of a world-machine.

19. _____ The author suggests that there is no logic to the arguments of those who are both atheists and believers in human morality.

20. _____ The author claims his argument uses logic and common sense.

COMPLETION   Choose the best answer for each question.

1. _____ Bertrand Russell eventually decided to sanction moral ideals even though: (a) no one else would. (b) his logic made them unnecessary. (c) they had religious values. (d) he was not an idealist.

2. _____ The author's strongest argument seems to be: (a) that most people believe in God. (b) every other argument is emotional while his is rational. (c) that life seems to follow a pattern. (d) that morality without God is impossible.

3. _____ The author's eventual belief in God implies a religious attitude that is: (a) rather traditional. (b) unrelated to tradition. (c) related to tradition but not traditional. (d) totally unique in its character.

4. _____ This passage says that man's moral life demands a belief in God because: (a) religion and morality are mutually dependent. (b) ethics without religion never can exist. (c) God demands morality. (d) no one can be moral who does not believe in God.

5. _____ One of the joys of believing in the God the author defines is the feeling that we have a: (a) friend in heaven. (b) father to keep us and protect us. (c) role in the divine plan. (d) logical belief.

6. _____ For an Old Man on the Throne concept, the author substitutes: (a) a machine. (b) Mind-will. (c) logic. (d) atheism.

DEFINITIONS In the following passage, each underlined word has a number. In the columns below, match the number of each underlined word with the letter of the word that is closest to it in meaning.

                                    1   2
The universe further contains consciousness. It has produced man. At least in

          3   4   5   6
him it discloses intelligence, a thirst for truth, sensitivity to beauty, a desire

      7   8
for goodness. And man is a component of reality. Whence it follows that no

                  9   10   11
explanation of the entirety can be acceptable if it does not illumine the exist-

              12   13   14
ence and nature of this most complex, challenging and mysterious of its

      15
components.

Column A   Column B
1. _____   a. receptivity
                                  b. yearning
2. _____
                                  c. awareness
3. _____   d. features, characteristics
4. _____   e. organization
                                  f. ability to know
5. _____
                                  g. morality
6. _____   h. fragility
7. _____   i. complicated
                                  j. from which
8. _____
                                  k. shows
9. _____   l. elements, parts
10. _____   m. worthy, reasonable
                                  n. the whole
11. _____
                                  o. quench
12. _____   p. strange
                                  q. made
13. _____
                                  r. offering
14. _____   s. clarify

15. _____

40 · Frank Lloyd Wright: An American Original

MERLE ARMITAGE

The greatest American architect was also a blustery man, confident to the point of arrogance, but capable of great charm. A famous American impresario, Merle Armitage, tells what it was like to have Frank Lloyd Wright as a friend.

The year was 1923. I believe it was autumn and am certain it was midafternoon. As I looked out the window of my Los Angeles house a most improbable car drove up—a 1920-model Cadillac, with a Victoria body, huge coach lamps on either side, folding top, and all. From this equipage stepped a small figure in a gray suit, over which was thrown a black cloak. The face was stern but composed as he grasped his stick and walked with assurance. Frank Lloyd Wright had arrived!

Right behind him was the driver of the car, his son Lloyd, an old friend. They had a problem. These were the first few days after the disastrous earthquake in Japan. The American press was full of the disaster . . . tidal waves, thousands killed, cities leveled, and hosts of homeless. But added to this nightmare, reports were seeping through that Wright's Imperial Hotel was ruined. And that just could not be!

Wright was indignant to the point of explosion. "Young man," he said, "the Imperial Hotel is NOT ruined. In fact it is not even damaged. I built that hotel to withstand *any* earthquake, and I want you to help me with the newspapers." Wright knew me as an impresario, with friends and connections high and low on newspapers, the wire services, etc. "I'm at your service," was my quick reply as I poured tea for the group. "When do we start?"

FRANK LLOYD WRIGHT: AN AMERICAN ORIGINAL From *The Texas Quarterly*, spring 1962. Copyright © 1962 by The University of Texas. Reprinted by permission.

That initiated a daily trip to every newspaper in town. We rode down the
street in that open Victoria waving to friends. I was not exactly comfortable,
for I felt I had a madman on my hands. Approaching city editors, Wright
would shake his stick at them; with fire in his eyes, he would shout, "I'm going
to sue you. This is blasphemy. The Imperial Hotel is not damaged and you
are going to pay *me* damages for what you are doing to my reputation."

After a week of tension and Wright's angry incantations came a cable from
his friend and patron, Baron Okura of Japan: IMPERIAL HOTEL UNDAMAGED
FEEDING HUNDREDS OF REFUGEES DAILY A TRIBUTE TO YOUR GENIUS. CONGRATU-
LATIONS.

If Wright had been demonstrative about the "lies" appearing daily, he now
became calm and solemn. But this did not inhibit that peculiar sardonic gleam,
an F. L. W. trademark. Particularly in a moment of triumph. He bore up well!

We gave him a dinner, just a few of us. My own recollection of this event
is that Wright took a giant step forward in his own self-confidence and self-
assurance. Most of us were full of hilarity, toasting the Master, and thoroughly
enjoying his success which was to mean so much. F. L. W. on the contrary,
while genial, was preoccupied. Was he fascinated with vistas that now had
opened . . . ? Could he now envision equally important projects in his own
America?

There were to be other dinners.

Years later, Lloyd Wright and I made an automobile trip to Arizona for a
week's visit with F. L. W. near Chandler. He had established a drafting camp
near the site where he prepared to build a hotel. The hotel was to be built
atop two low hills, and would span with an arch the arroyo that separated
them. We arrived in the vicinity of the camp one afternoon at about four,
when the desert is magical with long and brilliant shadows. Presently Lloyd
said, "Look at that!"

Far away on the horizon (distances are deceptive in the clear Arizona atmosphere) was a painting by Picasso! But when we stopped the car for a more
inclusive look, the vision took on the appearance of a landscape by Tanguy.
We fished a pair of field glasses out of the trunk and took a closer look. On a
desert knoll was a cherry-colored fence that must have covered an acre of
terrain. Above this cherry stockade, white sails emerged—the tents of the camp.
Dominating this colorful ensemble were several giant saguaro cacti, masts of
green and bubulous trunks. Who but Frank Lloyd Wright would have used
the desert, and captured its fantasy, in constructing a mere living quarters and
drafting rooms?

As we covered the eight miles (we checked our speedometer) to the camp,
its appearance changed and became more fantastic, helped, of course, by the
declining sun. That is a memory that will not fade.

Next day Lloyd joined the crew at the drafting boards as his fathers' assistant. I roamed the desert, read books in an improvised library, and occasionally inspected the plans for the hotel. Entrance to the proposed hotel, to be called San Marcos in the Desert, was over a road up the arroyo, under the arch. When the road reached an altitude almost level with the hotel it split, one road for guests going right, one for service and supplies going left. The arroyo was to have a concrete sluiceway against flash flood from cloudbursts, which otherwise would wash out the road.

I recall vividly those plans—low, horizontal structures that seemed to hug the tops of those two hills, connected by an arch, the sort of curve that seems to have been invented by F. L. W. It was a gentle curve, but dynamic, too, and the abutments were so constructed that you did not feel it was simply a bridge over the Seine. It had a magic of its own.

Dinner was the pivotal time of day. With the master at the head of the table, there was discussion of everything, except the day's work. That seemed to be a sort of forum, held early each morning. If F. L. W. thought some topic was too trivial for conversation he would subtly change the subject. He opposed, for instance, America's entanglements with foreign powers. "It can only lead to trouble; they do not understand us, their hatreds are centuries old."

But it was after dinner, when Wright made his appearance in the improvised salon (a piano looked exotic indeed under a tent), that Wright became the prophet. The mess of the American city was a dominant theme. "Here we are, with the broad acres of America, crowding ugly, unhealthy structures almost on top of each other. There is no room to breathe, no light or sun, no place for the spirit to breathe. And the traffic thus engendered! How can the people move?" Of course there was, and is, no simple answer to this problem. This is gregariousness carried to the ultimate! But to hear the voice of F. L. W. rise with indignation as he discussed and described our national folly was an experience. "The buildings are not even structures," Wright maintained, "just unorganic boxes held together with steel and concrete. Nothing natural, or beautiful, or really permanent about them."

At the final dinner before our departure, I presented F. L. W. with an album of records, as a tiny gesture of appreciation. He slowly unwrapped the package, with talk reminiscent of a little boy with his Christmas presents. But this mood changed to anger as he saw the contents. "Debussy!" he shouted in disdain. "Don't you know, young man, that there has never been any music written since Mozart!" My temper is quick, too. Throwing caution to the winds, I came back instantly with, "On that basis, there has been no improvement in architecture since some primitive put up a hut of four walls, with a thatched roof on it."

Lloyd quickly introduced a story, and in a few minutes we were laughing about a draftsman who had mistaken a Wright gesture of appreciation as an explanation of the dynamics of a curve! When we departed after a good breakfast the next morning, F. L. W. shook hands with me, and there was a wicked twinkle in his cordial eye. Two weeks later, I received an autographed copy of his just-published, first autobiography. In it he had written, "To my friend Merle Armitage, a good fellow in the desert." To his credit, Wright never held my remark against me.

There were many other meetings. I was present at one gathering of reporters when Wright told of stating, in court, that he, F. L. W. was the world's greatest architect. "Wasn't that a little immodest?" a courageous reporter asked. "Yes I suppose it was," Wright mused, "but you forget that I was under oath . . . had to tell the truth."

The last time Wright accepted my hospitality was in New York in 1952. Talking on the phone with one of my publishers, Charles Pearce, of Duell, Sloan and Pearce, I learned that F. L. W. had just arrived in the office. "How long will he be in town?" I asked. Charles said he would be in New York just one day. "Then you bring him and Duell and come to lunch at our apartment." Charles consulted the other two, and they accepted for one o'clock. It was then ten in the morning.

I phoned my bride Isabelle. Taking it slowly and easily, I announced that both Duell and Pearce had been invited for lunch, she said "Splendid, always wanted to meet them socially." But when I said, "and they are bringing Frank Lloyd Wright," she nearly dropped the phone. But her luncheon, as usual, was delicious.

As Wright and I had indulged in many heated arguments about modern art, I told Isabelle to be prepared for an outburst about the Klees, Picassos, Braques, and Matisses that were hanging directly over the dining table. But Wright took care of it all in one gesture. Walking over to the Picasso bull in bold, meagre outline, he pointed his stick at the head and horns. "Some people assume that thinking takes place here," he pontificated. "Actually, all cerebration begins here," and he moved his stick to the region of the genitals. That did it; we could now move gleefully on to other subjects, and did.

I shall never forget the stories F. L. W. told at that luncheon. "Some people say that we are just making little Frank Lloyd Wrights at Taliesin West," Wright said with scorn. "But just remember this, young man," he continued, "there are no *little* Frank Lloyd Wrights."

Again he talked of Madison, Wisconsin, and his Spring Green home, where so much tragedy had occurred. He had been en route from Chicago one late afternoon on his favorite C.&N.W. train. He noticed a new porter and, as the same porter had served him for twenty years, he regretted the change. When the train entered the suburbs of Madison, the new porter approached and asked F. L. W. if he would like to be brushed. "I'm just new on this run," he apologized, "And, Sir, may I know your name." Wright told him. The porter threw down his brush, slapped his knee, and exclaimed, "Godalmighty, I

302   MERLE ARMITAGE

knowed all the time you-all was a *face card*!" Wright said it was his most precious compliment.

There are inimitable anecdotes and pleasant memories. What do I think of Frank Lloyd Wright, the architect? I think of him as a great architect, of course. But more than that, I deeply feel that he is America's greatest artist. If that seems a bold statement, let your mind flit over any possible candidates. In the end, you will find there are no serious contenders. Many fine painters, composers, sculptors, poets, writers, dancers. But not a single individual of the stature of Wright. As a creative artist, he stands alone as a world, as well as American, figure.

This is how I see him.

First, two things must be said. Ours is a different world because he lived; all around us are structures that would not be there except for Wright. Changed, diluted, and caricatured they may be; basically, they owe their being to this one man. Second, Wright is indubitably the inventor of the modern American structure! All his life he fought to get his ideas accepted and, once accepted, he battled to preserve them.

If the purists maintain that he was influenced by Sullivan, by the Japanese, by Mayan temples, even by things seemingly as far removed as cubism and *art nouveau*, they are correct in principle and wrong in attitude. From this cauldron of stimuli and influences Wright distilled his *own* architectural personality. This personality is just as unique, strong, and dominant, and just as free of plagiarism, as the processes of heredity. These, plus his sense of landscape, site, and nature, are the basis of his architectural independence. As much as any man in this world can be free, Wright was a free man, and he paid a fearful price for it.

Early in life he actively resisted moral conventions. Later in life he resisted regimentation and ugliness. *All* his life he resisted mediocrity. In the passing of Wright, America lost a giant of the old school, a man not cowed by anything or anybody.

A paradox in action, Wright maintained an outward hatred of modern art but actually operated within the framework of its soundest principles. In presenting new colors and textures to the world of architecture, he also introduced a new vocabulary of form, as bold, correct, and revealing as the experiments of Cezanne, Picasso, and Kandinsky. There is much in Kandinsky and Wright that relates the one to the other—as well as to the temples of the Mexican Indians.

It must also be remembered that Wright was an engineer, which in the eyes of many architects gives a deceptive simplicity to his solutions of complex problems. Contemporary man cannot avail himself of slave labor to move his stone and build his temples. Very well, Wright used modern concrete to achieve similar ends. Concrete in blocks with simple, strong decoration, held together with steel. He achieved the solidity and mass of the temple, with a modern feeling for form and space.

Buildings by Wright are fortunately all over America, not nearly as many as there should be. We failed to fully recognize his genius. But where you do find his work, you find a milestone in architecture. *Architectural Forum* once published an article on Wright (June 1959) with pictures of buildings which demonstrated his progress. Beneath each of Wright's buildings was an insert of the popular architectural style of that exact period. A devastating comment.

Knowing Wright in the casual manner of our friendship, I was always and continually aware of his courage, courage on many levels. At the time of his Princeton lectures, for instance, there was no hope that he would ever design a major structure in this country. Yet the principles for which he stood were delineated with all the courage, confidence, and precision of a man about to take over the whole architectural future of our country. Though he seemed to be at war with everything, when you analyzed his belligerence you found yourself agreeing with him. The things he was against are the things that have robbed our democracy, with its brilliant promise, of its pristine best. Advertising has helped to build our economic strength, but its concomitant, the Madison Avenue attitude, has eroded and degraded our essential spirit. Wright continually struck at the Madison Avenue attitude.

Being with Wright was a stimulating, amusing, and enlightening experience. He seemed always to be arrogant, even when he smiled. But over the years when you examined this arrogance, you understood it. His iconoclastic ideas brought him an exasperating group of followers. Sometimes they became rather sticky and demanding in their adoration. Wright, being an artist, secretly resented being thus robbed of his time and energies. Both his clinging followers and the studied indifference of the entrenched and reactionary forces exhausted his patience. His anger lashed out at both, in much the same way that a storm vents its energy in lightning.

Within my personal reactions are the recollections of two structures by Wright that console, now that he is dead. I am mindful of all the others, beginning with Winslow House in Illinois, Midway Gardens in Chicago, the Imperial Hotel in Japan, the Johnson Wax Building in Racine, Price Tower in Tulsa, Florida Southern College in Lakeland, Beth Sholom Synagogue in Pennsylvania, down through the superb Kaufman House near Pittsburgh, and countless residences, to the Guggenheim Museum in New York.

But my mind goes back to Taliesin North, in Wisconsin, and Taliesin West, in Arizona. These are the sorts of structures you feel that God intended man to live in. As James Marston Fitch expressed it, "They are larger than life." Here, in these two buildings, splendor, excitement, strength, and gentleness are blended in a magical ensemble. A domain of peace, a dome of plenty.

Above and beyond any other structures he created, the two contain most of the meaning of the man: the best of Frank Lloyd Wright. This is the nobility I shall remember.

LENGTH: 3,120 WORDS

VOCABULARY

equipage   a carriage, especially when elaborately outfitted
impresario   one who sponsors performers or performances for entertainment
sardonic   wry, bitter, sarcastic
arroyo   a small stream or its dry bed
sluiceway   a channel for the rerouting of a stream of water
abutments   piers, supports
engendered   brought about, supported
gregariousness   sociability
inimitable   incapable of being imitated
avail   benefit, good
delineated   spelled out, shown, clarified
iconoclastic   irreverent, skeptical
entrenched   dug in, well established
reactionary   one who wants to return to old ways

40 · Frank Lloyd Wright: An American Original

SCORING: Reading time: _____ Rate from chart: _____ W.P.M.

PURPOSE	number right _____ × 4 equals _____ points
GENERALITIES	number right _____ × 4 equals _____ points
RETENTION	number right _____ × 2 equals _____ points
COMPLETION	number right _____ × 3 equals _____ points
DEFINITIONS	number right _____ × 2 equals _____ points

(Total points: 100)   **total** _____ points

PURPOSE   Which of the following phrases best expresses the purpose of the passage? _____

1. to clarify some specific events in the life of the original American architect
2. to communicate the essence of Wright's character
3. to eulogize a great architect

GENERALITIES   Based on the passage, which of the following generalities seem justifiable? _____ and _____

1. Architects take themselves seriously even when they are not working.
2. Eccentricity was a characteristic of Frank Lloyd Wright.
3. Music since Mozart is unrelated to Wright's architecture.
4. Armitage was impressed with the sheer force of Wright's personality.

RETENTION   Based on the passage, which of the following statements are True (T), False (F), or Not answerable (N)?

1. _____ During the Japanese earthquake, Wright was sure his hotel stood.

2. _____ Wright had first triumphed architecturally in America.

3. _____ The camp in the desert was picturesque.

4. _____ At dinner at the camp Wright never discussed his current work.

5. _____ Wright, with characteristic good taste, praised the American city.

6. _____ Mozart was Wright's favorite composer.

7. _____ Wright seems not to have enjoyed modern art.

8. _____ Armitage considers Wright both an architect and an artist.

9. _____ In every way except architecturally, Wright was a conventional man.

10. _____ Wright's work is located in specific, limited sections of the country.

11. _____ Wright's architectural style was beyond the prevailing style.

12. _____ An exasperating group of followers hung around Wright.

13. _____ Wright opposed the things that deprive us of our liberties.

14. _____ In general, people did not like Frank Lloyd Wright.

15. _____ Wright designed many public buildings, but no private residences.

16. _____ Armitage implies that Wright's personal life was smooth and pleasant.

17. _____ One constant feature of Wright's personality was his arrogance.

18. _____ Wright's general view was that architecture in America was poor.

19. _____ Armitage remembers best Taliesin North and Taliesin West.

20. _____ Wright had an imposing personal nobility.

COMPLETION   Choose the best answer for each question.

1. _____ Armitage's principal method of describing Wright is by: (a) telling what other people thought of him. (b) recounting personal anecdotes about him. (c) letting Wright tell the story himself. (d) being factual and essentially objective.

2. _____ The story about Wright's reaction to false reports that his Imperial Hotel in Japan had been destroyed showed that F. L. W. was: (a) most cautious. (b) highly insolent. (c) frightened for his reputation. (d) eminently sure of himself.

3. _____ From Armitage's picture we could assume that he: (a) did not like Wright's ideas. (b) liked Wright but not his ideas. (c) liked Wright and most of his ideas. (d) liked Wright's ideas and sometimes liked Wright.

4. _____ The fact that Wright was trained as an engineer rather than as an architect made some people: (a) feel sorry for him. (b) take issue with his ideas. (c) try to argue him out of his ideas. (d) think less of his achievement.

5. _____ Wright was opposed to American political involvement with foreign powers because he felt that foreign countries: (a) respected the United States out of all proportion. (b) were unaware of America's great strength. (c) would only hold America back. (d) hated and did not understand the United States.

6. ____ Armitage mentions the fact that Wright never reacted to his comment about primitive huts being unsurpassed by subsequent architecture in order to show that: (a) Wright was gallant enough not to hold it against him. (b) Wright agreed with him. (c) Wright was becoming deaf. (d) Wright felt the comment beneath his dignity.

DEFINITIONS In the following passage, each underlined word has a number. In the columns below, match the number of each underlined word with the letter of the word that is closest to it in meaning.

    1   2   3   4   5   6

I recall vividly those plans—low, horizontal structures that seemed to hug the

                        7   8   9

tops of those two hills, connected by an arch, the sort of curve that seems to

                10   11   12

have been invented by F. L. W. It was a gentle curve, but dynamic, too, and

     13   14

the abutments were so constructed that you did not feel it was simply a bridge

               15

over the Seine. It had a magic of its own.

Column A	Column B
1. ____	a. spirit
2. ____	b. diagrams, drawings
3. ____	c. gradual
4. ____	d. joined
5. ____	e. intensely
	f. buildings
6. ____	g. energetic
7. ____	h. remember
8. ____	i. painfully
	j. created
9. ____	k. touch
10. ____	l. stoppers
11. ____	m. curved structure
12. ____	n. arbitrarily
13. ____	o. reinforced sections
14. ____	p. parallel to the horizon
	q. variety, type
15. ____	r. become aware, think
	s. keep close to

Charts for Measuring Speed of Reading

how to find WPM

To find the speed at which a selection is read in terms of words per minute, divide the total number of words by the reading time in minutes. For example, selection 1 has 365 words. If it took 3.5 minutes to read the passage, the calculation is: 3.5 $\overline{)365}$ = 105 W.P.M. These charts give the actual words per minute figure for each selection.

3 minutes

SECTION I

TIME IN MINS.	SELECTIONS				
	1	2	3	4	5
1	365	350	320	540	280
2	183	175	160	270	140
2.5	146	140	128	216	112
3	122	117	107	180	93
3.5	105	100	91	154	80
4	91	88	80	135	70
4.5	81			120	
5				108	

wph

SECTION II

TIME IN MINS.	SELECTIONS							
	6	7	8	9	10	11	12	13
1	820	980	1,000	980	940	790	910	1,220
2	410	490	500	490	470	395	455	610
3	275	327	333	327	313	263	303	407
4	205	245	250	245	235	198	228	305
5	164	196	200	196	188	158	182	245
6	137	164	167	164	157	131	152	203
7	117	140	143	140	134	113	130	174
8		123	125	123	118	99	114	153
9			111					136
10			100					122

TIME IN MINS.	SELECTIONS									
	14	*15*	*16*	*17*	*18*	*19*	*20*	*21*	*22*	*23*
1	1,230	2,020	1,620	1,310	1,110	1,200	1,480	1,230	1,380	1,760
2	615	1,010	810	655	555	600	740	615	690	880
3	410	673	540	437	370	400	495	410	460	587
4	308	505	405	328	278	300	370	308	345	440
5	246	404	324	262	222	240	296	246	276	352
6	205	337	270	218	185	200	247	205	230	293
7	176	289	231	187	159	171	211	176	197	251
8	154	253	203	164	139	150	185	154	173	220
9	137	224	180	146	123	133	164	137	153	196
10	123	202	162	131	110	120	148	123	138	176
11		184	147							
12		168	135							
13		155								
14		144								
15		135								

TIME IN MINS.	SELECTIONS									
	24	*25*	*26*	*27*	*28*	*29*	*30*	*31*	*32*	*33*
1	1,210	1,750	1,350	1,850	1,600	1,780	1,660	2,050	1,800	2,180
2	605	875	675	925	800	890	830	1,025	900	1,090
3	403	583	450	617	533	593	553	683	600	727
4	303	438	338	463	400	445	415	513	450	545
5	242	350	270	370	320	356	332	410	360	436
6	202	293	225	308	267	297	277	342	300	364
7	173	250	193	264	229	254	237	293	257	311
8	151	219	169	231	200	223	208	256	225	273
9	134	194	150	206	178	198	184	228	200	242
10	121	175	135	185	160	178	166	205	180	218
11						162		186	164	198
12								171		182
13								158		167

TIME IN MINS.	SELECTIONS						
	34	*35*	*36*	*37*	*38*	*39*	*40*
1	2,400	2,650	2,155	2,110	2,710	2,190	3,120
2	1,200	1,325	1,077	1,055	1,355	1,095	1,560
3	800	883	718	703	903	730	1,040
4	600	663	539	528	678	548	780
5	480	530	431	420	542	438	624
6	400	442	359	352	452	365	520
7	343	379	308	301	387	313	446
8	300	331	269	264	339	274	390
9	267	294	239	234	310	243	347
10	240	265	216	211	271	219	312
11	218	241	196	192	246	199	284
12	200	221	180	176	226	183	260
13	185	204	166	162	208	168	240
14	171	189	154	151	194	156	223
15		177	144		181		208
16					169		195
17							184

Graph for Measuring Progress in Retention

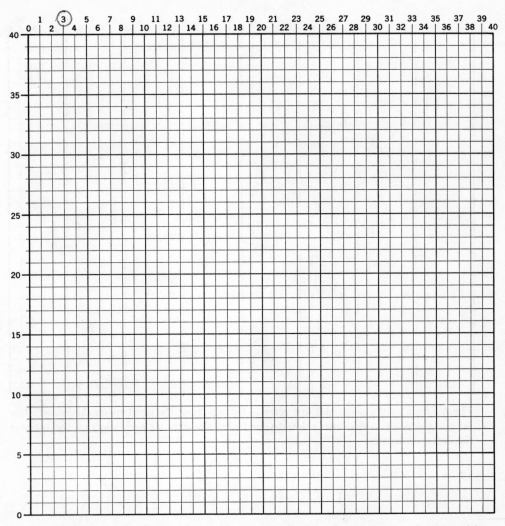

The numbers on the horizontal line refer to the selection; the numbers on the vertical line refer to the point score. Make a dot at your Retention score for each selection and connect the dots with a line.

315

Graph for Measuring Progress in Vocabulary Skill

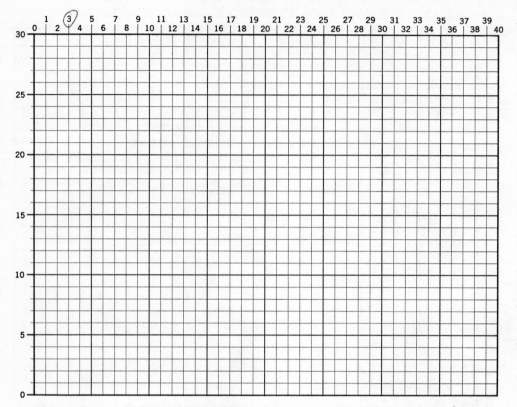

The numbers on the horizontal line refer to the selection; the numbers on the vertical line refer to the point score. Make a dot at your Definition score for each selection and connect the dots with a line.

316

Graph for Scores for Inferential and Completion Questions

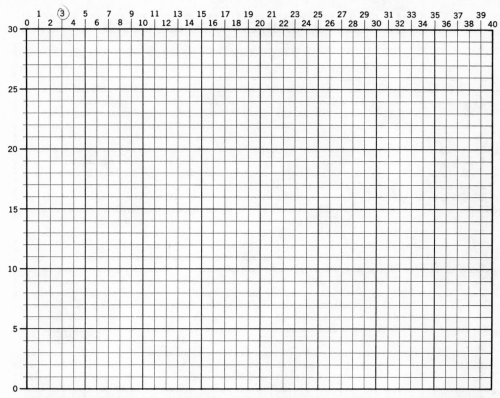

The numbers on the horizontal line refer to the selection; the numbers on the vertical line refer to the point score. Add the scores for Inference, Completion, Main Sentence, Generalities, and Purpose questions. Enter the total on the graph as a dot and connect the dots with a line.

Graph for Measuring Progress in Reading Speed in Words per Minute

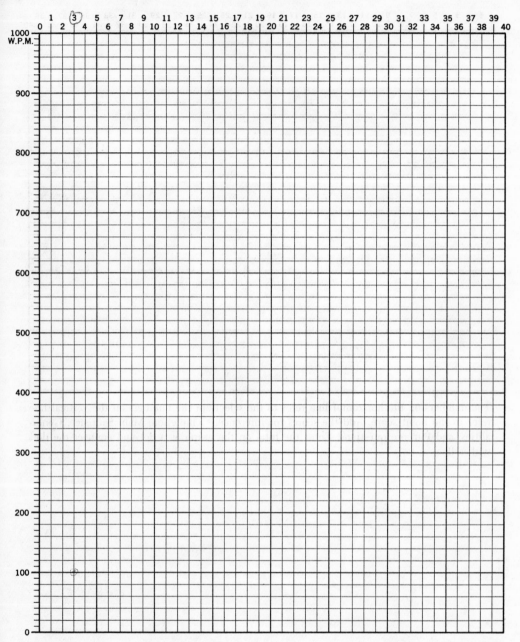

The numbers on the horizontal line refer to the selection; the numbers on the vertical line refer to reading speed in words per minute. Make a dot at your speed for each selection and connect the dots with a line.

Progress Chart

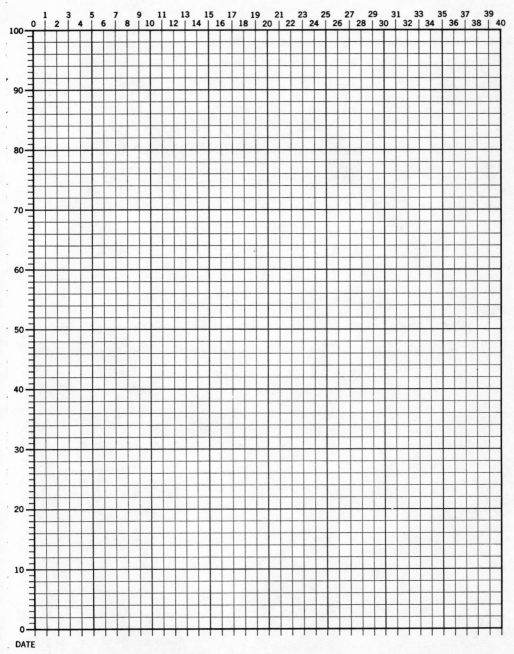

The numbers on the horizontal line refer to the selection; the numbers on the vertical line refer to the total point score of each selection. Check your progress by graphing your scores. Put the date of each exercise on the lower part of the graph.